CAMBRIDGE STUDIES IN SOCIAL
ANTHROPOLOGY

No. 8

MARRIAGE AMONG A
MATRILINEAL ELITE

Cambridge Studies in Social Anthropology

General Editors

M. FORTES, J. R. GOODY, E. R. LEACH, S. J. TAMBIAH

MARRIAGE AMONG A MATRILINEAL ELITE

A FAMILY STUDY OF GHANAIAN SENIOR CIVIL SERVANTS

CHRISTINE OPPONG

Senior Research Fellow, Institute of African Studies
University of Ghana

CAMBRIDGE UNIVERSITY PRESS

Published by the Syndics of the Cambridge University Press
Bentley House, 200 Euston Road, London NW1 2DB
American Branch: 32 East 57th Street, New York, N.Y. 10022

© Cambridge University Press 1974

Library of Congress Catalogue Card Number: 73-82452

ISBN: 0 521 20328 7

First published 1974

Printed in Great Britain
at the University Printing House, Cambridge
(Brooke Crutchley, University Printer)

CONTENTS

TABLES

Tables

To J. and E.

FOREWORD

There is now considerable evidence to support the conclusion that the processes of social change in ex-colonial countries lumped together under the label of 'modernisation' conduce to the abandonment of traditional family patterns in favour of a western-type conjugal family, at any rate in some sections of society. In Europe and America the study of the family is a major academic industry, drawing into its orbit social scientists, psychologists, and many other specialists, not to speak of various categories of social workers with practical interests. Much is known about the western conjugal family – which, it should be remembered, is obligatory in law as well as normative by custom. We have learnt to accept that internal harmony and stability are by no means to be taken for granted in western conjugal families. Internal conflicts and tensions are known to be common and to play a significant part in the manifestations of personal and social deviance that are so burdensome to developed societies.

By contrast we know little about the actual working of the conjugal family in developing countries where it is a recent innovation and not legally binding. Dr Oppong's book changes this situation completely and it is easy to predict that it will soon inspire many imitations. The problems Dr Oppong tackles are of passionate and even painful concern to the persons who collaborated in this study. This calls for the highest levels of professional skill and integrity if objectivity is to be achieved. Dr Oppong succeeds admirably in this without sacrificing the insight and sensitivity that were indispensable for her research.

In pursuit of her enquiries, Dr Oppong has borrowed widely from western family studies; but she marshalls these methods and concepts brilliantly in the service of her overall research design. By definition the conjugal family is centred on the relationship of marriage and Dr Oppong's main aim is to find out how this relationship works out in the segment of Ghanaian society on which she concentrates. To this end she uses the methods and concepts

ix

drawn from western family studies to find out how spouses distribute and manage the tasks, and allocate their respective resources of income, time and moral commitment, that are required for the family to maintain its distinctive character of an autonomous and exclusive unit. However, as an anthropologist, Dr Oppong knows that it is essential to examine any form of family organization, traditional or new, in its setting in the larger social structure and in its context of norms and values; and this is the basis of her research design.

Dr Oppong deliberately restricts her enquiry to a limited community of common culture, language and historical experience, the Akan peoples of Ghana. Furthermore, she concentrates on a limited social class within this community, which gives her a relatively homogeneous sample of people of the same occupational and economic status and similar life experiences. This enables her to adapt the intensive field methods of anthropological enquiry to her needs and to keep track of distinctive cultural and structural variables.

There are *a priori* considerations that suggest an inherent contradiction between the conjugal family pattern and matrilineal kinship institutions. Dr Oppong's book is among other things a striking test of this expectation, for which the Akan data are particularly adapted. There is a rich and comprehensive literature on the Akan peoples, the traditional marriage and kinship institutions being especially well documented in a succession of studies over the past half century.

Accordingly, it is well known that, traditionally, marriage was (and in village communities still is) the frailest of bonds and is secondary to the matrilineal kinship ties focussed in the unbreakable natal bonds of brother and sister, and symbolised by the law of 'nephew inheritance'. Spouses often resided apart, with their close maternal kin, on whom they had everlasting claims. This ensured virtual legal equality between the spouses, as regards control over personal income and freedom of divorce. But it also gave rise to chronic feelings of insecurity among wives, fearful of being left destitute as widows or divorcees by inheriting nephews.

Dr Oppong's investigations reveal an intricate state of affairs in the internal organization of the conjugal families of her respondents. They are caught up in conflicting pressures and aspirations; and the main source of this is the persistence, even among this highly educated, urban-dwelling, economically secure and privileged bourgeoisie, of traditional attitudes, loyalties and apprehensions.

Dr Oppong's case histories vividly portray these situations, which are further carefully evaluated by means of a number of ingenious quantitative indices and comparisons which she has devised.

Characteristically, it emerges that husband and wife rarely own property in common or have joint bank accounts. Each, by contrast, is apt to own some property jointly with close matrilineal kin, which, for the wives, is thought of as a hedge against destitution. Demands from such kin are frequent and cannot be resisted by most people. But there are reciprocal advantages. The wives, being themselves educated or professionally qualified, object strongly to housekeeping and insist on having paid outside employment. This means having servants to attend to the housekeeping and it is from rural maternal kin that young relatives are commonly recruited for this purpose. In traditional style, wives quote the insecurity of marriage, and fear of dispossession by the husband's maternal kin, as reasons for building up their private resources. Yet they dare not leave their husbands (even if they are known to have 'concubines') since 'fridgeful' men are hard to come by and the economically superior luxurious living conditions they provide are not willingly given up. Tension and frustration inevitably build up in these circumstances.

Among Dr Oppong's most interesting discoveries is that there is a scale of variation between families. At one end are families in which there is no pooling of resources or sharing of tasks or complete mutual trust between the spouses, who are unable to free themselves from the demands of kin and cannot thus achieve 'closure' of the family. It is in these families that tension and dissatisfaction spread. At the other end of the scale however, are families which appear to achieve the mutuality and sharing, the 'jointness' and 'closure' that correspond to the ideal western conjugal family. In these families it turns out that the husband and sometimes both partners, are commonly second or third generation educated people with salaried jobs. In the disharmonious families by contrast, the husbands are usually first generation educated and salaried men. Furthermore, unlike the families that, not being closed, continue to be open to the demands of kinship, the harmonious, closed families tend to isolate themselves from kin and community and resist external demands; and though the wives often have paid employment, they also willingly devote time to their housekeeping. In short it seems that the more a family is able to 'keep themselves to themselves' by reason of secure salaried employment in typically bourgeois style, and the more generations of such family life a couple can look back to for models, the better are the chances of their establishing and maintaining a successful and satisfactory conjugal family in the circumstances of a country like Ghana.

As for the future, Dr Oppong ventures no predictions. She is content to spread before us the data she has so brilliantly brought together. This is wonderful material for comparison with the data we have on the conjugal family in Europe and America and for testing many current theories about these data. Perhaps there is indeed something in the very nature and structure of the conjugal family, wherever it exists, that inevitably generates tension and frustration, regardless of the traditional background in a particular society. More particularly, it is only by such close study of limited and precisely definable problems in a culturally unitary population that significant conclusions can be reached about the processes of social change.

MEYER FORTES

PREFACE

This book is the revised version of a thesis submitted to the Faculty of Archaeology and Anthropology of the University of Cambridge in December 1970. The enquiries on which the study is based were carried out in 1967–8 in the centre and suburbs of Accra. They took me into many homes and offices of senior Ghanaian government employees and I am deeply grateful to all the husbands and wives who cooperated in providing me with the relevant data. Some even sat with me repeatedly month after month to discuss their own life histories, their families and their households.

Since the segment of the society within which the domestic relationships were examined is a relatively small and sophisticated one, great pains have been taken to transpose all cases documented, so that while they depict the reality of the social relationships observed and reported, they are not portraits of any identifiable individuals. Pseudonyms have been used throughout. It is sincerely hoped that no one will feel that an unwarranted intrusion has been made upon his or her domestic privacy.

Throughout the period of work I have been a Research Fellow of the Institute of African Studies of the University of Ghana and have benefited in numerous ways from the understanding help and encouragement of the Director, Professor Kwabena Nketia and from stimulating discussions, on various aspects of my work, with colleagues, both in the Institute and in other departments of the University. The latter include Dr E. N. W. Oppong, Dr M. Peil, Dr K. Arhin, Dr G. Woodman, and Dr G. K. Nukunya. I am also grateful to Mr G. Hagan and to Mrs C. Okali for reading through the complete typescript and for their useful comments. In addition Mr Arthur Johnson, also of the Institute of African Studies, helped in various ways.

During the first period of data analysis in Cambridge, and also during his several short and extended visits to Ghana, I was extremely fortunate to have the invaluable guidance of Professor Jack Goody, who supervised my post-graduate work. Without his kind encouragement and sympathetic advice over the years this book would never have been written. Also his wife, Dr Esther N. Goody has played an important part, first as a stimulating teacher during my undergraduate years and later as a helpful friend. Throughout, in working with the Akan, first as an undergraduate and then a graduate student in his Faculty, I have had Professor Fortes and his work to inspire me. To him I owe more thanks than I can easily express. I should also like to mention Professor Simon Ottenbeng, who examined the original thesis and made a number of highly pertinent comments.

Last but by no means least I owe a great debt of gratitude to Professor K. Little, formerly head of the Department of Anthropology now Professor of Urban African Studies, Edinburgh University, for the research reported here forms a contribution to a cross-cultural study of marriage organised by the Department of Social Anthropology, Edinburgh University, in which the Institute of African Studies, University of Ghana collaborated. Thus it was Professor Little's generous administration of a grant from the Social Science Research Council, which facilitated the collection and processing of these and other data referred to in this work. Through him I was given the opportunity to take part in very valuable discussions with members of his department in Edinburgh, including Dr Mary Noble and Dr Barbara Harrell-Bond, who were at the same time working on similar problems in Scotland and Sierra Leone.

In addition the opportunity which Professor Little gave me to attend a conference on networks at Leiden in 1969 incidentally led to a stimulating meeting with Dr Bruce Kapferer. This meeting prompted an exploration of exchange theory as presented by Peter Blau, an experience which has had an important effect upon the presentation of data in this book.

During the initial stages of the research I gained a great deal from reading preliminary drafts of papers in post-graduate and staff seminars in Legon, Edinburgh, Cambridge and Birmingham. Papers on the subject of conjugal finances have been read at conferences at Leiden Africa Studies Centrum in 1969 and the Institute of African Studies, Legon in February 1971. These and other related papers in which I have already discussed aspects of the domestic lives of Ghanaian Senior Civil Servants are listed in the bibliography.

In 1968–9 I held the Woodall Bye Fellowship at my former Cambridge college, Girton, and thus enjoyed the facilities of a congenial setting within which to carry out the initial processes of data analysis.

Preface

Finally I could not end these acknowledgements and omit a word to the Nananom, without whom this book would certainly never have been begun, Nana Kwame Waddie, Nana Kofi Waddie, Nana Amma Kyerewaa and Nana Yaa Pokua.

C. OPPONG

December 1973,
Legon

NOTE

The following customary notation is used to signify relationships:

M = mother	S = son	D = daughter
F = father	Z = sister	B = brother
W = wife	H = husband	

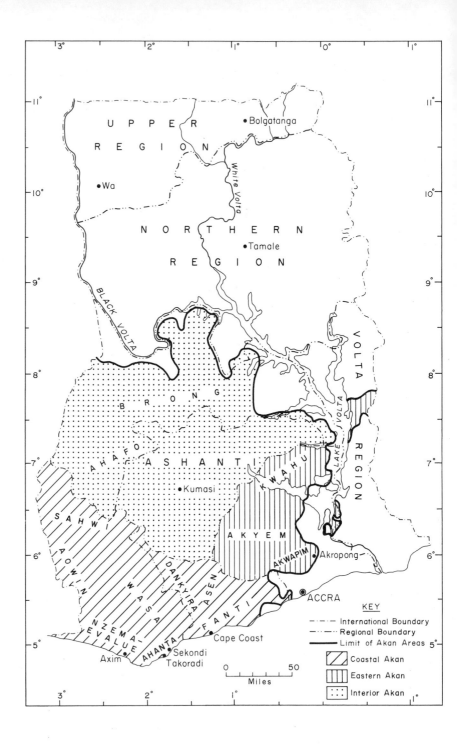

KEY
- –·–·– International Boundary
- –··–··– Regional Boundary
- —— Limit of Akan Areas
- ⧄ Coastal Akan
- ⦀ Eastern Akan
- ⠿ Interior Akan

0   50
Miles

1

THE PROBLEM

The present study has three interrelated aspects. First, it is offered as a contribution to the growing body of data on marriage and family life among urban, educated West Africans. As such it is concerned with the description of facets of conjugal and kin relationships among a section of the educated inhabitants of Accra, the Akan Senior Civil Servants. Secondly it is an exercise in methodology, in which the aim has been to evolve ways of documenting and comparing two major aspects of conjugal family relationships: the division of labour, resources and power between husbands and wives, and the extent to which the conjugal family is a functionally discrete unit in a number of domestic activity areas. This documentation and analysis has been carried out to facilitate the ultimate aim, the examination of marital continuity and change among educated, urban migrants from a region characterized by matrilineal descent and inheritance. Changes in urban family relationships have attracted much attention in recent years. Here a number of such domestic problems are presented. They were documented in Accra in 1967–8, a time and place characterized by marked social changes in many spheres of life, including the political, demographic and economic, as well as the domestic.

The central themes are familiar to anyone acquainted with the home life of educated Ghanaians. The practical problems involved are the frequent subject of popular debate in press reports, at society meetings and formerly in parliament. Similarly the academic problems, associated with the study of these effects, are ones of perennial concern to students of comparative family systems and to sociologists and anthropologists in general. They involve no less than the study of the processes through which customary norms and behaviour patterns persist in new social and geographical environments, and the social factors associated with change and conflict at the domestic level.

In the course of informal, preliminary investigations of conjugal relationships among educated Ghanaian couples in an Accra suburb in 1966, two types of emphatic statements were noted, which focussed attention upon certain problem areas. The first type of statement was that customary kinship norms and practices associated with matriliny considerably affect the domestic behaviour of educated, urban Akan men and women. A few men spoke of the financial strain they experienced in fulfilling their multiple obligations as matri-kinsmen and fathers. Apprehension was voiced by several Akan women concerning the potential financial insecurity of themselves and their children, since they did not belong to their husbands' 'families' and so did not, according to custom, share rights in their property, a factor which it was said, might easily bring a disturbing element of tension into the marriage. The documentation of such conflicts inherent in matrilineal systems, centring upon a man's obligations as brother, son, uncle on the one hand and husband and father on the other have a long history. Over forty years ago they were graphically described by Malinowski (1926:100–11) among the Trobrianders and Fortune among the Dobuans (1932: 1–21).

The second type of statement was that there is a marked difference between the marital and kinship ties and expectations of people from educated families, with one or more generations of educated forebears, who have worked as businessmen or salaried employees, and those who are first-generation educated, the children of illiterate farmers and fishermen. Coastal Akan, from communities exposed to the influences of education and salaried employment for several generations, and who consequently considered themselves 'enlightened', claimed that they expected a 'closer' marriage tie and a more 'independent' nuclear family than the Akan of the hinterland, who only began to have opportunities for widespread formal education a generation or so ago.

That both traditional modes of reckoning descent and length of exposure to formal education play an important part in moulding the changing patterns of domestic relationships of urban African migrants has been observed for some time. Over thirty years ago Wilson (1936: 549) and Richards (1940: 8–9) were making such observations. Recently Lloyd (1966: 30) has suggested that,

Within the elite (educated African) nuclear family the pattern of the relationship between husband and wife tends to be one of shared roles, greater intimacy and equality. Yet the patterns to be found in any one part of Africa will vary widely, according to the traditional relationships and perhaps to the levels of education found in the ascendant generations.

The Problem

In the present enquiry two different types of data are examined to see possible areas of continuity, strain and change. They include a survey of married men's reports of aspects of their domestic relationships, and a panel of twelve case studies of couples collected over extended periods of six to twelve months as well as extensive descriptive data collected through participant observation and interviews. All the data discussed in detail here were collected in Accra from Akan Senior Civil Servants and their wives. The modes of collecting and analysing the data from the cases and survey and the framework used for classifying them are described below.

The conjugal families selected for study, being those of professionals and administrators employed in the senior ranks of government service, form a relatively homogeneous population, in respect of type of occupation, level of education, wealth, and place of residence. At the same time the diverse origins and educational experience of themselves, their wives, their forebears and kin, are such that the sample provides a suitable laboratory for the controlled comparison of the effects on domestic life of matrilineal norms and practices and extent of schooling. This type of limited comparison of adjacent, economically homogeneous sectors of the Ghanaian population, to examine effects of matrilineal and other norms upon aspects of conjugal and kin relationships, has already been used to considerable effect in studies of local rural communities.[1]

It was intended from the outset that the survey data should assist as elsewhere in the 'synchronic analysis of the general structural principles' of the sets of relationships under discussion, and that they would be dovetailed with case study material. The latter was intended to be used to present what Van Velsen has called 'a diachronic analysis of the operation of principles by specific actors in the domestic situation' (1967: 149).

Published observations upon conjugal roles, urban families and migrants' kinship ties are now so many and are proliferating at such a rate that only those thought pertinent to the present study have been mentioned. The intention has been to provide sufficient references to put this study into a general framework and a particular context. The latter has been provided by a number of important studies of Akan kinship and marriage referred to below in chapter two.[2] Caldwell's recent population studies in Ghana, including those on fertility and rural urban migration, provide a valuable backcloth of relevant demographic data (1965, 1966, 1967, 1969). As regards the general framework of the study, comparative material on rural,

3

matrilineal kinship systems, subject to change, is offered by a number of studies, including the mammoth work by Schneider and Gough (1961).[3] Of particular relevance to the present theme is the latter's discussion of disintegrating matrilineal systems. Pioneering studies, on the changing family in urban Ghana, including the early works of Crabtree (1950) and Busia (1950) and more recently those of Caldwell (1968), Kilson (1967) and Mills-Odoi (1967). Many useful insights and interesting comparative material on changing urban family systems from various parts of the globe have been provided by amongst others Blood and Wolfe (1960), Goode (1963), and the several authors cited in the text. In particular Clignet's recent work *Many Wives Many Powers* (1970), which was read after the completion of this text, provides some interesting comparative data and conclusions for it deals with domestic changes taking place among the neighbouring matrilineal Abouré.

Relevant to the present problems and their conceptualization have been Herbst's (1952, 1954) modes of measuring family data; Bott's (1957) classification of conjugal relationships as *joint* or *segregated*; the classification of nuclear family systems as *open* or *closed*, discussed by Farber (1966) – following the earlier usage of such terms by Redfield (1947) and Weber (1947); and exchange theory as presented by Blau (1964).

Lloyd in his consideration of various social changes taking place in West Africa, has recently pinpointed some of the issues dealt with here, regarding the types of conjugal relationships between members of the urban, educated elite and their wives. These include for example the incidence of tension and the effects of parental educational levels upon marriages and of financial and other resources upon decision-making in the home (Lloyd, 1967: 172, 178–9, 181 etc.).

The data presented in this account were collected from Akan only. Their analysis at every stage has however, been considerably affected by the parallel consideration of similar data collected from the Ga and Ewe elements of the total population studied during the field-work period. Reference is made at several points both to comparisons of the different groups and to analyses including all three populations.[4]

I begin by describing the background of the study. First the general problem of the kind of changes taking place in urban African family life is briefly sketched, with particular reference to the conflicts associated with change in matrilineal kinship systems and the effects of education, migration and urban residence upon domestic life.

4

Then the dependent variables, the dimensions of conjugal and kin relationships which are the focus of the enquiry, and the mode of classifying data are defined.

Next an outline of the institutional framework of the conjugal relationships under analysis is presented and then the present social and economic positions of the actors concerned, the Akan Senior Civil Servants – both in the external occupational system and the internal domestic domain. The institutions examined include customary Akan marriage and matriliny, which have shaped the family lives of most Akan Senior Civil Servants, and the schools, universities and Civil Service hierarchy, which have provided the channels for their present careers.

Historical depth is given to this account of institutions, since time span, in terms of generations of exposure to the effects of education and the associated forms of salaried employment and residence patterns, is an important variable in the analysis. Thus I trace some of the historical and present-day factors, which have contributed to the widespread social and geographical mobility, now observable in Akan populations. Of particular interest are the differences among the Akan sub-groups, found in the littoral, in the east, and in the interior. The focus is upon education, treated here as the index par-excellence of individualism and mobility and of participation in the modern sector of the economy of privately disposable goods and skills; for the Civil Servant is seen as the epitome of the mobile, educated man.

In a similar way time-depth is given to the discussion of the present occupational, kinship and conjugal roles of the sample of married Akan Senior Civil Servants chosen for detailed study. The several processes through which they have reached their present positions over time are described; how they acquired the necessary professional and administrative experience to do their jobs; how all incurred binding social and economic obligations to members of their families of origin who reared and educated them, some only to parents others to any array of grandparents or parents' siblings. Next some of the ways in which they have chosen and married their wives and become fathers and heads of urban households are indicated.

The aim of this discussion is to provide some understanding of the kinds of bundles of material rights and obligations characteristically attached to the position of the Akan Senior Civil Servant. These include the status rights and privileges accruing to him as

5

high ranking government employee, in terms of salary, transport and accommodation, all of which put him in a category far above the mass of his countrymen with respect to income and living standard. They also include the persistent sets of social and financial obligations, as well as advantages, associated with his kinship ties, including those as son, brother and maternal uncle. They include thirdly his rights and duties as an urban householder, who must often provide accommodation not only for his wife and children, but also for the kin and affines and unrelated domestic helpers, who constitute one tiny part of the massive flux of migrants currently shifting into the capital of Ghana.

It is with all these facts in mind that the discussion can begin in Chapter 4 of the ways in which Akan Senior Civil Servants and their Akan wives allocate their resources in money and time in the domestic context. This allocation includes the day-to-day provision for the material needs of their households, long-term saving and ownership of property, which may provide future security for themselves and their dependents as well as the study of the division of domestic labour: who is responsible for, and who performs which kinds of housework in the home. In Chapter 5 is given an account of the conjugal power relationship and the ways in which decisions are made about the allocation of these resources.

In the description of budgeting arrangements, chore performance, and decision-making three concerns are paramount. One is conjugal 'solidarity', the extent to which couples act together, or in place of each other. The second is to examine the degree of functional individuation of the conjugal family, the extent to which kin or others perform household activities with the husband, wife and children or in place of them. The third is to locate and analyse tension and conflict in domestic relations, the areas of family functioning in which it typically arises, the kinds of outward forms it assumes and the ways in which it is avoided or resolved.

Chapter 6 concludes the study. Conflict areas are re-examined and shown to be associated with a number of changes currently taking place in the redistribution of several rights and duties in the domestic system. Subsequently these changes are viewed with reference to similar ones noted to be taking place elsewhere in urban populations.

The Problem

The proposition that there is currently taking place a world-wide series of changes in family patterns tending towards some type of individuated, nuclear family system, in which the keystone is the conjugal bond rather than ties of consanguinity has been advanced and discussed in a vast array of recent work. Among others, Goode (1963) referring to material describing rural and urban societies from several continents, has attempted a comprehensive documentation of this trend. Much detailed work has also centred upon the changing nature of the husband-wife relationship, the fact that in many societies the distribution of power, resources and labour between husbands and wives, both inside and outside the home, are altering. Studies such as those of Blood and Wolfe (1960) in Detroit, have indicated some of the important variables associated with these alterations and variations, for example the level of education, ethnic origin and type of occupation of the spouses. Moreover marriage is increasingly observed to be an individual contract rather than a compact between two bodies of kin.

There is ample evidence that in Africa in particular the effects have been immense of economic, demographic, political, legal and religious innovation upon systems of kinship and marriage. Some of these effects have been examined from the point of view of the changes in relationships between husbands and wives, or parents and children, as well as between members of the conjugal family and their kin. A number of general works have attempted to highlight and to document some of these trends.[5] Numerous monographs and papers have also described in more detail changes at the domestic level.[6]

Gough (1961: 640–1) has pinpointed what she considers to be the 'root cause of kinship change', precipitating the disintegration of descent groups and the functional individuation of the conjugal family. She suggests that this is the incorporation of societies into a 'unitary market system' in which goods, land, labour and other resources become privately owned and potentially marketable commodities and therefore may become fragmented and dispersed. This market system is the result of the introduction of international trade, wage-labour, cash-cropping and education. Economically and jurally men and women become increasingly independent of kin groups, as access to resources and positions of power depend more upon voluntary labour contracts and personal wealth, rather than rights

7

in jointly held family estates. The introduction of educational institutions, and of training which enables people to earn incomes and to fill new jobs, often channels talents away from the home areas and devalues the authority, knowledge and skills of the senior generation. In some cases other agencies assume the economic, political and religious functions of descent groups, leaving them with only a vestige of their traditional power. There are however instances documented in which such groups continue to operate relatively effectively in one or more areas of contemporary life, such as inheritance of property or succession to local, hereditary offices.[7] This is perhaps especially likely to occur in regions in which some highly valued good is at stake, such as modern cash crops, where land and crop are at a premium (Richards, 1940: 10; Watson, 1958: 221).

An effect of the large scale townward migration of individuals in search of new opportunities is a rapid increase in the number of first-generation city dwellers, living in conditions entirely different from those experienced in their youth. Not only are many of the new, urban migrants separated from most, if not all, of their kin, but there is a predominance of ethnically mixed neighbourhoods in many communities, even single houses containing people of different origins. Residential separation of spouses, parents and children, and the co-residence of distantly related people and strangers, over-crowding and the temporary nature of much accommodation, are common.[8] There is some evidence that household size may be related to income, people with larger incomes finding themselves housing a proportionately large number of kin.

Though people migrate to the towns to gain the rewards offered by the new educational and economic opportunities available there, effective links still join kin in the urban and rural areas. A considerable proportion of wages earned in labour centres is sent back to relatives in the villages and urban workers often maintain claims to financial security in their home villages in the form of buildings and plots.[9] In addition people in both urban and rural areas frequently see the advantages to be gained by sending their children to be reared and educated, either with kin or acquaintances in the town or country.[10] As regards domestic decision-making, family meetings may still take place and be attended by urban migrants. There is however a noted tendency for kin to have fewer controls over urban couples.

Since households of migrants are perforce relatively isolated from

8

kin, traditional patterns of kinship behaviour cannot continue to operate in their entirety. The range of kin with whom the urban migrant remains in effective contact is necessarily incomplete. These ties with kin have been seen as forming an egocentred network rather than a corporate group, comprising relationships the migrant may choose at will to activate and manipulate.[11] The lack of customary sanctions may be such that the migrant can afford to seek out some kin to carry out traditional kinship obligations on his behalf, while at the same time avoiding the acceptance of kinship obligations considered too onerous. For the urban wage-earner, personal choice is also important in choosing marriage partners, as well as kin with whom to maintain effective contacts. Though the force of customary sanctions may be breaking down, there is still evidence that in many communities bridewealth payments continue to be made, parental consent sought and given, and customary marriage rites widely performed. It is, however, the comparative ineffectiveness of the customary sanctions regulating marriage and family relationships in the towns, the individual's ability to choose to shirk responsibility and avoid obligations, allegedly resulting in the widely reported increases in marital conflict, infidelity, divorce, irregular unions, prostitution and illegitimacy, which has led some writers to deplore the state of disorganization and anomie thought to exist in some African towns. An important element in this situation may be the conflict in laws. Often there exists a plurality of legal norms and sanctions, based upon customary law, Christian Church law and statutory law which may be a copy of a colonial model.[12]

It is upon the matter of the city dweller's decisions, as to which domestic duties and family obligations to accept and which rights he or she wishes, or has the power to claim, that the crux of the problem of analysing the direction of social changes taking place in the family partly rests. The analysis of these decisions is vital to an understanding of the way in which the conjugal family is, or is not, becoming more functionally individuated and whether rights and duties based upon the conjugal tie are superseding those based upon sibling and filial bonds. The recognition and fulfilment of many domestic obligations, both conjugal and consanguine, requires the expenditure of money and time to provide the needed goods and services. Not only are the material resources in demand, such as income and living space, limited in the town, they are often pitifully inadequate to provide the necessities of life, even for close dependents. The personal conflict, ambivalence and even feelings of guilt which men feel, when faced with the problem of selecting which claims of kin to honour and which to avoid, have been frequently stressed.[13] Wife and children on the one hand and patrikin and matrikin on the other have at various times been labelled 'parasites', since they demand and consume the hard-earned income of the urban wage-earner.[14] Those who think that the man's income should be spent only on his wife and children see the claims of consanguines as a continual drain on his resources, while those who favour the opposite view, see wives as the useless drain and the kin group as the unit for common spending, saving and security, in situations where social security benefits, organised on nationwide bases, have scarcely begun.

The urban migrant has to establish his own ego-centred set of effective relationships and with regard to his available resources and power position, decide how to allot his scarce time and money and other benefits among them. To discover the source of some of the forces affecting his decisions it has been suggested that it is necessary to examine the pressures and other sets of people, to see how they try to wield an influence.[15] For though the general trends of changes taking place in African urban family life and their major correlates have been frequently indicated, the precise and detailed changes in family relationships and the position of individuals, the choices people are making in the domestic domain, their prescribed norms, expectations and activities, and the social factors influencing these, are less well documented and understood.

There is a widely held assumption that it is among the educated, urban workers that changes in family life have been most radical and shifted furthest away from traditional patterns. The particular categories of urban educated which are frequently noted as forming significant reference groups and are viewed as being in the vanguard of change, include the Civil Servants, the professionals and the university students destined to join their ranks. Two early, unpublished studies of urban educated West African couples in these categories, from Ghana and Nigeria, are those of Crabtree (1950) and Bird (1958). Emphasis has been placed in these and elsewhere upon the fact that changes in the family lives of such people appear to point towards the so-called 'Western' conjugal ideal of marriage and family life. Some writers even see the choices of the educated as being modelled on Western European stereotypes. Marriage among educated urban Africans is said to be increasingly based upon romantic ideas and companionate aims.[16]

10

In the socio-economically better-off areas of the towns, housing and circumstances are such that conjugal families generally co-reside and the number of kin who can reasonably live in the same small, two-bedroomed accommodation is limited. The resulting comparative residential separation of the conjugal family may be heralded as the emergence of the 'nuclear family'. But though the educated are thought to be at the forefront of change, on closer examination of the written evidence, the facts turn out to be relatively few, statements are sometimes imprecise and often based upon the unwarranted assumption that changes are unidimensional and in one vaguely specified direction. Accounts are often more heavily larded with references to changes in material culture, and 'style of life', than to changes in systems of domestic rights and obligations, since the former are more easily ascertainable.[17] As Gutkind (1962) pointed out, facts relating to the family in developing, urban areas of Africa are as yet few and far between, most are culled from more general works, but there is sufficient evidence to show that while the African, conjugal family may be radically changed in some ways in the new urban context, yet its members continue to retain traditional elements of their strong links with kin. When we consider only West African towns in the coastal areas, we see that a beginning has been made upon the detailed documentation of some of the changes taking place in educated, urban family life.[18] We are still far, however, from achieving the kind of sophisticated analyses which have been produced by anthropologists in the last few decades for rural systems of kinship and marriage in Africa.

MATRILINEAL SYSTEMS

Not only has it been stated that in the new African urban areas high achieved status in the new occupational system (where rank is to a large extent based upon educational attainment) is associated with radical change in domestic relationships, but it has also been proposed and to some extent demonstrated, that ethnicity, status ascribed by descent, is also an important variable affecting the kinds of changes occurring. As Goode (1963: 2) notes, family systems in various areas of the world may be moving towards similar patterns, but they begin from different starting points. A question frequently discussed is whether kin relationships in matrilineal systems can survive the impact of modern economic changes and the adaptations required by such innovations as labour migration and salaried employment.[19] There is undoubtedly considerable evidence to indicate that matriliny is particularly vulnerable to the spread of private property ownership and inequalities in the distribution of wealth. Evidence from at least fourteen different matrilineal societies subject to such changes, in Africa and elsewhere, including the Tonga, Bemba, Yao and Ndembu, has been compiled to indicate the extent to which the conjugal family is emerging, or has already emerged, as the key kinship group, with respect to residence, economic cooperation, legal responsibility and socialization, being linked to other elementary families by a narrow range of interpersonal kinship relations spreading out bilaterally (Gough, 1961: 631). For purposes of inheritance however there is a noted tendency for the matrilineage to split up into small groups of uterine siblings and their descendants rather than conjugal families. Although the trend seems similar in the several systems sufficiently well documented, the steps in the change process observed have varied and there are significant differences in the degree of change experienced, both within individual matrilineal kinship systems and between one system and another.

The one factor apparently common to all changing matrilineal systems is the strain engendered by the changes, that is between conjugal family ties on the one hand and relationships between matrikin on the other. Even within the traditional subsistence economic setting however, there is ample evidence that the conjugal family in matrilineal society is prone to a number of kinds of structural strain and problems. The phrase 'matrilineal puzzle' was coined by Richards (1950: 246) to refer to the inherent difficulty of combining recognition of descent through women with the rule of exogamous marriage, involving the question, among others, as to how descent groups can simultaneously retain control over both their male and female members, who are at once members of conjugal families and matrilineages.[20]

In the domestic sphere tension may be engendered over the use and distribution of scarce resources. As a result of the potentially conflicting claims, accusations of sorcery, poisoning and witchcraft, by the sets of people involved, both matrikin and in-laws, are said to be common. A number of authors, who have produced monographs about matrilineal systems, have concentrated to a considerable extent on documenting and analysing such tension, present both before and after widespread economic change and alterations in the modes of access to resources.[21] Role strain is often observed on the part

12

of men acting as brothers and husbands to two sets of people with conflicting expectations.[22] Conflict is frequently between two sets of would-be heirs, a man's children and his sisters' children.[23] Colson for instance has vividly illustrated the kinds of conflict situations occurring among the Plateau Tonga, under changing economic conditions, which have made possible the accumulation of wealth to support some individuals at a higher standard of living than their kin, and have enabled some to invest in capital goods and savings of permanent value. As an illustration she quotes the case of a headman who died and whose death was attributed upon divination to the hatred of his matrikin. They were angered that in a period of hunger he had bought sugar which he ate with his wife and children. 'Because of the hatred which they had for his wife, who shared these good things, they decided to kill him, so he died because of his property' (Colson, 1958: 117). Matrikin regard the wealth a man produces as part of his estate, over which they have rights of inheritance, to the exclusion of his wife and children, so they are resentful if a man uses this wealth to raise the standard of living of the latter.

The manifestation of such conflicts however, does not only occur within the rural agricultural setting, when opportunities for wage-labour and cash-cropping facilitate the accumulation of surplus wealth, but it is also observed in urban situations among educated salary-earners. Gough's comparison (1961: 649) of the matrilineal Nayar and patrilineal Tamil Brahmans of Tanjore district in South India provides a case in point, showing the kind of situations and tensions which may arise for urban migrants and how those experienced by people from an area practising matrilineal descent and inheritance appear to be aggravated. Both of these castes have combined salary-earning with land-owning. The urban Nayar salary-earner may spend much of his earnings upon his wife and children living with him and be reluctant to contribute to the investments of his natal matrilineage, since such contributions would detract from the amount of resources available for his own children. On becoming head of his own matrilineal descent group he may even be tempted to use profits from the group's estate for the benefit of his own wife and children. In such conditions, we are told, acute tensions arise between the matrikin of the male members. On the other hand among the urban salary-earners from patrilineal groups, investment in lineage enterprises and in the conjugal family are not in conflict to such an extent. As Gough points out, the greater apparent fragility of the matrilineal system may be basically due to the structure of the conjugal family, which is the typical domestic group set up by the socially and spatially mobile individual, migrating and working in the new labour market. While in the patrilineal system this unit may operate as a minimal segment of a lineage, the conjugal family in the matrilineal system can scarcely do so. An increase in conjugal family financial solidarity and loyalty is likely to be at the expense of the economic solidarity of matrilineal ties (Schneider, 1961: 16).

The general features of the direction and magnitude of changes taking place in African systems of kinship and marriage, consequent upon widespread migration, wage-labour, urbanization and education have been variously documented. A number of observers see the urban educated as being at the forefront of a series of changes, conceptualizing the process as being one of a growing similarity to the family systems of industrialized Europe and America, the outcome of a process of 'Westernization'. There is however a lack of detailed observation and analysis and as Goode (1963: 18–19) has warned,

Even the common assertion that many countries are now becoming 'Westernized' may obscure our view of these processes by leading us to believe the countries are changing under the impact of Western influence, whereas often the most important pressure is nationalist and indigenous.

Obviously it is necessary, in examining such domestic change processes, to take into account both the effects of external innovations and of indigenous pressures. There are indications that, in systems characterized by matrilineal descent and inheritance, change is more likely to be conflict-prone than in systems characterized by patriliny, since the conjugal family in matrilineal society is already subject to strain through the diverse loyalties and duties of the husband and wife. It is the strengthening of nuclear family solidarity and the incipient shift towards father-to-child inheritance, which has led observers to remark on the apparent trend towards 'patriliny' in matrilineal systems.

Before proceeding to examine the conjugal family relationships of a sample of educated urban migrants, from a society characterized by matrilineal descent, an explicit account is needed of the methods of data collection and the conceptual framework used in their classification and analysis.

The Problem

One of the initial decisions in the present enquiry was to avoid choosing between a qualitative or quantitative approach and to reject the separation of the two as a false dichotomy. Indeed one of the earliest sophisticated studies of African domestic organization which wedded qualitative with quantitative material was carried out among the Akan, so there was a relatively early case of this dual approach to serve as an example in the same ethnic area (Fortes, 1949b). Thus it was decided at the outset to collect and combine in the final analysis several kinds of data including a limited number of case studies of Akan couples, supplemented by further observational and interview data from Akan families and secondly a survey of married men's reports about themselves and aspects of their domestic relationships.

The Akan married couples selected for detailed study were contacted through the assistance of officials working in government institutions. The general purposes of the study were explained to them and they were asked to suggest suitable couples in which the husband was a Senior Civil Servant and both husband and wife were Akan. Altogether multiple interviews with eighteen couples were obtained in this manner. The data collected from twelve of these couples was considered sufficiently comprehensive for these case studies to be used as a panel for detailed analysis.[24]

The husbands in these couples were between thirty and forty-five years of age, university graduates, and employed in government institutions as professionals and administrators. Their wives, whose ages ranged from the late twenties to early forties, had all been educated or had some kind of vocational training beyond the elementary level. They lived in the suburbs of Accra and had families of two to six children, including toddlers and teenagers. They had been married for periods ranging from four to eighteen years and all but two of the couples had children under five. Ethnically the husbands and wives were distributed among the several Akan sub-groups, being Fanti, Ashanti, Brong, Akwapim, Akim and Kwahu. Only a few of their fathers had been in salaried employment. Several were illiterate, as were most of their mothers. Socially and geographically they were mobile people, without exception higher up the occupational and income ladder than their parents and separated from their home towns by more or less long journeys. All the husbands had reached their present positions by dint of shifting from one institution to another, both in Ghana and abroad, to gain higher educational qualifications and better jobs. Thus the systematic field work began with the repeated interviewing, relatively unstructured and in depth, of a number of Akan husbands and wives. Obviously from the nature of the situation, the kinds of people under study and the topics of interest it was impossible to rely solely upon participant observation for the systematic collection of the case study material required, though much incidental relevant information was collected in this latter manner. The answers to questions had to be the main material for analysis. The interviews held for collecting the data were of the type which has been termed 'focussed' – that is most of the topics were selected by the interviewer but the questions were mainly such that the responses were left free. Domestic activities among the urban educated are obviously of such a private nature as to require a process of informal probing, if information relevant to a particular study is to be gained. These interviews were mainly held in private with individual husbands and wives in their offices and homes or with couples together. Often when rapport was good the interviews developed into the kind of 'non-directive' interview in which the respondents were raising their own topics for discussion which were almost always pertinent to the main themes of the enquiry.[25] Frequently the topics raised aroused considerable personal feelings. The first topic of the interview for each spouse was usually his or her own personal life history, including data on family of origin, education, travels, jobs held, marriages and present occupation. This led on to the collection of data on each spouse's kin, their places of residence, occupations, schooling and maintenance of contact with the respondent.

With the wife the history of the household was also discussed, from its gradual setting up, through its various changes in place and composition, to the present setting. This included births of children and changes in household composition occasioned by the coming and going of kin and servants. A number of topics were raised with each spouse, including contacts with neighbours, colleagues, spouse's colleagues, voluntary associations and friends. With regard to current family practices questions were asked about the following – the family budget, decision-making, child-care, chore-performance and spending of leisure. The concern was the spouses' use of their resources in time, and material goods and their allocation to a number of roles. Throughout the interviews with the spouses an attempt was made to note all open and oblique

16

expressions of each spouse's attitudes to his or her own and spouse's roles.

In the preliminary stages these repeated interviews were carried out:

(a) to provide descriptive case studies of families;

(b) to help in the formulation of a relevant conceptual framework for the classification of both case and survey data;

(c) to serve as the basis for the construction of a more highly structured questionnaire;

(d) to gain insight into what might be the relevant social factors associated with differences and changes in aspects of the conjugal relationships under scrutiny;

(e) to evolve suitable indices for quantifying and comparing the dependent variables under study, that is aspects of conjugal and spouse-kin interaction;

(f) to generate hypotheses regarding correlations between one set of variables and another.

Certainly the case studies provided, as had been envisaged, intimate descriptive accounts of the histories of a number of conjugal families from the points of view of both the husbands and wives. They provided qualitative material about domestic organization – the household division of labour, budgeting and decision-making. What however proved to be crucial was that they indicated in addition, with varying degrees of vividness, how the actors *felt* about themselves as husbands, wives, workers, parents, kin and affines and also how they *felt* about the other people in their domestic groups and their kin and in-laws. In addition the importance of reference groups of various kinds and their significance to the dissatisfied actor's way of talking about his or her own behaviour and that of the partner was seen. In other words valuable data was provided about the *orientations* of the husbands and wives towards their own domestic roles and those of the other members of their role sets. Moreover as the data began to be analysed they revealed potential areas of conflict between husbands wives and kin as well as illustrating modes of conflict resolution and avoidance. Indeed because the interviews occurred over extended periods of several months to a year it was possible to document the course of one or two domestic conflicts and events leading to changes in the relationships of some of the husbands and wives.

In retrospect it was perhaps this aspect of the panel study which was the most valuable; that is it provided 'dynamic' data; information not only about the changes in conjugal relationships and households during the months of interviewing and in the previous years which were recalled, but clues were given as to certain underlying aspects of the family systems under study – the nature of structural tensions and change. For the types of configurations of relationships were indicated which were potentially conflict prone and unstable due to internal and external pressures, as well as those which appeared harmonious and unlikely to change. At the same time actors' strategies were revealed which they used with a view to enhancing their own positions by increasing their shares of desired rewards and if necessary alleviating any felt sense of dissatisfaction or insecurity. Thus the nature of the material collected led to the consideration of domestic tension, conflict, power and change. Indeed these emerged as some of the central themes in the case studies and it was from the consideration of these that Chapter 5 evolved. Because data of so many kinds were collected from both husbands and wives it was possible to assess however roughly the levels of tension manifest in particular relationships and the pressures towards change and the directions in which change was desired. These data were collected – through formal questioning, informal probing and observation on a wide range of topics and the recording of incidental comments – revealing attitudes, aspirations, regrets, dissatisfactions and intentions, as well as the recording of past and present events. Unfortunately the crucial nature of tension levels and expressions of conflict was only fully realized at an advanced stage of the field work, after the survey described below had been designed and carried out. Thus no quantitative data was collected in the subsequent survey of Senior Civil Servants which might have given an indication as to the more general incidence and manifestations of such conjugal conflict.

One very serious problem which arose upon completion of the panel study was how to utilize the material to the full, while at the same time completely retaining the anonymity of the informants as promised to them. I have as far as possible tried to do both with varying degrees of success by transposing all the interview data given, that is changing all names and details which are not absolutely relevant to the context of the situation. Thus the *dramatis personae* have been changed somewhat but the glimpses of domestic dramas and actors' comments and relationships with each other have been portrayed as far as possible as they appeared to be in real life. It is however this paramount consideration of retaining the anonymity of the respondents which has prevented the fuller and more detailed presentation of these cases.

The qualitative data from this panel study of couples, in which both husbands and wives were interviewed repeatedly over relatively long periods of time, was supplemented by information given during single and multiple informal interviews held with individual husbands and wives in the same occupational categories. Overy forty such husbands and wives were interviewed altogether including several Ga and Ewe as well as Akan. These people were contacted in various ways, some through acquaintances, others through visits paid to government organizations. The same kinds of topics were dealt with as in the panel study but of course in a more curtailed manner. Sometimes only one or two out of the many topics listed above were touched upon. Data selected from some of these interviews have been used to illustrate the points made in Chapters 3 and 4 regarding achievement of Senior Civil Service status, getting married and forming a household and then ways in which resources are allocated.

The survey of Senior Civil Servants was not begun until the interviewing of the panel of couples was well under way and the main lines of enquiry had been decided upon. The sample selected was comparatively homogeneous. The survey was of the kind which has been called 'analytic, relational...set up specifically to explore relationships between particular variables...less oriented towards representativeness and more towards finding associations and explanations' (Oppenheim, 1969: 9). In other words the sample chosen was not selected for its random representative character nor was it meant to be used to make inferences about the total Senior Civil Service population of Ghana, but it was designed to obtain data for what has been likened to 'the poor man's experiment'. Propositions about the possible interrelationships between certain variables arising from the study of individual case histories could be explored on a somewhat larger albeit more superficial body of data. The independent variables of primary interest were ethnicity and the educational experience of the couples' forebears. The dependent variables were the dimensions of conjugal and kin relationships chosen for measurement and comparison.

Thus questionnaires were distributed to Senior Civil Servants working in a number of selected government institutions in Accra. (See Appendix for a copy of the questionnaire.) These included a bank, a hospital and several secondary schools and government departments. They were chosen partly with a view to including men in different professions such as medicine, accountancy, law and education as well as administration. Three hundred and forty eight questionnaires were delivered, both by post and personally together with letters explaining the general purpose of the survey. Of these self-administered questionnaires nearly seventy per cent were returned, half of them by post and the rest were collected after one or more personal calls. One hundred and eighty of the questionnaires returned were from married men.

Men below the age of twenty-five and over fifty, and earning salaries of less than ₡1,360 or more than ₡4,500[26] were eliminated from the original sample, so as to exclude the extremes of age and status ranking.

The data from the eighty five Akan civil servants who responded has been used in Chapter 3, which discusses their origins, achievement of educational qualifications and government jobs and getting married. In the subsequent chapters only the data from the sixty-one Akan husbands with Akan wives has been tabulated.[27]

THE CONCEPTUAL FRAMEWORK

The two variables which require specification for our present purposes are the degree to which the conjugal family forms a functionally discrete unit and the extent to which the husband and wife share domestic tasks, resources and decision-making with each other. Much of the terminology adopted in descriptions of the conjugal family in particular cultural environments has been found inadequate for the detailed documentation and comparison of types of husband–wife relationships and the nature of the links between spouses and their kin, either cross-culturally or in an urban environment with a heterogeneous population and characterized by rapid social changes. Widespread concern over this lack of adequate analytical tools is indicated by the stress placed in a number of recent writings, upon the problem of the clarification of terms, which remains one of the first difficulties the research worker encounters, either in the attempt to synthesize previous accounts or to present his own field material (e.g. Adams, 1967).[28]

A major concern in the description of family systems is to document which actors, in their several roles as spouses, kin and affines of various categories, are actually or potentially responsible for the performance of a number of vital domestic functions. Since many rights

20

and duties may be held by more than one person, each area of functioning needs to be examined separately to see who are the actors who may serve as potential substitutes for, or act in consort with, each other, in the holding of particular rights and duties and performance of specified tasks. This kind of analysis has been carried out in the most detailed manner for stable, rural, kinship systems, in particular those characterized by unilineal descent groups. In such studies the sets of kin who share rights and responsibilities with regard to land-ownership, use and inheritance, debts, maintenance of children, care of widows and so on, are very precisely defined, often according to status by descent – for instance the delineation of the groups of classificatory siblings with a common grandparent or more remote ancestor, who are coparceners to an estate or potential parent surrogates to each other's children (e.g. Evans Pritchard 1940; Fortes 1945, 1949).

The examination of the incidence of the sharing of rights and duties and the potential substitutability of actors in the domestic domain has not been confined however, to the study of lineage systems alone. Examples of the habitual substitution of individuals acting in the parental and filial capacities with respect to child-training, termed fostering, has been provided recently among the Gonja of Northern Ghana by Esther Goody (1966, 1969).[29] The difficulties inherent in comparable analyses of urban domestic life are only now beginning to be met (Gutkind, 1963: 165). Some of the discussions of the content and norms of the relationships between urban-dwellers and members of their kin networks however, point in this direction, such as the studies of the maintenance of adult, married children by their parents and vice versa (e.g. Sussman, 1953). In such cases attention focuses upon the extension of rights and obligations attached to conjugal, parental and filial roles across the boundaries of the elementary family. This is essentially what is required for studies of the continuity of 'extended family' norms and activities and any kind of precise quantification and comparison of the functional individuation of conjugal families.

Adopting the earlier usage of Weber (1947)[30] and Redfield (1947), the terms *open* and *closed* have been used, to refer to the presence or absence of this phenomenon (Farber, 1966).[31] In pursuit of precision and objectivity however, we need to admit at the outset that, just as societies may differ in the extent to which they prescribe or act out *closed* conjugal family relationships (Farber, 1966: 80), so in societies undergoing rapid social change, like the one under study, there may be differences in the degree of *closure* exhibited by neighbouring conjugal families, subject to a variety of social pressures. Moreover, the degree of *closure* apparent for different functions may vary.

Accordingly in this study a number of activity areas have been examined in which there may be the assumption of rights and obligations by kin, such as in rearing each other's children, maintaining one another, and joint ownership and management of resources. Thus in the survey of Senior Civil Servants questions were asked about the frequency and amount of remittances sent to help and maintain kin; about the number and categories of relatives' children who had been educated and whether property was jointly owned with kin (see questions 12, 13, 14, 15, 16, 23 in the questionnaire in the Appendix pp. 162 ff). At one point an index of financial *openness* or *closure* in these several areas was devised by scoring the various responses to these questions. This index was meant to give an overall indication of the extent to which husbands were educating and maintaining kin and owning property with them. (The mode of calculating the score is given on p. 165 of the Appendix.)

The extent to which spouses act as substitutes for each other, sharing rights and duties and the performance of tasks was also examined. Relevant to the method of the enquiry is the analysis by Herbst of Australian family data (in Oeser and Hammond, 1954), in which three quantified variables were used to describe and compare conjugal relationships. These included the sharing and joint performance of several kinds of tasks, the type of power relationship and the degree of tension apparent. A subsequent work in this area, that of Bott (1957), carried out on London families, went a step further in its attempt to relate a variable aspect of the conjugal relationship, degree of *segregation* of roles, to the kind of relationships obtaining among people in the spouses' social field. She referred to marital relationships as being *joint* or *segregated*, depending upon the predominance of complementary, independent or joint types of organisation. She used 'complementary organisation' to refer to cases in which the activities of husband and wife were different and separate, but fitted together to form a whole. 'Independent organisation' was used to indicate cases in which activities were carried out separately by spouses, without reference to each other. 'Joint organisation' meant that activities were carried out by husband and wife together or the same activity was carried out by either partner at different times. Herbst and a number of subsequent contri-

22

butors to the subject have stressed the importance of separating out a number of activity fields when attempting such classifications of conjugal relationships. Bond (1967) for instance, using data collected from an Oxford housing estate, demonstrated that there may be considerable variation in the degree of *segregation* observed for different kinds of conjugal activities. Similarly Platt (1969) has pointed out the difficulties inherent in regarding *jointness* as a single dimension of conjugal relationships.

In this study, in assessing the *joint* or *segregated* nature of the conjugal relationship for a particular area of functioning the question asked was whether the husband and wife used a resource or performed a task interchangeably, together or separately. This included the division of labour in the home, the joint or separate management of money and goods and whether the wife, as well as the husband, was employed and spent money on the household needs.

Thus the questionnaire incorporated a number of questions intended to elicit this kind of information. Once more an attempt was made to devise suitable indices for the comparison of degrees of *jointness* and *segregation* in several areas of behaviour. Husbands were asked to indicate how often they had done seventeen different household chores since they married (question 29, see Appendix p. 164). Their responses were totalled to give a chore participation score (see Appendix p. 165). Secondly an index of the wife's participation in financial provision for the household was devised, based on her husband's responses concerning the relative amount she contributed to eight basic domestic items including food, transport, clothes and fuel (see question 18 in the questionnaire p. 163, and the Wife's Financial Provision Score Appendix p. 165).

As it had become obvious from the interviews that patterns of financial provision for the household were likely to be quite different from those concerning financial management another index of the spouses' financial behaviour was devised; this time to indicate the extent to which husband and wife spent, owned and saved jointly. This was devised from responses to questions about knowledge of spouse's spending and joint ownership of property or accounts (see questions 20–3 pp. 163–4 and the Financial Management Score p. 165).

As mentioned above, unfortunately no index was devised to assess or compare the incidence and levels of conjugal tension among the married civil servants included in the survey.[32] They were however asked a question about modes of decision-making in their households (see question 19 p. 163). From their responses to this a rough classification could be made as to whether they said they reached their major household decisions after joint discussion – a *syncratic pattern*; whether the husband decided some issues and the wife decided others – an *automomic pattern*; or whether the husband said that he decided all the main issues – a *husband-dominant* or *autocratic pattern*.

Using the two variables concerned with the substitutability of the roles of spouses and kin, four types of conjugal family systems, associated with any chosen activity area are distinguishable. The types are tabulated below in the form of a two way property space.

Table 1.1. *Types of conjugal family role systems*

Husband and wife hold domestic
rights/duties jointly.

		Yes	No
Spouse and Kin hold domestic rights/duties jointly.	Yes	Open/ Joint	Open/ Segregated
	No	Closed/ Joint	Closed/ Segregated

After choosing a number of areas of family functioning, such as child-rearing, domestic chore performance, financial provision for conjugal family members and so on, detailed items of data may be classified in such a way as to facilitate, not only synchronic description of individual conjugal family systems and the distribution of selected traits of conjugal relationships in a given population, but also the study of changes observed, revealing the direction in which changes are taking place, in one or more areas of behaviour or norms, whether to a more or less *closed* or more or less *joint* pattern. Similarly such a framework for classifying data may assist in the assessment of the functional relationships between different types of behaviour. Thus the present data, both descriptions of single conjugal families from the panel study and the distribution of certain traits from the survey, have been classified and examined in this way. As well as providing an account of the 'normal' behaviour patterns in the selected population this exercise has also served partly to demonstrate the directions and correlates of change.

Such an approach to the classification of data avoids a number of confusions based upon assumptions implicit elsewhere, such as that *closure* and *jointness* are necessarily correlated. For instance Farber (1966: 80) appears to assume that a *closed* conjugal family system is correlated with 'togetherness' in household tasks, in leisure, in emotional support and decision-making. Secondly it makes no assumptions as to the directions of change. It was rather thought from the beginning that change, if it obtained, might be in any direction, depending upon the traditional 'starting point', and the pressures causing the changes. In addition it is assumed that husbands and wives have a limited amount of finite resources, and that choices have to be made continually with respect to the allocation of these in the fulfilment of certain potentially conflicting domestic rights and obligations.

The focus of the study, the dimensions of conjugal and kin relationships to be examined and the mode of classifying data, have now been defined. In Chapter 2 a brief paradigm of elements of the customary Akan institutions of matriliny and marriage is first presented, with particular reference to the two variables in which we are interested; that is the degree of *segregation* of interests and activities in the conjugal relationship and the extent to which the conjugal family is an *open* or *closed* unit according to the criteria outlined. Next some of the innovations effecting change in traditional Akan institutions over the past four hundred years are indicated. This forms the baseline, as it were, for the subsequent study of domestic relationships among educated city dwellers, who come from the several Akan regions.

NOTES

[1] See Goody J. (1956, 1958, 1959, 1961, 1969) and Goody J. & E. (1966, 1967).

[2] A selection of Akan literature is given in the bibliography.

[3] See also Richards (1939, 1940, 1950); Mitchell (1956, 1962); Turner (1957); Colson (1958); Marwick (1965); Long (1968).

[4] Oppong (1969a & b, 1970, 1971, 1972).

[5] These include among others Phillips (1953); Forde (ed.) (1956); Southall (ed.) (1961) and Lloyd (1967).

[6] The following are examples of these Hunter (1936); Richards (1940); Barnes (1951); Marris (1961); Bernard (1968).

[7] For example Ashanti chiefship described by Busia (1951).

[8] The following have variously commented upon these phenomena, Hellman (1948); Busia (1950); Banton (1957); Acquah (1958); Southall & Gutkind (1957); Reader (1961); Mayer (1961); Pons (1969).

[9] See Wilson (1941: 40, 52); Barnes (1951: 85).

[10] For instance Banton (1957: 207) notes the numbers of children sent to live in Freetown to attend school, who are lodged as wards with acquaintances of their parents. See also Marris (1961: 56–66) who comments on the percentage of children fostered by kin in a Lagos sample, and Comhaire (1956b) on the rearing of Leopoldville children.

[11] See Southall (1961: 34) also Gutkind (1962, 1965a, b & c).

[12] For discussions of such conflict of laws see Phillips (1953) and Allott (1969).

[13] For example see Richards (1940: 27).

[14] The question of 'parasitism' has been discussed among others by Busia (1951); Baker and Bird (1959) and Comhaire (1956: 49).

[15] For an example of a discussion of urban networks and change in relation to migrant Xhosa see Mayer (1961) Part v.

[16] Thus Jahoda (1959) in analysing Ghanaian newspaper letters, writes of the 'adoption of Western norms (and) values', by young Ghanaians and 'the taking over of the notion of romantic love and marriage as a partnership of like-minded individuals'. Similarly Little (1965) refers to West Africa, 'where to an increasing extent educated young people apparently want a companionate marriage on Western lines'. Again in analysing the responses of a number of young Sierra Leoneans the latter comments that the data, 'seem to confirm that in Freetown the attitude of educated young people towards marriage is strongly Western' (1966).

[17] Thus the Smythes have given a highly detailed description of the material culture of the Nigerian elite in Chapter 9, 'How the Elite Live', of their book (1960: 137–53).

[18] Recent examples of such studies may be found in Lloyd (ed. 1966) and Miner (ed.) (1967). Caldwell's demographic surveys have revealed areas of attitudinal change in Ghana (e.g. 1965, 1966, 1968).

[19] Douglas (1969) has recently enumerated several of the 'prophets of doom' of matriliny. See Long (1968: 3).

[20] This is the first of Schneider's criteria for the maintenance of matrilineal descent groups. 'Matrilineal descent groups depend for their continuity and operation on retaining control over both male and female members' (1961: 8). He also goes on to enumerate a number of sources of friction and strain including the following facts that: (a) 'there is always potential conflict between the bonds of marriage and the bonds of descent' (1961: 17); (b) 'the bonds which may tend to develop between a child and his father tend to be in direct competition with the authority of the child's matrilineal descent group' (1961: 21); (c) and again 'In matrilineal descent groups the emotional interest of the father in his own children constitutes a source of strain.'

[21] Monographs in which such psychological and social strains and tensions have been vividly documented include Malinowski (1926); Fortune (1932); Mitchell (1956); Turner (1957); Colson (1958); Field (1969) and Marwick (1965).

[22] See for example Mitchell (1962: 30) and Long (1968: 193–4).

[23] Kluckhohn and Leighton (1946: 60); Alland (1965: 495–502).

[24] The remaining six cases were considered inadequate for this purpose. For one reason or another the data collected were insufficient. Two couples after a number of interviews had more or less declined to continue by making it increasingly difficult to arrange any further appointments to see them. In the remaining four cases the data collected was not comparable in kind and quantity to that collected from the twelve panel couples either because the couple had no children and had not been married very long or because they were contacted towards the end of the year's field work and the data collected were incomplete.

[25] Attempts to use formal interview schedules during interviews with these couples were not found to be satisfactory, since they disturbed the intimacy and rapport essential in the recording of such domestic detail over a prolonged period of time.

[26] At the time of the survey the value of the cedi was approximately one dollar.

[27] The Ga and Ewe materials collected at the same time have been analysed elsewhere

and when relevant to the text they are mentioned, especially in so far as they serve to highlight differences between the matrilineal Akan couples and the rest. The total number of Akan respondents in several tables is only 58 or 59 instead of 61, owing to the fact that all questionnaires were not fully complete.

[28] For a fuller discussion of this dilemma see Oppong (1971b).

[29] Cf. also an account of fostering among the neighbouring Dagomba (Oppong 1974).

[30] Weber defined *open* and *closed* relationships as follows, 'A social relationship...will be known as *open* to those on the outside, if, and insofar as, participation in the mutually oriented social conduct, relevant to its subjective meaning, is, according to its system of authority, not denied to anyone who is inclined to participate and is actually in a position to do so. The relationship will be known as *closed*, on the other hand to those on the outside, so far as and to the extent that within the range of its subjective meaning and the validity of its authority the participation of certain persons is exluded, limited, or subject to conditions' (1962: 97).

[31] Farber (1966) has pointed out that the distinction between an *open* group and a *closed* group has long been useful for describing variation and change in family life. He defines the terms in relation to nuclear family functioning as follows: 'When family relations are relatively *open*, the spouse and parent roles extend beyond the nuclear family to other kinship groups in the community. (The spouse and parent roles refer to rights and obligations about authority, family division of labour, child care, and financial support.) In societies characterized by *open* families the roles of uncle, aunt, grandparent, brother, sister, and cousin embody rights and obligations for enacting some spouse–parent roles in families of procreation other than their own. The borderline between the individual's own family of procreation and a kinsman's family of procreation is not well defined' (pp. 79–80).

[32] A study of potential areas of marital strain and tension has however been made using data collected during the field work period from a sample of university students. The data analysed there are prescribed norms for conjugal roles (Oppong, 1972a) rather than actual behaviour.

2

CUSTOM AND INNOVATION

The Akan of Ghana number some three million or more and constitute over two-fifths of the total population of the country.[1] They inhabit the southern half of the country stretching from the coast in the south, to the Gonja state in the north, and from the Volta in the east to the Ivory Coast border in the west. They are divided by differences of dialect into a number of subgroups. The dialect groups include in order of size – Asante (Ashanti), Fante–Agona, Boron (Brong), Akyem, Akuapem (Akwapim) Kwawu (Kwahu), Wasa, Nzema–Evalue, Ahanta and Sahwi (Sefwi).[2] They are mainly farmers, those on the coast being fishermen, and live traditionally in nucleated settlements occupied by members of a number of exogamous matrilineages, which are localized segments of dispersed matriclans. Culturally the peoples comprising the Akan are homogeneous to a high degree. Their traditional political, economic, legal, religious and kinship systems, their geography, material culture, history and art have been documented by many writers, both indigenous and foreign.[3]

MATRILINY

As Fortes has noted (1970a: 138) the Akan have long been well known outside West Africa, as much for their matrilineal kinship institutions as for their political and military exploits. The tracing of matrilineal descent is important in almost every aspect of their social life, in establishing personal status as royal, commoner, or slave; in validating the right to succeed to political office; in claiming citizenship of a particular state; in the utilization of lineage farm land and houses and in the inheritance of property. The most inclusive matrilineal descent group (maximal lineage) found in a community has important political, religious, legal and economic functions. Its members have a single legal personality *vis à vis* outsiders, in the sense that they are corporately responsible for each other's debts and wrongs, and borrowing between members is not considered to create a debt.[4] It has a male and female head, who represent it in their ritual and political capacities. Common lineage property includes a house, where the lineage head may live and lineage meetings be held. In a room in this house the blackened ancestral stools, consecrated to past lineage heads, are kept and receive libations and sacrifices. They form an important focus of spiritual unity. The lineage also has its own deity, cared for by a priest or priestess of the lineage. The disposal of dead members is a prime responsibility of the lineage and the head supervises the performance of funeral rites. While the strongly sanctioned exogamy rules and incest prohibitions demonstrate the unity of the living descent group, beliefs about the life after death among the lineage ancestors indicate its spiritual continuity.

Segments of the most inclusive matrilineage in a community are defined by reference to a recent common ancestress, to whom members trace matrilineal descent. These are often said to be people whose maternal grandmothers and mother's mother's brothers, were brothers and sisters and grew up together with one mother in one household. It is in this 'family' unit that control over people and property are effectively held at the domestic level.[5] The head of this group is a *wofa*, mother's brother, not a lineage head. He is the guardian of dependent members, accepting and offering marriage payments, and in former times arranging cross-cousin marriages and holding the power to pawn junior members when necessary. The elementary units of which this lineage segment and the maximal lineage is formed consist of uterine siblings, brothers and sisters and the sister's children, who perpetuate the group as heirs and successors of their maternal uncles. The absolutely binding tie within the matrilineage is that between mother and child. The relationship between children of the same mother is one of equality and solidarity, a unity expressed in the classificatory kinship terminology. Their properties are considered to be joint, their loyalty and trust in each other paramount over all other interests.

Land, houses, gold, cloth, and other goods may be classified as stool property, family property and private property.[6] The first category includes the profits of trading, court fines, gifts, death duties, gold and timber concessions, which go directly to the stool treasury (Danquah, 1928: 197–8, 206–7). The main category of family property is lineage land, used by lineage members for their food farms. Rights in individually acquired property of all kinds tend to be severely restricted and to consist of limited usufruct during the owner's life-time. Ability to dispose of property such as farms, by gift or will, depends upon the knowledge and public consent of the owner's matrilineage. Property which remains to be inherited at death becomes either stool or matrilineage property.[7]

As well as being the unit for the ownership of property, with control over the disposition of member's individually acquired property, the matrilineage segment is also the unit within which inheritance occurs. The real successor to any deceased person is the mother, if living. The heir chosen to act as custodian of the property and also successor to the responsibilities of the deceased is the oldest surviving sibling, or, failing that, a sister's child. The sibling group for this purpose, comprises the children of full sisters, with a common maternal grandmother. Bosman in 1705 commented on this as an 'odd adjustment of the right of inheritance'.[8]

MARRIAGE

The absolute prerequisite to legitimate childbirth is the performance of a nubile girl's public puberty ceremony, in which both her paternal and maternal kin play a part. After this has been performed she may marry, but whether she formally marries or not, her children will be socially acceptable lineage members. The partners to most marriages have tended in the past to come from the same or neighbouring communities and cross-cousin marriage is reported to be a preferred type of union. The former fact enables spouses to reside with matrikin and yet fulfil their conjugal rights and duties. The latter is said to help resolve any latent conflicts of loyalties between conjugal and filial ties on the one hand and relationships between matrikin on the other.

A marriage contract is sealed by the giving and acceptance of drinks, the normal procedure for witnessing and sealing a transaction, and may be publicized by a wedding feast. The essential element of the marriage contract is the gift of 'drinks' (*tiri nsa*) by the head of the groom's lineage to the head of the bride's lineage. This is accompanied by the handing over of small gifts to close kin, father and matrikin as well as a gift to the bride herself. In the actual bestowal of women as wives, fathers have about as much say as mothers and their brothers (Fortes, 1970a: 213).

The marriage transfer gives to the husband exclusive sexual rights and claims to the domestic services of his wife, and to the wife, rights to economic support for herself and her children. Though

most marriages are monogamous, all unions are potentially polygynous and we are told that permanent cohabitation or procreation
with a minimum of formalities or public rites may be practised
with relatively little prejudice to the social status of the wives and
children concerned.[9] If parents do not marry then public recognition
of paternity on the father's part may give the child full birth status
rights.[10] Just as conjugal relationships may be entered with a
minimum of formality, so they may be, and often are,[11] broken
with comparative ease. Divorce is effected by the refunding of the
tiri nsa payment, through the husband and wife's guardians and
lineage heads. Accounts may also be reckoned to find out which
party is in debt to the other. Whichever partner is in debt pays
the other the due amount, so as not to be accused of accumulating
wealth from another's matrilineage.[12] The wife is not at liberty to
remarry until this bill of expenses and the *head money* are repaid.
Although divorce rests entirely with the couple it is always preceded
by a family meeting, attended by the heads of the two lineages
concerned, who hear the grievances and try to reconcile the couple.
Husbands and wives are not regarded as two persons in one as
a result of the marriage contract. The interests of the husband,
apart from their conjugal life, are not thought to be part of the
wife's business. She is considered to have her own separate rights
to look after. This contrasts strongly with the concept of the lineage
unit as one person. Moreover, married people customarily have no
joint property, each retaining his or her own goods, and they may
not inherit each other's property at the death of one intestate.[13]

Even joint productive effort does not result in joint ownership,
for property a wife helps her husband to acquire and maintain,
belongs only to the husband.[14] Spouses are not liable for the payment
of each others debts, except those incurred by the wife for purposes
of maintaining herself and children.[15] As Sarbah remarks, wives
are of different 'families' from their husbands and can acquire and
hold property apart from them and they have their own 'families'
to fall back on. The economic rights of wives and children consist
essentially in rights to maintenance, accommodation if necessary,
and medical care. Those rights, are not extinguished by death. The
only legitimate means whereby a wife or child may obtain part of
or rights in a man's property, are by gift or will before his death,
ratified by the matrikin or through the claim to maintenance and
accommodation from the deceased's heir. Sons have the right to
a life interest in a dwelling house built by their father and the right

to occupy his family home during their good conduct (Sarbah, 1897: 90, 105). Indeed foremost among the moral responsibilities of an heir is the care of his dead brother's or uncle's widow and orphans. The heir is even referred to by them as husband and father, and should act as such, to the extent of cohabiting with the widow. Should she however, choose not to remarry into her husband's matrilineage, she ought still to be provided with the necessities of life (Danquah, 1928: 161). But if a wife or child dispute that they have a right to inherit a share of the property they may have helped to acquire, they are unlikely to succeed, for a wife has no interest in property built by herself and her husband on his family land, except as an occupant (Sarbah, 1897: 191–3). In fact a widow may even be compelled to return all the gifts she has received from her husband.[16]

THE HOUSEHOLD

In the relatively stable towns and villages the majority of the population has traditionally tended to live in households inhabited by matrilineage segments, that is uterine descendants of a common grandmother or great-grandmother, married adults living with their matrikin, rather than with their spouses.[17] It is in the farm hamlets at a distance from home-towns that conjugal families tend most frequently to co-reside. The normal practice, when spouses live in different houses in the same community, is for the wife to stay with her matrikin by day, sending cooked food to her husband, and going to sleep in his house at night, except when she is menstruating. This domestic residential pattern, whereby several female matrikin generally co-reside, facilitates the assistance of one by another and sharing of household chores and child-minding.

The majority of adults are gainfully employed. Women as well as men farm, especially in the southern Akan area, where planting of food crops remains to a great extent the responsibility of the women.[18] The heavy involvement of women in agriculture may trace back to the period when men were mainly hunters and warriors. The idea that the man provides the meat and the women the food, dies hard. On the coast, where men fish, women are engaged in fish-selling as well as the cultivation of food crops. Though women work outside the home, on the farm and in the market, it is not customary for men to do any household chores. There are usually several adult women in each compound responsible for these tasks, who are helped by the children in the household. The outcome of the women's hard work and enterprise as farmers and traders, their control of property separately from their husbands and the social and economic support of their matrikin, is that Akan women are widely noted for their social and economic independence.[19] Some elderly women head their own houses of matrikin. In fact matrilineage membership, with its attached permanent rights in the use of land and houses, provides enduring security for women and their children. The customary ambition of Akan women, for themselves and their daughters, is to bring forth and strengthen their lineages.

MATRILINEAL AND CONJUGAL OBLIGATIONS

In his capacity as matrikinsman, senior brother or maternal uncle, an Akan man has considerable responsibilities for the maintenance and training of the dependent women and children under his care. The latter include his mother (own and classificatory) and sisters (full and classificatory), younger brothers and uterine nephews and nieces.

As a husband he has wives to maintain and in addition he has an important part to play in the technical and moral training of his own children, in providing them with the assets needed for the transition to responsible adulthood, even though, as a general rule, he is unable to pass on to them his own rank, office and property.[20]

Ideally a boy should be with his father in his formative years and in practice he often is, though to some extent responsibility for children is divided between their fathers and their mothers and mothers' kin.[21] Both in his paternal and avuncular roles an Akan man has important functions with respect to the allocation of resources and the wielding of authority. Women, in their roles as matrikin owe their primary allegiance to their mothers, siblings and mother's siblings, and in their roles as wives to their husbands. A number of customary mechanisms serve to minimize any potential elements of strain, experienced by both men and women, in their multiple roles as kin and conjugal family members. These include partial avoidance and respect between in-laws, and cross-cousin marriage arrangements. The latter strengthen the spouses' claims upon either paternal or maternal kin and combine what may be conflicting roles.[22] Another important traditional mechanism for tension avoidance is the separation of interests of spouses, achieved both by segregation of their property interests and duolocal residence, all of which also serve to maintain the strength and unity of the lineage.

Should domestic conflict arise and remain unresolved, conjugal and affinal ties may ultimately be ruptured by separation and divorce, but matrilineal ties can scarcely be broken, and tension, if it arises, may find an outlet in witchcraft accusations.[23] Witchcraft is believed to operate mainly in the matrilineage and may highlight jealousy concerning the distribution of resources.[24]

TRADITIONAL NORMS

The *closed* and permanent kinship unit with a single legal personality, members sharing responsibilities, rights and tasks with each other, is the matrilineage or segment of it. To this children are recruited on the basis of matrilineal descent. Attachment to it is necessary for economic and social survival. The conjugal family on the other hand is legally, economically and residentially an *open* unit. Child-training, material provision, management and control of property and domestic chores are habitually carried out in a lineage context. Kin assume responsibilities and take an active, sometimes predominant part, in all these areas of activities. None of these functions is customarily carried out by individuals entirely alone in their capacities as husbands, wives and parents.

The main functions of the conjugal family are the regulation of the transient processes of sex, subsistence and socialization, but all of these can and often do take place outside this group. Marriage does not necessarily involve the setting up of either residentially or functionally discrete conjugal families. Within the conjugal relationship however, spouses generally share two responsibilities, the training and rearing of their own children, and material provision for their needs, but the control and ownership of property and the performance of domestic tasks are quite *segregated*.

Now, having briefly described some of the salient features of the traditional system of conjugal and kin relationships among the Akan, I shall give an outline of the entry of the coastal, eastern and interior Akan communities into a 'unitary market system'. A number of revolutionary social changes have taken place in Akan society which, in spite of the persistence of customary law, have had profound effects upon domestic institutions. These changes have been more far reaching and of longer duration in some regions and in some social strata than others.

Custom and Innovation

For over four hundred years the coastal Akan people, in particular the Fanti, were exposed to the effects of contact with European traders. From the fifteenth to the nineteenth centuries European merchant companies were attracted by the lucrative trade in slaves and gold. They built and inhabited forts along the coast which in turn attracted migrants and resulted in the establishment of urban settlements, already quite large by the beginning of the seventeenth century. Elmina castle was the earliest monument to the trade, built towards the end of the fifteenth century by the Portuguese. Later Dutch, English, French, Danish and Swedish traders competed in acquiring slaves and gold along the coast of present Ghana. In the process they built thirty or more forts along the three hundred miles of coastline.[25]

A number of town dwellers served at the forts as artisans, soldiers and slaves, while others came to trade. Europeans took local women as concubines and wives, giving rise to a local population of mixed descent. During the eighteenth century the Fanti were in effective control of the trade with the interior and in their role of middlemen became associated with European influence more than any other group. It has been observed that nowhere else have such small and transitory communities, as those set up by the foreign trading companies, so changed the life of the local people who surrounded them.[26] New forms of wealth and ownership were introduced into the society. Individuals began to earn considerable private incomes through their own trading ventures and deployment of their labour and skills. Even at the beginning of the eighteenth century, Bosman remarked about the new wealthy class of Africans, who had European-style houses, clothes and other goods and had by then, 'acquired a great reputation for their riches, either devolved on them by inheritance or trade'. Increasingly high social status and riches became attainable through personal success in trading ventures, as well as being ascribed by descent.

An important event was the opening of schools at the coastal forts to enable local people, in particular the children of mixed European and Fanti descent, and of the wealthy traders, to become literate. Some of these children were subsequently employed as messengers and clerks, others going abroad for higher education. As early as the sixteenth century the Portuguese started a Catholic school at Elmina, from which one or two children were sent to Portugal

35

for further studies. This school however did not last long, but in 1880 new Catholic schools were reopened there.[27] In the eighteenth century the Dutch and English opened schools and one or two more pupils went on to Holland and England.[28]

Other missionaries took up the teaching task, in particular the Methodists, and by the end of the nineteenth century there were several schools in coastal Akan towns.[29] Cape-Coast, the original English colonial headquarters, became one of the main educational centres, which it remains to this day. One of these schools is now over two hundred years old and Cape Coast has citizens whose fore-bears have been educated for several generations.

It was through participation in these two new systems, the economic and the educational, through the personal acquisition of wealth and learning, that a new set of coastal Akan people evolved, comparatively wealthy and educated, with standards of living and modes of life different from most of the rural coastal population. As Priestley points out the individualistic aims and activities of such men were soon seen to be a potential challenge to the corporate family and its claims (1969: 23).

Within the category of educated men however there were wide gaps in wealth and social position, for though children were sent to school, with the intention that education would give them an opportunity to enter more highly paid jobs in the exchange sector of the economy, a proportion of the school-attenders were unable to find the kinds of jobs they thought they were fitted to do, and remained unemployed, some even sinking back into illiteracy.[30]

Priestly (1969) has recently traced the history of a series of such men and women, the Fanti family of Brews, who by the nineteenth century were adding their quota to the new category of west African professional men, who had their higher training abroad (Foster, 1965: 64). Like a number of other such coastal families they had their European ancestry, which could be traced back to a merchant. She has outlined some of the ways in which such trading families with education began to differ from their contemporaries. One of the crucial differences was that they held individually acquired property, which fathers began not infrequently to leave to their own children, in spite of the still continuing norm of matrilineal inheritance. The practice of leaving written wills also began to emerge.[31] Not only was there this emphasis upon father to child inheritance, by the end of the nineteenth century, but also a growing minority of legally monogamous marital unions, which were blessed in church and registered under the Marriage Ordinance of 1884, with literate wives bearing the title of 'Mrs'.

By 1850 then, revolutionary economic and educational changes had taken place in a chain of coastal, urban Akan settlements, which influenced residential patterns, property-holding, patterns of inheritance, all of which had undoubted effects upon the kinship ties of the people concerned. By the second half of the nineteenth century there was in these coastal communities a considerable number of European-trained professional men, teachers, lawyers, journalists, doctors and ministers of religion, whose names are now well known in the history of Ghana.

Until this period however, there had been no similar economic or educational innovation in the other Akan areas. It was only at this time that schools were first opened in the eastern Akan area, when the Basel mission moved from Accra to Akropong.

THE EASTERN AKAN

The Basel missionaries from Accra opened schools, first among the south eastern Akan on the Akwapim ridge and later northwards in the Akyem and Kwahu areas in the eighteen-forties. The new converts lived in separate Christian communities, called 'Salem', near the missions. The influence of old family ties and custom as a result began to be weakened and Christian marriages were first celebrated in these areas in 1853. The emphasis of the missionaries was upon education of the young, their aim being to build up Christian communities of people dedicated to a new way of life.[32] They trained teachers, catechists and artisans, developed agricultural and trading institutions, and built roads. All of these increased the range of employment open to the new school-leavers, broadening the available avenues to social and spatial mobility.

The single revolutionary event of this period was the planting of cocoa in Akwapim, the first export of cocoa to Europe from Akwapim being in 1885. By 1903 over forty-four thousand acres of cocoa were under production. The period 1900 to 1930 has been called the 'golden age' of agriculture for it was during this period that cocoa exports were high and many Akan acquired wealth and property in a short space of time (La Anyane, 1963: 38–40). The introduction of cocoa cash-cropping into the south-eastern Akan area and its steady expansion north westwards, entailed widespread migration of farmers to find more land for the cocoa plantations. Some of the effects of this migration have been described by Hill (1963). The spread of cocoa farming was such that by 1960 over one third of all employed Akan men, including half of those in Ashanti and Brong Ahafo, and over one fifth of Akan women, were working as cocoa farmers (Gil, Aryee and Ghansah, 1964).

THE HINTERLAND AKAN

The Akan peoples of the interior, chiefly the Ashanti and Brong were involved in the coastal trade in the nineteenth century and earlier, through providing and buying goods from the coastal market. The Ashanti court policy however successfully curtailed the growth of a powerful, wealthy, independent middle class, such as arose on the coast, partly by keeping the bulk of the trade north and south in the control of the King, chiefs and their subordinates, and partly by enforcing the rules that the Ashanti king was the ultimate heir of his subjects and also had a right to a third share of any treasure found. In addition the overtures of the missionaries, the harbingers of schools, were rejected.[33] The area therefore remained virtually isolated until the twentieth century from those innovations effecting revolution on the coast, and the Ashanti and Brong and their neighbours were at first almost entirely excluded from the kinds of positions open to educated men in the modern colonial, political and economic systems.

By 1905 the Wesleyan and Basel Missions combined, had only seventeen schools and less than five hundred pupils between them in Ashanti. There was apparently strong opposition to sending children to school. It was only after 1910 that the expansion of education in the hinterland got under way. The pattern was similar to that observed in the south, where a massive increase in the demand for school places followed upon the incorporation of segments of the population into the new market economy, through trade and cash-cropping.[34] For cocoa-growing, like the coastal trade, offered new opportunities for amassing wealth. Some of this was passed on to children in the form of cocoa lands and money. Some was invested in children's education, so that they were trained to take up occupations other than farming. As Foster notes (1965: 126 fn. 29), in cocoa areas rural as well as urban children were sent to school, in contrast to the coastal pattern, in which urban children predominated. The demand for schools was notably associated with

38

the realization of what benefits salaried employment could bring, especially white collar government jobs, for from the beginning the government was a major employer of school-leavers. Thus Fortes (1948: 32), in describing the demand for schools sweeping the interior Akan areas in the 1945 period, pointed to the strong economic element behind this demand, mentioning amongst other things the goal of Civil Service employment with its rewards manifestly better than those accruing to farmers and unskilled workers.

HIGHER EDUCATION

So far, in outlining the development of educational institutions in the coastal, eastern and then the hinterland areas among the Akan, only primary school establishments have been mentioned. Secondary schools followed a similar pattern in that the first were opened on the coast. The Wesleyans opened a secondary school for boys in Cape Coast in 1876, which later became Mfantsipim school. By 1900 there were four secondary schools. Three were in Cape Coast and one of them in Accra. These schools were originally totally staffed and supported by local people, and were important because they opened the way for professional and university training for their students. They provided the intermediate steps in the ladder leading to the most highly regarded occupations, the legal and medical professions and the senior ranks of the Civil Service. Many secondary school leavers, who did not go on to higher institutions, went into the Civil Service. Thus by 1935 over 30 per cent of the students from Achimota Secondary School had entered government employment and possibly a larger proportion from Mfantsipim did the same (Foster, 1965: 135).

More recently the expansion and spread of secondary schooling has been such that by 1960 there were one hundred and one secondary schools with over 20,000 pupils in the whole of Ghana. Among the Akan students recruited to these, the best represented groups continue to be the Coastal Fanti and Eastern Akwapim the most under-represented a number of southwestern minority groups including the Nzima, and the northeastern Brong (Foster 1965: 146).

In 1948 the University College of the Gold Coast was founded, also near Accra, later becoming the University of Ghana, Legon, and in 1951 the College of Science and Technology was founded in Kumasi, while the University College subsequently the University of Cape Coast was founded in 1964. Until after independence

39

however, the number of University students graduating locally was small and many still continued to go abroad to get degrees, but in the sixties, the volume of graduates increased rapidly. The annual output of the University of Ghana more than doubled from less than two hundred to over five hundred graduates. The students leaving the new Colleges of Science and Technology in Kumasi and of Education at Cape Coast swelled the ranks of degree holders, the majority of whom found employment in Government institutions, the ministries, schools and colleges, and public corporations.

GOVERNMENT EMPLOYMENT

Since the beginning of the colonial era, the part played by the government and other public agencies as employers of labour has been a major one. In 1951 the public sector of salaried employees contained 41 per cent of all recorded employees. By 1958 it was calculated that over half of all employment in the modern sector of the economy was by government and the rate of growth of employment has since been higher in the public than the private sectors. Thus Foster (1965: 146) estimated in 1965 that the government then controlled no less than 60 per cent of the employment outlets to which secondary school leavers are orientated.

Initially the majority of senior government appointments were held by expatriate Englishmen, but gradually the numbers and proportion of local employees increased until at independence they composed 70 per cent of the total. Thus while in 1925 there were only twenty seven Africans with 'European' government appointments and in 1950 less than two hundred, by 1955 this number had increased to over a thousand and in 1960 it had reached over two thousand and continues to increase. Thus the Ghanaian Senior Civil Service is, in its present proportions, a product of the nineteen-sixties, though local men have been holding such posts for the last fifty years or more.[35]

Since many of the Akan come from areas longest exposed to educational opportunities, they have always formed a significant proportion of this higher educated, Senior Civil Service population. However the considerable timelag in the expansion of educational opportunities and demand northwards, witnessed by the higher incidence of illiteracy among the interior Akan than among the south eastern populations, has meant that the eastern and coastal Akan have produced a comparatively higher number of secondary school and University graduates and so can boast in the main a higher percentage of well-qualified employees in the professional, administrative, managerial and technical categories.[36] The sharpest contrast in educational opportunity and achievement is that between the southern Akwapim with 9 per cent in higher employment and the northern Brong with only 2 per cent.

POPULATION CHANGE

In the last couple of decades the shift of rural populations to the towns in Ghana, in search of paid employment in the private as well as the public sector, has been phenomenal (Caldwell, 1969). Between 1960 and 1970 the population of Accra increased tremendously. By 1960 over a third of the Akan population had moved away from their natal homes into other districts and regions and nearly one in four were living in urban areas. The factors leading to this widespread dispersal of matrikin, include the movement of farmers to find new land, as well as the migration of the educated to find employment in the growing urban centres, mainly in the south east. The proportion of people in the Akan subgroups affected by this migration varies. The areas with the largest percentage of migrants are the coastal Fanti and eastern Kwahu and Akwapim districts. The subgroup with the most stable population is that of the Brong, only 22 per cent of whom had moved in 1960. Thus while one quarter to a third of the eastern Akan subgroups and Fanti were classified as town dwellers in 1960, less than one in five Ashanti, Ahafo and Brong were in this category. At the time of the 1960 census there were about seventy thousand Akan living in Accra, where they formed 16 per cent of the population of the capital. They were either self-employed or working in government service, commerce or industry.

LEGAL CHANGE

With this migration and urbanization, and the increasing availability of sources of income beyond the control of the individual's lineage head and chief has come gradual legal change, including the recognition of the individual's ability to acquire, possess and dispose of private property. On the coast as early as 1871 the courts accepted the possibility that an individual could own a substantial interest in land (Sarbah, 1897: 204). But even at the turn of the century

41

Sarbah could still write that, 'With the exception of the coast towns (where written wills were recognised) private property in the strict sense does not exist...the head of the family owns the whole of the property (Sarbah, 1897: 60–61).'[37]

The growth of the legal recognition of private-property ownership and the corresponding paralleled diminution in the extent of lineage land ownership in the Akan area and its gradual spread northwards, especially in the period 1910 to 1930, during the great cocoa boom, has been referred to by several commentators. It would appear to have been inextricably linked with the spread of cocoa growing and the associated migration of farmers, in which large numbers of individuals amassed wealth by their own effort and bought property for themselves with the proceeds. Woodman (1966) has carefully documented this process, in a discussion of the factors influencing the development of customary land law in Ghana.[38] As a result of such changes it is now legally accepted, throughout the Akan region, that an individual owner of property may freely dispose of it *inter vivos* or by will. The latter has only been legally as well as morally binding since 1932. Thus from being an inalienable ancestral heritage, land has become a commercial object, subject to sale, purchase and transfer.

The customary law however, of joint matrilineage interest in property, still applies to that part of people's privately acquired wealth, which has not been disposed of by gift or will, except for the small minority of Akan discussed below, who are married under the Ordinance or who are the issue of an Ordinance marriage. Land and other properties continue to pass to the 'family' of the deceased and to become 'family' property, that is property of the matrilineage segment. Most legal authorities support the view that the inheriting matrilineage segment is composed of the mother of the deceased and all persons male or female descended from her in the female line.[39] Sisters as well as brothers are included in this inheriting group. It is only in the total absence of such matrikin that a man's children have any right to inherit his personally acquired property, similarly spouses continue to be barred from such rights of inheritance.

There is massive evidence of discontent at the continuation of this matrilineal inheritance system. While such discontent was widespread on the coast by the nineteenth century (Priestly, 1969: 184) conflict resulting from diverging claims and interests is only reported to have occurred on a wide scale in the interior after the spread of cocoa plantations in the early decades of the twentieth century.[40]

One manifestation of the seriousness of such conflicts consequent upon economic revolution was the thriving witch finding cults.[41] In the towns discontent was recorded twenty years ago (Busia, 1950: 43–6). Dissatisfaction and conflict have arisen in those areas in which through migration, education and employment, personal property has become important.

Various attempts have been made at several levels by individuals, by churches, by local courts, by government and by judges to counter the effects of matriliny.

The vexed question of the property rights of members of the conjugal family has been debated by the Akan chiefs at the Confederacy Council on several occasions, first in 1938 and again in 1941 and in 1942, when eventually the Asantehene made the proposal, passed by the chiefs, that witnessed gifts of personal property *inter vivos* should be valid, whether approved by the matrilineage concerned or not.[42] Again in 1948 the Ashanti Confederacy Council ruled that one third of a man's property should be inherited by his widow and children. But since this proposal was not sanctioned by the Governor at the time, it did not become law and decisions of the local courts based upon it have been reversed upon appeal, as it is not a legally enforceable custom. This has also been the case in areas where churches have attempted to change the customary law of their congregations with respect to inheritance of personal property.

On the coast in the fort towns in the early days of the missionaries, the usage arose among the converts of recognising English law, so that the wife, married in church, took the husband's name and at death the wife and children took one half of his moveable property (Sarbah, 1897: 43–4). Similarly among the Eastern Akan in Akwapim and Akyem it became the practice, under the Basel missionary influence, for Christians to divide the estate of a deceased member into three parts, a third to his wife, a third to his children and a third to his matrikin, his house going to his wife and children who, according to church custom, would be residing with him. According to Danquah (1928: 184–5) this rule had a strong hold on the Christian converts and such claims were upheld in the local courts. Indeed the Akim Abuakwa State Council attempted to make this the customary law for inheritance in the area. But as in the case of the Confederacy Council ruling this has not altered the legally enforceable customary law, though it may have reflected an actual change in practices current in local areas subject to strong missionary influence.[43]

The common way of materially benefiting wife and children, which is becoming increasingly current, is that of making a gift before death, a practice which may be upheld in court, should the matrikin appeal against it.[44] Fortes (1970a: 206) has given quantitative evidence of the increasing extent to which cocoa farms are being passed to their owners' sons in this way, varying from 25–44 per cent of the farms in the areas he examined; a reflection of the increasing scope of fathers to give material recognition of their affection for their sons.

The shift of public opinion in favour of conjugal family rights was indicated by the recommendations of the Inheritance Commission, which sat in 1958. These suggested that the wife and children should receive a share of the property, as if they were members of the family. Later two abortive Marriage Divorce and Inheritance Bills, published in 1962 and 1963, would have included wives and children in the inheritance group, but the bills were withdrawn on a variety of grounds after much public discussion and argument, a fault probably being that too many different kinds of proposals were included in single bills.

In spite of the fact of repeated failure of attempts to change the law and the fact that what have amounted to new local customs have not been given legal sanctions, some developments have occurred, as Woodman (1971) has pointed out, in the kinds of decisions made in the courts of recent years, which have sought to increase the material security of the conjugal family members, both widows and children. There is evidently a widespread desire for some modification of the matrilineal family situation, so as to give a man's wife and children an interest in a definite portion of his estate at death. The right to maintenance and education, though legally enforceable is not felt by many to be enough. The stumbling block is lack of agreement on two issues; the extent to which a husband and wife's financial interests should be recognised as *joint,* and the extent to which the conjugal family should remain financially *open,* both in the recognition of the precedence of claims of matrikin, and with respect to the financial claims of offspring born outside it.

Up to the present time the customary dictum that legally man and wife have no community of goods and may not inherit each other's property, at the death of one intestate, is still as true as when Bosman recorded it. Reiterations in court that it is the wife's duty to help her husband and that if she helps him, the produce of their joint labour belongs to him alone in his lifetime and to

44

his matrikin at his death, as well as the circulation of harrowing accounts of the dispossession of widows and orphans by the matrikin of the recently deceased, give ample proof, if any is required.[45] The only special legal case is that of the minority of couples married under the provisions of the Marriage Ordinance.[46] According to these if an Akan husband of such a marriage dies intestate his property should be divided so that his matrikin inherit three-ninths of his self-acquired property, his children four-ninths and his wife two-ninths. The second main difference between marriages registered according to provisions of the Ordinance and those contracted according to customary law is that the latter are potentially polygynous, whereas legally at least, the former are not, since bigamy in its various forms is a criminal offence.[47]

It is however an openly acknowledged fact that some husbands married under the Ordinance are actually parties to other 'conjugal' relationships and the offspring of such may be completely legitimate in the legal sense that they have rights to inherit a share of their father's property at his decease, whatever the degree of public recognition given to their mother.[48]

There is then a minority of unions contracted in which relative solidarity and *closure* of spouses' financial interests are given legal sanctions. Very few people however contract such marriages, about four per cent of the Akan as a whole. They are in the main educated salaried workers, many of whose parents have also been educated and employed. Few are illiterate or farm workers.[49] Thus, it is that such unions are most common among those sectors of the Akan population longest and most widely exposed to education and salaried employment.[50] Registered marriages are thought to enhance the prestige of the partners and their families.

THE CONTINUITY OF CUSTOM

There is evidence of the widespread persistence of traditional marriage traits, especially in the hinterland areas less widely exposed to change. The continuing high proportion of divorcées found among Akan women indicates the actual fragility of conjugal unions, while the high incidence of cohabitation without customary, legal or ritual procedures denotes a persistent lack of emphasis upon formal marriage. Thus at the time of the 1960 census, 11.6 per cent of Akan women were noted to be divorcées, the highest percentage for women of any ethnic group in Ghana.[51] Similarly the percentage of common law unions was higher than the national average reaching 12 and 13 per cent in Ashanti and Brong Ahafo. In addition the pattern of duolocality of spouses remains a current norm for a significant part of the Akan population. For instance in the Ashanti region only 58 per cent of married women live in the same houses as their husbands and only three quarters of married men live with at least one of their wives.[52] As Field (1948: 59; 1960: 24) noted, both in the nineteen-forties and in the nineteen-fifties, the simple conjugal household is difficult to find, for not only do spouses continue to have separate residential arrangements, but frequently non-nuclear kin are co-resident in the household. As regards differences between the urban and rural Akan populations, registered marriages, both Ordinance and Christian, are more common in town, where divorce is less frequent. The incidence of duolocality does not differ significantly in urban and rural areas.

Some mention has now been made of continuities and changes in marriage patterns with regard to types of contract, divorce and residence of spouses. What of evidence regarding conjugal rights and duties? It has already been indicated above that Akan women have customarily made an important contribution to financial provision for themselves and their children by farming both for food and cash crops as well as trading, and at the present time less than a quarter are housewives unemployed outside the home.[53] This pattern of participation in the labour force and joint provision for their dependant children by wives and mothers continues in the urban environment where wives still supplement the weekly spending. It has even been reported common for the wife to take a large measure of responsibility for the upkeep of the home. Indeed many are said to contribute more than their own subsistence to the family exchequer.[54] With regard then to the fulfilment of economic responsibilities by men as husbands, there is little or no recorded evidence that men are increasingly accepting financial responsibility for their wives, who remain relatively financially independent and act as joint providers for their children. There is however evidence that men are increasingly shouldering responsibility for their own children, at the expense of obligations to care for children of matrikin. For example Fortes, on the basis of the analysis of the payment of middle school fees for a sample of Ashanti school children, demonstrated that thirty years ago men were accepting responsibility for the payment of their own children's school fees more often than for those of their sisters. The latter was only taken on as a duty when the father failed. Moreover there was a noticeable increase in this acceptance of paternal responsibility in communities more exposed to the effects of social and spatial mobility (Fortes, 1963 and 1970a: 207). As Danquah has pointed out, already by the 1920s the role of guardian and educator of a child had changed. It was becoming no longer a matter of simple upkeep, but beginning to require active improvement of the child's condition, through proper training in school to fit the child for the new positions in the expanding economy. In fact he went on to prophesy that,

of one thing we are sure, if among the small private families of limited means the system of maternal succession ever breaks down, it will be due largely to the increasing difficulties and responsibilities involved in the care and training of children (1928: 192).

Increasingly it is to his own children that a man chooses to devote this attention. The element of choice is partly related to the fact that modern education and the upkeep of the school child is costly. Thus the number of children a working man can endow in this way is limited.

On the other hand mobility has been seen to lessen the extent of fulfilment of obligations expected by non-nuclear kin, though this may still be considerable. Thus Fortes noted (1947: 164) that getting away from the home village frees the enterprising Akan from many constraints which operate in the village, where most people are his kin and where he is subject to many social obligations. However kinship obligations persist over distance and through time and as Fortes points out such movement may merely reduce kinship duties and not end them. For example, he noted, 'It is a common thing in Kumasi to find a man from a village with his house full of kinsfolk, chiefly schoolboys and girls, who have come to live with him and on him in order to find work or schooling in Kumasi.' Similarly Busia noted in a coastal urban, mainly Akan community, Sekondi Takoradi, that town dwellers' dependants increase in number with rises in salary. Some of the dependants are the unemployed, who come to town in the hope of finding jobs (Busia, 1950: 21, 24). With the increases in individual earning and private ownership of resources however, and the dwindling importance of rights in jointly owned property, the kinship obligations inherent in the latter have tended to dwindle (Field, 1960: 27).

Marriage among a Matrilineal Elite

CONCLUSION

The aspects of customary Akan marriage and matriliny relevant to our theme have now been briefly described and some of the significant historical events, the results of foreign intervention, have also been indicated. These include the advent of international trade and schools, the introduction of cash-cropping and the massive increase in opportunities for salaried employment consequent upon the formation of colonial government and administration. In the wake of these several innovations have followed a number of radical changes, which have altered the context and basis of domestic life. These are widespread migration, the dispersal of kin groups; social mobility, with increasing disparity in living standards and life styles between households; the diversification of means for achieving individual status rights and resources; urbanization, new residence patterns, and last but not least, new laws affecting changes in the legal rights and duties applicable to the marriages and family life of the few. A number of customary Akan norms however, have been seen to die hard, and the forces of change have been observed to be more marked and prolonged in some Akan regions than others, in particular among the coastal Fanti and Eastern Akwapim.

Akan Senior Civil Servants are in that sector of the total population personally most affected by the types of changes enumerated, since they are themselves highly educated migrants, living mainly in the major urban centres. Their standard of living is vastly higher than that of the majority of their countrymen, and their style of life among those most radically influenced by foreign customs and technology. In the chapter to follow some of the obstacles crossed by them in the climb to this occupational status are discussed and also some of the hazards of the social and spatial mobility it frequently entails.

NOTES

[1] At the time of the 1960 census they numbered 1,439,470 men and 1,525,110 women.

[2] See B. Gil, A. F. Aryee & D. K. Ghansah 1964, *Special Report E. Tribes of Ghana.* Census Office, Accra.

[3] These include Sarbah (1897); Danquah (1922, 1928); Rattray (1923, 1927, 1929); Field (1948, 1969); Fortes (1948, 1949, 1950, 1954, 1963, 1970a & b) and Busia (1951, 1954).

[4] The following often-quoted sayings express succinctly the corporate unity of the lineage, 'Abusua baako mogya baako. Abusua baako nipa koro.' One lineage, one blood. A lineage is one person.

[5] See Rattray (1929: 62); Fortes (1970a: 169).

[6] See Sarbah (1897: 47ff.); Rattray (1929: 330ff.); Fortes (1970a: 170).

[7] Cf. Gough (1961: 451): 'I suggest that with matrilineal descent and settled subsistence cultivation only land newly brought under cultivation can ever be controlled by individuals.

48

Custom and Innovation

Once it has been inherited, land will be held by some order of matrilineal descent group, although district or state, may have an over right in land.'

[8] Bosman (1967: 203). See also Sarbah (1897: 86–7) and Danquah (1928: 183).

[9] See Sarbah (1897: 124); Danquah (1928: 148); Fortes (1970a: 209). See also Rattray (1927: 94), 'the (marriage) rite is in itself of the utmost simplicity...in exceptional cases even these meagre ceremonies and gifts may be dispensed with, and a mere declaration of a man and woman, before witnesses of their intention to live together as man and wife, followed by cohabitation, may constitute a valid union'.

[10] There is however a note of ambivalence in the Akan attitude to 'illegitimacy', for Danquah notes: 'the issue of the illegal connexion (between a girl and socially unaccepted lover) will be "illegitimate", not that the child would be disinherited or in any way inconvenienced in its general progress in life, for illegitimacy of children is unknown in our institutions' (1928: 148). George Hagan has pointed out (personal communication) that the public recognition of paternity may even take place after the death of the *genitor*. In a case he witnessed the son himself took the necessary drinks, on his deceased father's behalf, to his mother's family head, thus earning himself recognition as a son, at his father's funeral.

[11] Danquah (1928: 156): 'It cannot be exaggerated how easily and rapidly marriages may be dissolved with little trouble'. Fortes (1948: 34) likewise comments upon the high incidence of divorce. A similar pattern is noted in other matrilineal societies, cf. Fortune (1932: 9, 278): 'marriages dissolve matrilineages remain'. Also Mitchell (1962: 29); Schneider and Gough (1961: 14).

[12] Sarbah (1897: 54, 126). According to Danquah (1928: 195) everything the husband has given to the wife since the marriage payment of *aseda* must be returned by her. This may even include cloth which wore out long ago: 'consequently while husband and wife are living together there may be constant dread on the part of the wife to make use of things given to her by her husband, else she may one day be divorced bankrupt' (1928: 153).

[13] Various writers have commented upon this state of affairs over the years including Bosman (1967: 201) 'Married people have no community of goods, but each hath his or her particular property'...'on the death of either the man or the wife the respective relatives come and immediately sweep away all, not leaving the widow or widower the least part thereof', and again, 'property of a wife is distinct from that of a husband'. Rattray reiterates this, (1927: 102) 'A married woman's property is distinct and wholly separate from her husband's nor can he possibly become her heir nor she his': cf. property relationships of spouses in other matrilineal societies e.g. Bemba, Cewa, Yao etc. (Mair, 1953: 7, 95–6).

[14] Sarbah (1897: 60) 'Whatever a wife helps her husband to acquire is the sole property of the husband.'

[15] Sarbah, (1897: 136): 'There is no obligation on the wife to pay any part of her husband's debt'...'While a husband is living with his wife or is providing for and maintaining her, he is not liable for her contracts debts or liabilities except for maintenance.'

[16] Rattray (1927: 173–4) observes when the heir is a woman, 'The heir, widow and clan of the widow meet. The widow produces all the gifts she had received from her late husband and whatever had been handed to her with the words – take and look after for me – and then hands them to the heir.' As he notes the latter may give some of the gifts to the deceased's children, but this is optional.

[17] For a sophisticated analysis of residence patterns in two Ashanti towns see Fortes (1970b).

[18] A number of observers have commented on the industry of Akan women, e.g. Fortes (1947: 163): 'It is taken for granted in Ashanti...That a woman will earn her own living or a large part of it.' See also Field (1960: 30): '(women) are, unless quite devoid of drive – economically independent'...'most women produce more than they consume'.

[19] Note also the high degree of equality between male and female members of the lineage (Fortes, 1950: 256).

[20] For discussions of paternal responsibility see Danquah (1927: 188–9, 191); Busia (1954: 196–99); Christensen (1954: 95); Fortes (1970a: 203); cf. Fortune (1932: 13–14).

[21] See Fortes (1963); cf. Richards (1940: 89).

[22] See Rattray (1927 Chap. XXIX); Fortes (1950: 281–2; 1970a: 213–15).

²³ That it is possible to sever ceremonially ties of matrikinship has been pointed out by Mr G. Hagan, who cited Ashanti Court Record No. 26 I.A.S. Legon, as an example of the procedure of 'cutting the pad' or 'cutting the broom'.

²⁴ As Rattray has pointed out, 'a witch is powerless to use her or his enchantment over any one outside the witches clan' (1927: 28).

²⁵ For a brief account of the history of this period see Fage (1959). As Claridge observed, 'two centuries of trade with Europeans increased the importance of the coast towns and raised them from the position of tiny fishing villages to that of populous trading centres' (1915: 55).

²⁶ Lawrence (1969: 29). The latter has provided a description of the English forts, their architecture and some insights into life in them. For an account of the Danish forts see Norregard (1966).

²⁷ A brief and useful history of the educational system of Ghana is provided by McWilliam (1959). For a more detailed account of the early development of education see Part 1, 'The Historical Background', in Foster (1965).

²⁸ One of these, Philip Quarque, the first African minister of the Church of England, returned to be a schoolmaster and missionary for fifty years.

²⁹ These included Anomabu, Accra, Winneba, Salt Pond, Kommenda and Dominasi. For an account of the activity of the Methodist mission in this area see Bartels (1965).

³⁰ As Foster notes (1965: 68), 'At one extreme were the wealthy literate merchants and at the other a large group of semi-literate "Cape Coast Scholars" able to find only the poorest type of menial employment or none at all.'

³¹ There is evidence of this change in the frequent litigation in nineteenth century records (Priestly, 1969: 184).

³² For an account of the endeavours of the Presbyterian Church in Ghana between 1835 and 1960 see Smith (1966).

³³ For a recent discussion of the above two points see Arhin (1968a & b). See also Morton–Williams (1969: 94).

³⁴ For a detailed discussion of educational expansion in relation to economic and political change see Foster (1965).

³⁵ Indeed Gardiner (1970: 13–14) has recently pointed out that in the nineteenth century many local people were Justices of the Peace etc. and some served as Colonial Secretary, Controller of Customs, Solicitor General and in other capacities but by the turn of the century virtually all senior posts had been emptied of Africans. By then, 'British authority had to be demonstrated in the person of British officials.'

³⁶ In 1960 while almost half of the Akyem and Akwapim were literate less than 20 per cent of the Brong were.

³⁷ Even in these coastal towns at a person's death however all such personally owned property descended to his successors as ancestral property. It was only in his lifetime that he could dispose of it. Thus Sarbah (1897: 100) pointed out the necessity for people married under the Ordinance of making wills according to the law of England.

³⁸ See especially chapter 5, 'Factors influencing the development of customary law'. See · also Busia (1951: 125–31) and Field (1960: 29).

³⁹ See Woodman (1966: 390–4). There is legal argument however, some authorities supporting the earlier custom recognising rights of a more inclusive matrilineage which, as Woodman points out, would further encourage the persistence of the inalienability of property and the perpetuation of corporate matrilineage rights.

⁴⁰ For discussions of this see Field (1948: 118); Fortes (1948: 34); Christensen (1954: 182); Lystad (1959: 196).

⁴¹ See Fortes (1947: 170); Ward (1956); Goody J. R. (1957); Field (1960).

⁴² See the account of this in Busia (1950).

⁴³ See Ollenu (1966: 144, 147) and Woodman (1965: 399).

⁴⁴ Danquah (1928: 185). 'A rich man would in these days of economic agriculture, provide well for his children by apportioning to them in his lifetime substantial parts of his property.' See also Field (1948: 118); Sarbah (1897: 43–4).

⁴⁵ See Ollenu (1966: 255). See Yaotey V. Quaye unreported judgement of Ollenu J. in the High Court Accra delivered on 16 Oct. 1961.

⁴⁶ The legal position of couples married 'in church', whose unions have only been blessed and not registered according to the provisions of the Ordinance is an ambiguous one as regards property rights of the spouses. Many people think that the spouses' legally enforceable rights are the same as for the participants to Ordinance marriages which is not so, though it may be so in effect if, in the community in which they live, a variant of the tripartite system of inheritance is the accepted norm and remains unchallenged.

⁴⁷ The penalty laid down in the Criminal Code for contracting more than one Ordinance marriage is seven years (section 440). The offence for marrying a second wife under the Ordinance while being married by customary law carries a penalty of five years imprisonment (section 448). The case of contracting a customary marriage to a third party, while being married under the Ordinance, carries a penalty of two years (section 449). However as more than one lawyer has pointed out, cases of bigamy which have reached the courts are hard to find and since being married under the Ordinance makes a man incapable of contracting another legally valid marriage, whatever other conjugal relationships he establishes may be said to be less than marriage. It is noteworthy that post Enumeration Survey Data disclose that even for official census purposes some men admit to a plurality of wives, when married according to Christian or Statutory law. See Allott (1960: 214, 217–18). Cf. Southall and Gutkind (1957: 68).

⁴⁸ See the case in 1959 of Coleman and Shang, Ghana Law Report 1959 Part 111 p. 390. Note that besides these provisions regarding monogamy and inheritance rights there is another way in which the Ordinance marriage seeks to give a further degree of unity to the conjugal pair, for while a partner to a customary marriage can be called as a witness for or against a spouse, a partner in an Ordinance marriage cannot be so called (Allott 1960: 211).

⁴⁹ An analysis of the occupations of partners to 2333 marriages contracted at the Accra City Council between 1960 and 1967 showed that of the brides 39 per cent reported they were seamstresses, commercial or clerical workers; 33 per cent that they were vocationally employed as teachers and nurses etc. and 2 per cent were professionals. Of the husbands 25 per cent were commercial workers; 29 per cent vocationally employed and 23 per cent professionals. Of the wives' fathers 42 per cent were in the above categories as were 32 per cent of the husbands' fathers. (Account must be taken of the 25 per cent and 30 per cent respectively of fathers who were deceased, retired etc.)

⁵⁰ Twelve per cent Akwapim, 7 per cent Akyem, 6 per cent Kwawu, 5 per cent Fante, 3 per cent Asante and Ahafo and 2 per cent Brong. See Gil, Aryee and Ghansah, (1964: 126).

⁵¹ See Special Report E.P. EX. Table 4.13B. Marital Status by Major Tribe, Sex etc. (Gil, Aryee and Ghansah, 1964), cf. Ewe women 3.8 per cent, Ga women 6.7 per cent.

⁵² Data extracted from the Post Enumeration Survey. Cf. Volta Region 72 per cent of married women live with their husbands and 85 per cent of married men live with their wives.

⁵³ In the 1960 Census only 23 per cent of Akan women were listed as homemakers. Of the employed women 70 per cent were farmers (22 per cent cocoa farmers) and 18 per cent sales workers (Gil, Aryee and Ghansah, 1964: 103, 110, 122).

⁵⁴ See Crabtree (1950: 49, 130) and Busia (1950: 20).

3

GOVERNMENT SERVANTS AND KINSMEN

Akan Senior Civil Servants in Accra are on the one hand fully incorporated by their occupations into the modern economic system, and on the other are kinsmen, with home towns and villages scattered in communities at distances varying from thirty to as many as three hundred miles from their places of work and residence. From these two positions stem their main social and economic rights and obligations, affecting the material resources at their disposal in the conjugal family context.

OCCUPATIONAL STATUS: MATERIAL PRIVILEGES

Many of the privileges associated with the Senior Civil Servants' way of life, which have ensured their maintenance of a high social status and comparative financial security and luxury, are remnants of the colonial heritage, formerly enjoyed by the expatriate British. These privileges included relatively high salaries of between approximately ₵1,360 and ₵5,000 or more, free medical care for self, wife and children, car loans and access to subsidized, partly furnished accommodation, with gardens, piped water and electricity, as well as pensions on retirement. On their salaries they can afford the amenities of modern urban life, such as refrigerators, television sets, imported food and clothing, and so maintain themselves and their immediate dependants on a standard of living far above the national average. The economic gap separating them from the majority is indicated by the fact that the average annual income of people working in public and private establishments with more than ten employees is less than ₵400.[1] Their salaries are therefore three, four or more times higher than the average and the gap between the high and low income groups, according to current trends, is not decreasing.

What they possess is mainly privately owned and paid for with their government salaries. Much of what they use, houses, furniture and cars, is either government property or bought on a hire purchase

52

Table 3. 1. *Percentage of Akan Senior Civil Servants owning property jointly with kin by region of origin**

Region	%	N
Coastal	30	(23)
Eastern	51	(35)
Interior	44	(16)
Total	43	(74)

* The tables in this chapter are based on the replies of the 85 Akan respondents in the Senior Civil Service Survey described above. The variations in the total number were due to several no-responses.

scheme, until recently through a government loan. Some say they have difficulty in saving to accumulate property such as farms and houses, since the cost of living is so high and their responsibilities so many. A sizeable minority have shares in family properties, in addition to their salaries, especially those who come from the rural cocoa-producing areas (see Table 3. 1). Some even use part of their salaries to build houses and make farms with their relatives.

The ladder required for climbing up the Civil Service hierarchy is higher education, gained in secondary schools and universities in Ghana and abroad. The acquisition of the certificates and diplomas, necessary for promotion to those ranks, was not easy for most Akan youths fifteen to twenty or more years ago. Very few had government scholarships to pay their secondary boarding school fees, which were about as high as a junior Civil Servant's income. The rest were supported through school by their parents and relatives. Since only a fortunate few had fathers with higher education or wealthy, bene-volent maternal uncles, it was a hard struggle for many. As is indicated in Table 3. 2, it was the young men from areas where schooling began at an early date, who were more likely to have the social and financial support of highly educated fathers. Meanwhile the majority of those from the interior Ashanti and other subgroups were the first in their families to achieve such positions.

Because of the lack of financial support and opportunities, at the moments when they were needed, it was not unusual for young men to work between the various stages of their educational careers, with the result that many attained their present positions, either by a slow process of promotion from the junior ranks, or after obtaining a degree relatively late in life. For all, even scholars from

53

Table 3. 2. *Education level of fathers of Akan Senior Civil*
Servants by region of origin (percentages)

Region	Nil	Elemen-tary	Post-elemen-tary	Total %	N
Coastal	17	52	31	100	(29)
Eastern	36	28	36	100	(36)
Interior	56	44	0	100	(18)
Total	34	40	27	100	(83)

Cape Coast, the old centre of learning, higher education entailed travel, in many cases abroad, for periods ranging from one to as many as ten years. Except for those few from privileged homes in the coastal towns, success brought about radical changes in living standards and conditions, especially for men reared by illiterate kin, who were farmers and traders in the rural areas, far from the modern conditions of urban life, and those whose fathers had only elementary education and worked as storekeepers and clerks in the provincial towns. Achievement of the new occupational status entailed far-reaching social and spatial mobility, causing wide gaps in terms of both distances and modes of living between many of the Senior Civil Servants and their relatives.

KIN TIES AND FINANCIAL OBLIGATIONS

Like most of the urban migrants in Ghana, Akan Senior Civil Servants continue to maintain close contacts with many relatives in the regions, some of whom come to stay with them or to pay visits, while those living in the home towns are seen on trips back home. The number of relationships maintained varies, as does the content, being social, economic and ritual. Funerals and Memorial Services for the dead, and the Christmas and Easter holidays are important times when kin reunite. Widely ramifying ties are recognized by most, but sometimes close relatives, such as paternal half-siblings, lose contact through dispersal and seldom if ever meet. As might be expected, in a situation in which relatively well-to-do urban, salary earners maintain close contacts with numerous kin, many of whom are financially less secure, a majority have frequent requests put to them for help, especially those from the interior

Table 3. 3. *Percentage of Akan Senior Civil Servants whose kin frequently request help by region of origin*

Region	%	N
Coastal	54	(28)
Eastern	58	(35)
Interior	74	(19)
Total	61	(82)

Table 3. 4. *Amount of money Akan Senior Civil Servants send to kin monthly by region of origin* (percentages)

Region	Nil	₵2–10	₵10+	Total %	Total N
Coastal	3	55	41	99	(29)
Eastern	15	42	42	99	(35)
Interior	5	53	42	100	(19)
Total	8	51	41	100	(83)

(see Table 3. 3). Elderly parents, grandmothers and aunts need money for their maintenance and medical expenses. Sisters and cousins (MZD) want help either to educate their children, or themselves, to buy a sewing machine or to start in trade. Brothers also want money to pay college fees, to start a farm or to help build a house. Naturally all demands are not met and excuses are frequently given, such as the difficulties of settling down in a new house in town, of trying to buy and maintain a car or of paying children's school fees. Almost all however, do remit money amounting to several cedis a month to kin, as well as giving sporadic amounts on visits home, at funerals and on festive occasions (see Table 3. 4).

A few short accounts of their early careers given by middle-aged Akan Senior Civil Servants illustrate some of the processes associated with the achievement of the new status goal, including the struggle to succeed, mobility, the repayment of obligations to parents and guardians and the financial responsibility to maintain and educate relatives inherent in the roles of elder brother and maternal uncle.

The first three accounts concern first generation educated men, whose mothers were either divorced or widowed before they attended school. The next two are examples of men sent to school by educated fathers and also assisted by kin. The last two are men whose kin on both sides, including grandfathers, and in one case even more remote forebears, had been to school.

MR BOATENG

Mr Boateng was the first among his relatives in Brong Ahafo to go to school. He describes his father as a 'polygynous, fetish-worshipping traditionalist', who only decided to send his son to school after he had been overcharged by a letter-writer in Kumasi. When he had been in school for a couple of years his father died and his father's relatives would take no responsibility for his education nor would his mother's relatives. It was only through his own exertions and the help of his mother and elder sister that he was able to continue. During his primary school years he lived with his maternal grandmother. His mother, then living with her second husband in another village, used to come every year to help him and his sister to start a new farm. He needed to sell sixty pesewas-worth of his farm produce each year to pay his expenses. At that time a head-load of plantain only cost two pesewas. Once he helped his cousin (MZS) to distil *akpeteshi* (a local 'gin') for a month to earn the 60p. Sometimes he collected fallen kola and sold it at six pesewas a basket or went as a contract labourer making onion beds. A large one would earn him 50p. At Middle School the fees were ₵1.20 a year, so he was busy all the time. He had hoped that his late father's brother would take an interest in his education, but he refused to pay his secondary school fees and in the end, seeing his industry, a local contractor offered to help and gave him lodgings in his vacations. He also won a scholarship which paid the fees. On leaving secondary school he worked as a travelling salesman and then as a primary school teacher for a year, before going to university. After that he went abroad to do a professional course.

While at school not only did he work to pay his own way, but he also earned enough money to send his younger maternal half-sister to school, after his mother's second husband had refused to send her. Since he returned from Britain he has been educating the rest of his mother's children (as well as his own four). One sister is now in training college while another sister and two brothers are in secondary school, he is also providing for his eldest sister's two small children in primary school, as she is separated from her husband, a driver, who has refused to send them to school. He also sends several cedis each month to his mother and grandmother.

MR AMOAKOH

Mr Amoakoh was the seventh and last child of illiterate farmers from Akyem. His father died just before his birth and his widowed mother was left with nothing, as his father's matrikin came and took everything his father ever had. His mother's brothers took pity on him when he was of school age, sending him to primary school and paying his fees till he won a half scholarship to secondary school. His maternal uncles refused to pay the extra ₵80 *per annum*, so he taught for a time and then got another secondary school scholarship, which again was worth half of the fees. The rest he paid from his savings. Seeing his determination and success in school, his uncles agreed to pay the remaining fees, but they refused to give any further help after he left secondary school, so instead of going to university he went to the technical branch of the Civil Service. Ambitious to continue his education, he passed an examination to do a college diploma for two years. Then he returned to the Civil Service for several more years in a higher grade post. After that he got a scholarship to go to England and take a full professional course.

Now he has returned he feels a moral obligation to give all the assistance he can to his own sisters and their children. They have no wish to live with him permanently, but they do come and stay from time to time. Among the financial responsibilities he has undertaken so far are, school fees of about ₵70 *per annum* for five years for a sister's son, who has now gone on to a university and the same amount for another sister's son, who has just begun secondary school. Others of his sisters' children are doing well at school and from time to time he meets their requests which amount to ₵40 or so *per annum*. If any wish to continue on to higher education he will be ready to help. He spends a further ₵40 *per annum* on his late mother's sister and her daughter. Because of these and other sums he gives sporadically and regularly and the knowledge that he may be called upon at any time to shoulder further responsibility for his mother's kin, (he says) he is unable to make a proper monthly budget.

Marriage among a Matrilineal Elite

MR OSEI

Mr Osei's parents divorced when he was still a baby and his father took no further interest in him. Until he was about fourteen he and his mother lived in her senior brother's house, together with his uncle's own children and about five of his other nephews. By the time he finished primary school, first his mother and then her brother had died, so that when he started secondary school at Cape Coast it was his mother's maternal uncle, then a chief, who paid his fees. During the holidays he used to stay with his mother's cousin (MMZS), a storekeeper in Accra. His great uncle thought he had gone far enough on leaving secondary school, and since his mother was not there to plead his case for him, he had to go and find employment as a junior civil servant. He worked in Accra, Kumasi then Tamale. He kept looking for an opportunity for further studies. Eventually an application for post-secondary technical training was successful and he set off abroad for two years. After returning he again worked in the Civil Service first in the Northern region and then the Volta Region. His next studies were aimed at getting the Higher School Certificate, necessary for entry to university. After he had passed the university entrance requirements he worked for a few more years before entering the university of Ghana. By the time he had finished his degree course Mr Osei was over forty.

He now finds his Senior Civil Service salary stretched to the limit, for as well as educating his three children by his first wife who are all in secondary school and his three by his second wife, attending primary school, a number of his matrikin expect him to give help by educating their children and providing accommodation for them in town. He therefore contributes to the secondary school fees of his maternal half sister's two children and helps towards the cost of maintaining two of his mother's daughters in training college and commercial school. He is thus contributing towards the education of ten dependant children.

MR KISSI

Mr Kissi came to his present administrative post by the devious route of being a teacher, clerk, technical officer and then junior administrator. He has been abroad several times in the course of his training and work. He considers his own background to be

58

unusual, as he was educated by his own father and he knows that it used to be difficult in Ashanti in the nineteen-twenties and thirties for fathers to send their own children to school, because of the pressures of their matrikin, who thought a man should rather care for his nephews. He remembers that his father educated seven such 'nephews' and younger 'brothers' as well as his own four sons. As a result of the good care his father and father's sister took of him, he is now known as coming from his father's town, since it was there that he stayed with his father's sister to attend school. His father a storekeeper and farmer is still alive, his mother lives with his father and also trades a little. Mr Kissi prides himself on being like his father, an educated man and staunch Presbyterian, having one wife and no 'outside' children.

He has never stayed in his mother's home town for more than an odd night and knows fewer people there than in his father's town. However he keeps in contact with them by attending their funerals and sending them presents of money and biscuits at Christmas. The only help he has been asked for, which he gave was to help his mother's only sister's son to get a training and a job. He thinks they hesitate to make any claims upon him as they realize they did nothing to further his education. On the other hand his father's kin do feel they can make claims upon him, since his father educated him. Recently a father's brother's son arrived after finishing school. He needs a job. Mr Kissi helped him earlier with his schooling. He has also helped his father's sister's daughter's daughter, by paying part of her fees at a vocational training school. Two of that same father's sister's sons have stayed with him to attend school. He feels it is justifiable that his father's relatives should make more claims upon him than his mother's. In fact he has named a daughter after his father's sister because she looked after him so well when he was attending school. He has also helped his own brothers when they have been in need, such as by giving his elder brother money to pay medical expenses, his younger brother building materials and another brother money to see him through his last year at university.

MR KUSI

Mr Kusi, a lawyer, was in primary school when his parents separated. He was educated by his Fanti father, a clerk, and was looked after by his father's sister, a baker in Takoradi. He went on from primary to secondary school and then abroad to university on scholarships, when he returned he entered the Civil Service and has now been working for over ten years.

He is having considerable difficulty meeting his several family commitments. After his Ashanti mother separated from his father, she remarried and had four more children. Mr Kusi calls her husband a 'typical Ashanti', in that he does not educate his own children and since his mother has no senior brothers to go to for help (her only brother is young and poor) he finds he has to provide for his mother's children including two in secondary school. Since two of his sisters have had children with men like their father, who do not care for their own offspring, he has also been forced to help them and accept responsibility for two nephews in primary school and a niece, who stays with him while her mother attends training college.

He now describes his own position as lying 'between two stools'. Whereas the family formerly centred upon a man's mother, it now centres upon his wife and children and he feels he has been caught in a position in which he has to provide for both. He thinks that the family system will have changed within the next fifty years, but in the meantime he is suffering. In his opinion coastal Akan men are better fathers than those from the interior. He refuses to provide for more distant kin such as his mother's sisters and their children, who on occasions have made many demands on him. This has the effect of isolating and cutting him off to some extent.

MR GYAMFI

Mr Gyamfi, in his late thirties, is an administrator of some experience, who was fortunately able to complete his education while still in his twenties. His maternal grandfather was sent to school and subsequently worked for the missionaries in his town. He built his house in the Christian quarter and broke away from the traditional Akan pattern by living together with his wife and children. Mr Gyamfi admired him very much and tries to emulate him in his family life. Unfortunately his grandfather's children did not follow the pattern he set. His daughters continued to live with their parents after marriage and his sons married more than one wife each.

Mr Gyamfi's own father was also an educated man, a junior Civil Servant, but he died before Mr Gyamfi had finished his education. While attending school he stayed at first with his parents, then with his mother's parents and her sisters and then his mother's brother. He won scholarships to pay for his fees through secondary school and university.

Since he became employed he has found that his kin on his mother's side, in particular the offspring of his maternal grandmother, with whom he lived as a school boy, make considerable demands upon him. He is at the moment the socially and economically best off among the men. Of his mother's brothers one is sick, one dead and one retired. His own elder brother is abroad and so people look to him when they need support. Many financial claims are made and he finds it hard to refuse them. His mother and grandmother are the only people to whom he makes regular monthly payments. He does not want to establish a practice of making a regular monthly payment to anyone else. Besides sporadic gifts to people in his home town, he pays the school fees and expenses of a mother's sister's daughter amounting to about ₵150 a year and gives another ₵300 *per annum* to his mother's sisters as well as paying funeral expenses and debts. He has helped one brother to set up in business, another lives with him and works in town and the youngest one, attending secondary school, stays with him in his vacations and is given about ₵100 a year to pay his expenses. His paternal half siblings, whom he considers to be closer relatives really, exert less economic pressure upon him than more distant maternal kin. He does not see them often and they have not asked for help.

In spite of advice to the contrary he intends to keep his wife and children with him and to provide for them, eschewing polygyny and other traditional Akan practices.

MR BLANKSON

Mr Blankson is a lawyer, as were his late father, father's brother and father's father before him. His great-grandfather was a merchant. He grew up in his parent's household in Cape Coast with his six older brothers and sisters and attended primary and secondary school as a day scholar. His educated mother, was the daughter of a Reverend Minister; she was a housewife and traded in cloth. Mr Blankson's father was educated first in Sierra Leone and then in Britain. He saw that all of his children received some kind of professional or vocational training. Two sons became lawyers and two doctors, all trained in England. Of his three daughters, one a seamstress is divorced and lives with her widowed mother, another is a teacher, married to a secondary school headmaster, while the third is a nurse married to a doctor. Mr Blankson frequently sees those of his brothers and father's younger brothers and his 'cousins', who are working in town. He sees many of his relatives on his regular trips to his home town to attend Masonic Lodge meetings, funerals and Memorial Services. The only financial help he gives to kin is a monthly remittance to his widowed mother and divorced sister, who live in his late father's house and are not in any need.

SONS AND BROTHERS

These several accounts illustrate that the many ambitious youths from the Akan areas, struggling to get an education in the nineteen forties and fifties, needed considerable family support, as well as tenacity and talent. Some succeeded with only minimal aid from close female kin, as did Mr Boateng, others with help from their maternal uncles, as did Mr Amoakoh and Mr Osei, while yet others were supported by fathers, who had themselves been to school. Very few, like Mr Blankson, simply followed in the family tradition, supported only by their fathers and reared only by their mothers, living permanently in the well-appointed family home. The majority had to rely upon a variety of help, from grandparents, older brothers and sisters and parents' brothers and sisters. Thus all accumulated, during their childhood and adolescence and even later, since their education was so extended, debts of obligation to those who supported them, sometimes in the face of opposition. A few were obligated only to their own parents, the majority to a wider range of kin and occasionally to an unrelated guardian. As a result now, virtually without exception, Akan Senior Civil Servants recognize a duty to reciprocate and help those who once supported them, especially since they are now in positions of relative affluence. Moreover their parents and guardians are elderly and some of them are in need. Thus almost all, give money in the form of regular monthly remittances or sporadic gifts to kin (Table 3. 4).

A striking difference is noticeable however, between the positions of those sent to school and college by their own educated fathers and the rest, for the latter tend to have depended for help upon a range of matrikin, to whom they now feel a sense of moral obligation. The accounts of Mr Kissi, Mr Kusi, and Mr Gyamfi indicate the dwindling sense of responsibility to the mother's relatives. In the

Table 3. 5. *Percentage of Akan Senior Civil Servants who have educated relatives' children by region of origin*

Region	Any*	Brother's child	Sister's child	Own sibling	N
		Relationship to Civil Servant			
Coastal	41	12	27	4	(26)
Eastern	59	14	37	14	(34)
Interior	61	6	50	39	(18)
Total	54	12	37	17	(78)

* Any relationship including nephew, niece, sibling, etc.

case of Mr Kusi there is a definite 'isolationist' policy. In Mr Gyamfi's case there is a conscious refusal of requests beyond a certain range. While the accounts of Mr Kissi and Mr Blankson indicate a change in the expectations and needs of matrikin, so that while numerous social and ritual contacts may continue, economic claims and obligations have become negligible. On the other hand owing a debt to father for education received in the past may give the patrikin a sense of right to help in return as Mr Kissi points out. Similarly the fact of being reared by a maternal surrogate, such as the father's or mother's sister, leaves an important sense of obligation to her and her offspring as well.

In their capacities as elder brothers and maternal uncles (full and classificatory) many assume some financial responsibility for the maintenance and education of younger brothers and sisters and siblings' children. As is indicated in Table 3. 5, more than a third in the Senior Civil Service sample have educated their sisters' children, and almost one in five their own younger brothers and sisters. Just as men from the rural interior have more financial demands made upon them by kin than those from further south, especially from the urban, coastal communities (a greater proportion of whose fathers are educated), so they apparently shoulder far more economic responsibilities, in their roles of older brothers and maternal uncles.

As the accounts given illustrate, the extent to which demands are made upon men in these capacities depends upon a number of factors. Two main factors appear to be the presence or absence of younger siblings and sisters' children in their families of origin

63

and secondly whether the latter have fathers and older brothers or uncles, willing and able to support them. Thus a man with several younger brothers and sisters, and no father to make adequate provision for them, either as a result of their mother's widowhood, divorce, conjugal separation, or marriage to a man of inadequate means, may have responsibilities as did Mr Kusi. Similarly it is men with one or more sisters, lacking a husband's support in the task of training their children, who are likely to be faced with heavy financial responsibilities to their nephews and nieces.

Many complaints are voiced about the lack of ability or desire, on the part of the fathers of their mothers' and sisters' children to undertake these responsibilities. Individual accounts and survey responses thus support what is generally maintained – that as a result of a variety of claims many Akan Senior Civil Servants are partly or wholly supporting two or three related adults and children, besides giving numerous sporadic amounts when necessary. Financial help to parents and guardians is a constant feature, but the amount of help given and the range of kin beyond them, who benefit from it, would appear to vary very much from region to region and case to case according to the circumstances. A noticeable fact is that, consciously or unconsciously, many are following or rejecting the examples set by their own parents and guardians in their domestic situations. They frequently describe their own domestic predicaments and goals with reference to these. In addition they refer to the ethnic subgroup stereotypes of the traditional, interior or educated coastal father and to the customary expectations of Akan mothers and sisters. There is great awareness of change, in particular of the difference being 'educated' makes to family life, and also recognition of cultural differences between people originating from various communities.

We have now briefly recounted some of the salient aspects of the economic positions of Akan Senior Civil Servants. Their main source of income is their government job, only a minority actively retaining shares in family properties. In the course of achieving their present occupations they have become indebted to parents and guardians, whom they now in turn assist. They also often find themselves supporting younger dependant siblings and nephews and nieces, who may be on a similar path to educational success. There is no doubt that some men are under considerable financial strain to make ends meet, as they attempt to satisfy a number of demands of kin, as well as various other commitments and to maintain a style of life commensurate with their new social status. Individual accounts of personal experiences have illustrated the considerable differences in the financial and social positions of individuals. Survey data have indicated areas of regional variation. Both point to the fact that education in the parental and previous generations is an important factor associated with differences in the expectations and obligations attached to kinship roles. The next task is to describe briefly how Akan Senior Civil Servants have become husbands and fathers; the types of marriages they contract, whom they marry and the birth and rearing of their children, before describing the location and composition of their new urban households.

HUSBANDS AND HOUSEHOLDERS

Nearly all Akan Senior Civil Servants become husbands first according to customary law and then many go on to marry in church or in the registry office, months or sometimes even years later. Few of their parents before them had their marriages registered (see Table 3. 6). Indeed only about four per cent of all extant marriages in the country have been contracted in this way. Unions contracted under the Marriage Ordinance can only be dissolved by divorce procedures in the High Court. Educated women and their parents in particular are known to favour the registration of marriages more than do men.[2] This is partly because the provisions of the Ordinance give a measure of security to wives, widows and orphans, not provided by customary law. The rights of the widow in the event of the husband's death intestate have been mentioned above, as has the fact that plural marriage is illegal, and children born to other women, during the existence of the Ordinance marriage, are illegitimate, in the sense that they have no legally enforceable right to inherit a share of that part of their father's property left to his Ordinance wife and her children, should he die intestate. In addition the increased difficulties and consequences of divorce, such as the wife's right to claim maintenance costs, may be considered as conferring an additional measure of security for women. There is moreover the prestige element of being called 'Mrs' and being known by the husband's name. On the other hand the husband may not feel that the provisions of the Ordinance enhance his own position sufficiently to outweigh the possible social and economic costs involved in such weddings. These include the reception, which it is customary for the groom, and not the bride's parents, to pay for. Thus in some

Table 3. 6. *Type of marriages contracted by Akan Senior Civil Servants (ASCS) and their parents (P) (percentages)*

Region	Customary ASCS & P	ASCS Registered, P Customary	ASCS & P, Registered	Total %	N
		Type of Contract		Total	
Coastal	31	38	31	100	(29)
Eastern	27	46	27	100	(37)
Interior	37	58	5	100	(19)
Total	30	46	24	100	(85)

cases the registration of the marriage may be preceded by a period of strain, during which the wife presses the husband to enhance her own status in this way, which he may only be willing to do after they have lived together for a time and he feels sure that he wants to make the relationship a permanent one and has funds for the reception.

The following three examples illustrate, among other things, how the process of getting married has sometimes been quite prolonged, and the kinds of influences in marriage arrangements, which may be exerted by the older generation. All three instances are of men who have achieved educational, occupational and marital statuses quite different from those of their fathers and grandfathers before them, who had only elementary education, if any, and were polygynous. These husbands are monogamous and live with their wives. Mr Amoah readily admits that he has only undertaken the first stage of what he considers to be the complete marriage rites. He intends to complete them step by step, as he is able to save the necessary outlay. Mr Kweku, has already entered two customary marriages, the first at the instigation of his father, the second of his own accord. After his unhappy first experience, he appears cautious of committing himself to the legal formalities of a registered marriage straight away, and comments that he intends to wait first and see how his marital relationship develops. Mr Arthur had been customarily married for seven years, and had become the father of three children, before he decided that the time was ripe to register his apparently successful marriage.

Government Servants and Kinsmen

MR AMOAH

Mr Amoah in his late thirties and his wife in her late twenties are both Eastern Akan from the same village.

He was a certificated teacher working at a primary school in Accra and she had just left Middle School when they married. His paternal half-brother was sent by his father to see his wife's parents and matrilineage head. Two bottles of whisky and money, in all about ₵20, were given to them. His wife did not join him immediately but stayed to get her cooking utensils ready with a further ₵20 he gave to her. She joined him after a month or so and then, when it was time for her to have her first child, she went to stay with her mother for six months, returning later with their son. During the next five years of marriage as two more children were born, Mr Amoah studied at home, gained entrance to university and took a degree. While he lived in the university for three years his wife went back to stay with her mother. After graduating he got his present post as a secondary school teacher with a bungalow provided with his job. His wife and three children joined him there. He now says that the second stage of the customary rites remains to be performed. He expects that it will cost him about ₵36. After that he hopes to have the church blessing and may subsequently decide to have the marriage registered.

MR KWEKU

Mr Kweku's first marriage was to his cross-cousin (FZD), whom he had known since childhood. Twelve years ago his father, a wealthy cocoa farmer, first suggested the marriage. He himself opposed it, but his father continued for five years to try to persuade him, saying that the bulk of his property would pass to them in the form of a marriage settlement, if only he would agree. The final pressure was applied when his father promised to remarry Mr Kweku's divorced mother, if only he would consent to the marriage. In the end he agreed and his father had the customary rites performed on his behalf, while he was studying in England, and sent the girl to join him there as his wife. Eighteen months later they had a child. At the end of the year Mr Kweku brought the child back to Ghana and took her to be cared for by his father's sister, the child's maternal grandmother. That same year his own mother died and he felt he could no longer continue with the marriage partly because, having been brought up in the same house as his wife, he felt as if she were a sister and was afraid that on returning home it would cause great embarrassment if his wife were mistaken for his sister. His cousin stayed on in England to learn hairdressing and sewing; while he came to take up his present administrative post. Though he has now lost contact with his cousin, he continues to see their child every few months and remits money towards her upkeep. He has no intention however, of removing her from where she is. His father, of course, is annoyed. He had not given them any property before the marriage broke up.

Three years after the separation he met a typist working in the same office block and courted her for twelve months. They are now customarily married. He sent a friend and a brother to inform her parents of his intentions, giving them ₵16.80. He later sent a dozen bottles of soft drinks, a dozen bottles of beer as well as whisky and schnapps and money totalling ₵60 and gave his bride ₵120 to buy cooking utensils and cloths. When she first came to stay with him they held a party for his colleagues and friends. The bride's mother came to help her to do the cooking. He may register the marriage; but first he will wait and see.

MR ARTHUR

While working in Cape Coast as a junior Civil Servant, and living in his father's house, Mr Arthur performed the customary rites to marry his wife. He had first met her nearly ten years previously through her brother, a good friend and secondary school classmate of his. When they married she continued working as a nurse in Cape Coast, living in her father's house, as they had no house of their own. Moreover Mr Arthur thought they should gain some experience before setting up house together. A few months after the marriage he was posted to Sekondi 47 miles away, and visited his wife at weekends. He was later posted to Kumasi, 138 miles north of Cape Coast, while his wife went to Accra to do a midwifery course. They left their first baby with the wife's mother in Cape Coast. From Kumasi he was transferred to Bolgatanga 337 miles further north, where his wife, together with her divorced sister and their two small children, joined him. Mrs Arthur continued nursing and bore another child there. They lived in Bolgatanga for a total of four years until his application to study for a degree at the university at Legon was successful. While he was at the university his wife did a further nursing diploma in Accra and again left their three children with her mother and sister in Cape Coast. During Mr Arthur's first year at the university, seven years after the performance of the customary rites, they celebrated their marriage in church and registered it. He felt constrained to take his step then, partly because his wife had been complaining for some time and also because he thought it would be more in keeping with his new status. They held a reception for about a hundred people, for which his wife helped him to pay.

Mr Kweku's case is interesting in indicating that a father may continue to exert pressure on his son to make a cross-cousin marriage, with a view to transmitting considerable property to the couple and their offspring, property which would otherwise remain under matri-lineage control. All three instances show how typical it is of those whose education has been prolonged, for childbirth and marriage to precede the completion of studies and achievement of the Senior Civil Service post. There have been some Akan Senior Civil Servants however, especially in the younger age groups who, being fortunate enough to go straight from secondary school through university and even post-graduate training, have achieved their occupational ambitions before marrying and having children. In the following two examples the husbands had been working one or two years in the Senior Civil Service before they married, one as a lawyer and the other as an administrator. Both of their parents and one of their grandparents also had monogamous registered marriages.

MR STONE

Mr and Mrs Stone both come from the same coastal town and had in fact lived close to each other during their childhood, but it was not until they were both working in Kumasi during the late nineteen-fifties that they met each other, through mutual friends, and courted. The next year they became engaged in the customary manner. Mr Stone and his parents met his wife's relatives and took them drinks. He also gave a bible and ring to his fiancée. This was felt by the husband to be a formal announcement of the intention to marry, rather than a customary marriage. The following year they registered their marriage in their home town. Afterwards they provided refreshments for a reception in a public hall, sharing the expense between themselves. The next day the wife's brothers provided a wedding lunch in one of their houses for relatives and friends, and they attended church in the morning. They spent a few days visiting people and then returned to their jobs in Kumasi, where they set up their home together. Within six months they had their first son.

MR JOHNSON

Mr Johnson and his wife both came from Cape Coast and attended the same secondary school, he being a few years her senior. They used to join in the same school and holiday leisure activities during their teens. They lost contact for about six years when he was doing his university course in Germany and she was doing her nursing training in Scotland. In fact they had both been back in Ghana for a year or two, working, before they met each other in Accra, where they courted for a few months and then got engaged. He went to see her mother and provided drinks and an engagement ring. The following year they had a church wedding and then went straight to the Volta Region where the husband had been transferred. Within two months Mrs Johnson was the mother of twin boys.

These examples indicate that for a few, in particular those whose own parents' marriages were registered and monogamous, the presentation of drinks to the wife's guardians and the giving of gifts to the bride are increasingly seen in terms of an 'engagement', a promise to marry, rather than as an actual marriage, and that though conception may occur during this period, the couple are not very likely to be co-resident. Living together in such cases tends to follow the registration of the marriage. Few men whose own parents had registered marriages marry their wives only according to customary law. It is the husbands in the most prestigious occupational groups, such as the medical doctors, who are among those most likely to marry in church and under the Ordinance.

WIVES AND CHILDREN

Wives tend to have a similar cultural and educational background and training to their husbands in that they are mainly Akan and have been to school (See Tables 3. 7 and 8). In the survey over half were secondary or vocational school leavers, about a third had elementary education and a minority were university graduates. The majority of wives work full-time outside the home, many as primary

Table 3. 7. *Origins of Akan Senior Civil Servants and their wives*
(percentages)

Husband's region	Wife's Origin				Total	
	Same Region	Other Akan Region	Other Ghanaian Region	Foreign	%	N
Coastal	52	10	27	10	99	(29)
Eastern	71	14	12	3	100	(35)
Interior	37	27	20	16	100	(19)
Total	57	15	19	8	99	(83)

Table 3. 8. *Education of wives of Akan Senior Civil Servants
by region* (percentages)

Husband's region	Wife's educational level			Total	
	Primary Middle	Secondary Vocational	University	%	N
Coastal	31	55	14	100	(29)
Eastern	40	41	19	100	(35)
Interior	21	79	0	100	(19)
Total	33	54	13	100	(83)

Table 3. 9. *Occupations of wives of Akan Senior Civil
Servants by region* (percentages)

Husband's region	Wife's occupation				Total	
	Vocational	Clerical	Other	Housewife	%	N
Coastal	45	21	25	10	101	(29)
Eastern	27	14	32	27	100	(37)
Interior	32	11	5	53	101	(19)
Total	32	16	24	28	100	(85)

school teachers, nurses and clerks, but a few are employed at home as full or part-time seamstresses and traders (see Table 3. 9). They continue the tradition of the partly self-supporting rural Akan women. They are able to take on such employment, even when mothers of babies and young children, by delegating most of their nursing and housework to a variety of helpers as will be discussed below. Couples usually have a child within the first year of marriage and not infrequently before the religious or state ceremony is performed. This was illustrated in the cases above and is indicated by the reports of the husbands in the survey according to which over forty per cent of their first-born children were conceived before the performance of the traditional Akan marriage rites. Since child-bearing is seldom postponed until circumstances are 'convenient', and the mother or father has finished studying or they have found suitable accommodation, many first and second children were born abroad, while their parents were studying in foreign institutions, or were born while their parents were living in separate accommodation because of their study or work contracts. Some were sent to grandparents during such periods, as in the case of Mr Arthur's children.

About one in five fathers in the survey were like Mr Kweku, in that they had children born to them by other unions, either before or during their present marriages. There are indications that this feature may be more common among the Akan from the interior than those further south, since among the interior Akan respondents in the survey over a third had such children, in contrast with one in ten of the coastal Akan. This is possibly associated with the fact that quite a few of the former are first generation educated and have only achieved Senior Service status by a long and arduous route, and one or two have even divorced wives with elementary or no education to marry vocationally trained women more easily able to fit into the new social and economic environments.

Although bigamy is contrary to church law and the Marriage Ordinance, a proportion of unions are, for some intents and purposes, polygynous. Common law unions and extra-conjugal liaisons, producing children whose paternity is acknowledged, are recognized as not uncommon in the higher socio-economic group in the city, to which the Senior Civil Servants belong.[3]

THE HOUSEHOLD

The Akan Senior Civil Servant's household in Accra generally includes his wife and most of his children, together with one or more relatives and in-laws and domestic helps. For instance in twenty of the households visited during the course of study, which ranged in size from six to fifteen members and housed couples who had been married for an average of ten years with 3.2 children, there was found to be one wife's relative per household and one husband's relative in every second household, as well as 1.2 paid domestic helps.

This picture of the composition of their households tallies somewhat with that drawn by Caldwell (1968: 61) for a larger sample of urban dwellers with a wider range of educational levels. Moreover, as the latter demonstrates, the majority of such co-resident kin and affines are junior siblings and siblings' children. Only a minority are adults, and of these very few are of the senior generation, that is parents and parents' siblings of the husband and wife. Various types of exchange relationship obtain between the household head and his wife and these co-resident kin and strangers. Some are dependants, such as the young people seeking an education referred to above, to whom the householder may feel a sense of obligation. Some are the distant kin and strangers, who come to help with the chores in return for maintenance and wages as discussed below. Not only do kinship obligations and domestic needs have an important effect upon the composition of the household, but so do the husband's and wife's educational and occupational statuses. The pursuit of further studies after marriage and the exigencies of Senior Civil Service life, such as transfers and promotion, often entail travelling both inside and outside the country and the consequent temporary separation of husbands and wives and children.

The following examples illustrate some of the ways in which kinship and occupational positions influence the setting up and composition of households. The first, that of Mr Smith, is an example of the type of residentially isolated, conjugal family unit, headed by men, who have no dependent kin needing or wanting to stay with them and whose wives' own relatives are all educated and employed and so unavailable to come and help with domestic chores. They have however, as is common in some old, educated coastal households, a maid, who belongs to a family of servants attached to the wife's maternal home.

73

MR SMITH

Mr Smith, an accountant, and his wife who is unemployed, are a third generation educated Fanti couple who have been married for seven years. Immediately after their registered church wedding the husband went to the United States to do a professional course. The wife and her mother went to live with her 'uncle' (MMZS) for six months, until her baby, born two months after the wedding, was old enough to fly with her to join her husband. They spent four years alone together in the U.S., where their second and third children were born. When they returned to Accra, two and a half years ago, the wife's mother came for a few weeks at the birth of the fourth child. Otherwise the only people who have lived in their household have been maids and stewards. The present maid, obtained by the wife's mother from Cape Coast, is the daughter of a woman who served the latter for many years and is said to be considered a kinswoman. Their stewards have been illiterate youths from northern Ghana. The couple's many educated relatives frequently pass by for a drink and chat, but none come to stay. Neither of them has any younger brothers or sisters.

The second household, that of Mr Amponsah, is an example of the common practice whereby young men, at a transitional stage in their careers, find it convenient to lodge for some months or years with a senior male relative. If their educational level is low and their relationship to the householder not very close, their role may be that of domestic help. If they are highly educated, like Kwame, in this case, then they may be treated as equals, dining and sharing leisure activities with the husband and wife.

MR AMPONSAH

Mr Amponsah, an administrator in his early thirties, has been customarily married for a few weeks to a nurse in her early twenties. They both have educated fathers and come from the Eastern Akan area. When his new bride moved to stay with him there were already two of his 'relatives' living with him. Kofi (his MZHDS), a middle school leaver in his early twenties, had been with him for about a year. He does the housework in return for a subsistence allowance, while he looks for a job in town. Kwame (his FZS) is a graduate in his late twenties and has lived with Mr Amponsah since he got a job in a government department nine months ago. He would find it difficult to set up a household on his own, as he has still not saved up enough money to buy furnishings, a refrigerator and other things.

The third household illustrates the type of situation in which conjugal family members are residentially separated during several years of early marriage, through the spouses' educational careers. This is particularly common among those men who have reached middle-age before attaining their occupational goal.

MR ANSAH

The Ansahs have spent most of their eight years of married life apart. Mr Ansah met and courted his wife when he was a junior civil servant, just about to go to university, and she, fresh from nurses' training college, was living with her parents. They met and married in their home town, first according to customary rites, and then at the insistence of the wife's father, a catechist, in church. The marriage could not be registered as Mr Ansah already had a 'customary' wife trading in Sekondi, by whom he had three sons.

Within a couple of months Mr Ansah left for university and his wife worked with a private midwife in her home town until her first child was born at her parents' home. As soon as the baby was three months old she went to work at a hospital fifty miles from her home town. Her mother accompanied her and stayed for two months and her cousin (FZD) stayed with her there for a year to help care for the baby while she worked. Each month her husband travelled by lorry from the university to visit her. Her mother when she left, sent a maid to stay with her, a neighbour's daughter of about thirteen.

A month before her second baby was due Mr Ansah's wife stopped work and went to stay with her parents for her three months' maternity leave. When she returned to her job with her two infants, her mother was unable to accompany her and she had no maid living with her at first. She had to leave her two children with a friend and neighbour while she continued working. After a few months her father sent her a girl, the daughter of one of the labourers on his cocoa farm. The following year she managed to get a transfer of job to her home town, where her maternal grandmother could care for her children, while she continued to work. Her third child was delivered in her maternal grandmother's house. By then her husband had finished his course, got a job in Accra, and rented accommodation from an acquaintance. She went there to join him, taking her own brother to attend school as well as a maid and her three small children. The husband already had two of his sons by his first marriage staying with him to attend school and his sister's son, who was going to a technical school. By the following year the Ansahs were also accommodating the wife's sister, who was attending commercial school and the husband's third child by his first marriage.

The continuation of studies by husbands and wives long after marriage has not only entailed conjugal separation for long periods in some cases, but it has also entailed the rearing of children of such marriages by their kin. Thus in the Boakyes' case their children were first cared for by their maternal grand-mother and a foreign foster mother before being sent to day nurseries, at three years old.

MR BOAKYE

Mr Boakye, an administrator in his late thirties, comes from Kumasi, and his wife, a teacher in her early thirties, from Sekondi. They met in Accra ten years ago, when Mr Boakye, who was on leave, visited the ministries with an old class-mate of his from Adisadel, the cousin of his future wife. They courted briefly until the end of his leave when he returned to Ho, where he was posted. A few months later he visited her parents to give the customary drinks. She continued living in Accra with her niece (BD).

Five months after the customary rites had been performed, his wife bore their first child at her mother's house. Mr Boakye in the meantime had his niece (MZD) living with him to do the cooking at his bungalow. The baby was born in June and in the September Mr Boakye, accompanied by his wife, went to England, where he had a scholarship to do a post-graduate diploma. Their daughter was left with the wife's mother. Mrs Boakye enrolled to train as a teacher in England. At Christmas they had a registry office wedding with a few Ghanaian and English friends for a luncheon reception, after which they spent a weekend in Brighton with the husband's brother. A month after the wife had completed her first year's training, they had their second child. Mrs Boakye nursed him for three months and then took him to an English 'foster mother', who was already caring for three other children. They both continued their courses, visiting the child on Saturday afternoons. At the end of their second year's stay in England their third child was born. Mr Boakye, who had completed his period of training, travelled with a couple back to Ghana, taking the two children with him to his wife's mother. Mrs Boakye returned the following year after finishing her course and they moved into their present bungalow with their three children. She found herself a teaching post within two weeks of arrival. Mrs Boakye's sister's daughter came to stay with her to attend a technical school and help with the children. Her mother sent her an unrelated maid to help. Her husband's nephew also came to live with them to attend middle school. The eldest daughter was sent to a local day nursery at three years of age.

SETTING UP A CONJUGAL HOUSEHOLD

Very few couples among those interviewed had, like the Smiths, set up house alone together immediately or soon after marriage. This was either because of the co-residence of kin and in-laws, as in the case of the honeymoon couple, the Amponsahs, or the husband's protracted studies at home or abroad, which might cause separation for months or years, as in the case of Mr Ansah and Mr Boakye, or transfer in the course of work, as for example in Mr Arthur's case. Many householders, like Mr Armah, have either their own relatives, including brothers and sisters and their children (own and classificatory) or in-laws staying with them from the initial stages of the marriage onwards. Some of these, as has already been indicated, are educated relatives who would have difficulty in finding lodgings elsewhere in town. Many are in search of employment, and are either fresh from school or are illiterates. Some have come to attend school, or to get medical attention. Others, especially the wife's kin, come to give domestic help. The number and type of such co-resident kin vary from household to household. Only seldom are senior brothers or sisters or parents-in-law resident. They generally come during family crises such as birth or ill-health.

A further problem which may hinder the setting up of a separate co-resident conjugal household is that of finding accommodation, a difficulty encountered by Mr Ansah. Government bungalows are in short supply, and housing in general in great demand and expensive. Thus prior to marriage, and afterwards, young professionals and administrators in the city frequently have to find a temporary place to stay with friends or relatives until, if they are fortunate, a government bungalow is allocated to them. A few couples live in the flat or house secured through the wife's job, as nurse or teacher (as did Mr Arthur, p. 68).

A colonial custom followed until recently, and which partly continues due to staffing problems, is that of changing the posting of government senior officers from one station to another every eighteen months or so. For the expatriate Civil Servant this used to mean a reposting after every tour of duty and home leave. For the local officers this has often entailed frequent transfers from one region of the country to another, with all the domestic upheavals and problems this entails. As a result of this many experienced Civil Servants have had to move on several occasions, never settling anywhere for long until their present posting in Accra. The strain of these continual shifts is sometimes felt most by the wife, who has her perpetual problems of packing and unpacking, of finding domestic help, and a job if she works. The temporary nature of much accommodation may contribute to the fact that couples often do not spend much time and money on decorating and beautifying the houses in which they are living, since they neither own them nor are likely to live in them for long. A household history illustrates the kind of situation brought about by this mobility and also once more indicates the range of kin who may be temporary residents in such households.

MR ARMAH

The Armahs are now in their early forties. They had their first baby in England seventeen years ago, when they were both studying and working there. The wife trained as a State Registered Nurse and midwife, the husband took a degree in economics. On their return to Ghana the husband went into government service and was subjected to frequent transfers from one district to another. They first stayed in a bungalow in Accra for three months, where the husband's great maternal uncle sent them a girl aged ten to serve them. This girl stayed with them for three years. The wife's mother also brought a girl (MZDD) of the same age, who stayed for four years. Both girls learnt how to do household chores. The Armahs next moved to Tamale, where they stayed for less than a year. While there they were joined by the wife's mother for three months after the birth of their second child. They were subsequently transferred to Sekondi-Takoradi where they stayed for six months. At the end of this period they proceeded on their two months annual leave, first to the wife's parents on the coast and then to the husband's kin in the interior. The husband's next posting was to Accra once more, where the fourth child was born. The wife's mother and two of her sisters were then staying with them, as were two of the husband's sisters attending school in Accra. It was while they were in Accra at this time that the husband's mother's sister came to stay for medical attention. Their fifth transfer was to Sekondi-Takoradi once more. They travelled together with their children, the two maids and a steward. While they were there one of the husband's maternal half brothers came to stay to attend school and has remained until the present. After a few months in Sekondi, they went on leave to stay with the husband's relatives. There the wife lost one of her maids, as the grandmother wanted her back. Then the husband resumed work again in Cape Coast where the wife lost her second maid to her own sister, who had just had a baby and needed a competent maid to help her. In exchange she gave her a less experienced girl. During that period, when she had lost her two competent maids, the wife's teenage sister, who had just left school, was a great help. She stayed for one year until she went to training college. In the meantime their first child was sent to attend school in Accra and stay with the wife's father. The second child began to attend a local nursery school. While they were still in Sekondi-Takoradi a distant 'niece' of the wife (MMZ-DSD) aged about fifteen, who was playing truant was sent to her to attend middle school. It was the wife's mother who asked if the 'niece' could stay. She remained with them about two years. At about the same time another 'niece' (FMZDDDD) of the wife came to stay with them for three months, as her parents were sent on a sudden transfer.

A month later Mr Armah himself was unexpectedly asked to go to Tamale on transfer for six months. His wife moved with her children to stay with her father during that period. Mr Armah stayed in Tamale with his two brothers, a sister and a maid. After that they went abroad for two years as he had the chance to do a specialist course in England. They left two of their four children with the wife's parents. While they were abroad Mrs Armah did a sewing course, which enabled her to set up as a seamstress in Accra, where they were posted on their return. Their household now includes the husband's two brothers, whom he is educating, a sister's child, attending primary school and the wife's sister's daughter in her late teens, and their own five children. Their fifth child was born four months after they returned from abroad. The wife's niece (ZD) still lives with them and has a job in town. The youngest child is now two and a half and attending nursery school. An unrelated girl of about twelve years old, sent by the wife's mother from her home town, and a steward aged about seventeen from the Upper Region help Mrs Armah with the chores while she runs her dress-making business.

The Armah's case is particularly interesting since it graphically illustrates the mobile character of Civil Service employment, which has meant that some government servants and their dependants have been shifted from region to region every few months, with the result that couples have scarcely had the time or the incentive to convert rented accommodation into a home. It also shows the effects upon the household composition of both the husband's obligations to his kin and the continual flow of domestic helpers from the wife's side. The residential pattern, as well as the location, of the domestic group, are seen to be continually shifting, people coming and going for longer or shorter periods. Altogether at some time the couple have had eight of the wife's kin living with them and seven of the husband's.

Since house-room in the city is so scarce and costly and dependants often so many, accommodation is frequently full to capacity. Bungalows and flats, either built under the colonial régime for the expatriate bachelor, or planned more recently with the small nuclear family in mind, usually have two bedrooms and yet they not infrequently house ten or more people. Overcrowding becomes so acute in some cases that children have to sleep on mats, relatives have to sleep in the servants' quarters (attached to most of the older types of accommodation) and many bedrooms have three or more occupants. Few houses have empty rooms ready for the visitors who arrive. The households of Mr Hammond and Mr Acquah described below indicate the kind of overcrowding which may result.

In the first example a couple, both teachers, have housed and sent to school a number of young dependent relatives. There are now fifteen adults and children in their three-bedroomed house. Because of the overcrowding some of the school-boys sleep in the servants' quarters in the yard of the house. In the next instance visitors have also had to overflow into the servants' quarters. The maids sleep in the sitting room and all of the couple's four children often have to sleep in their parents' bedroom.

Government Servants and Kinsmen

Mr Hammond and his wife, both in their early forties, come from a coastal town. Their fathers were junior Civil Servants and their mothers traders. He is now an education officer, having risen up from the junior ranks, and she is a primary school teacher. Since their marriage fifteen years ago they have supported quite a few dependants as well as their own six children. Altogether sixteen relatives have lived in their home, eight of the wife's and eight of the husband's including the following:

Wife's relatives

MZDS – in his early teens stayed with them for six months after they married to attend school.

MBDS – a teenage boy has stayed with them for the past year to attend the local middle school.

MZS – a youth has finished attending fifth form at secondary school waiting to get a place in a sixth form. He has been with them six months.

MZDS – has been with them two and a half years attending middle school. He stayed with his maternal grandfather till he died and then, since he was giving trouble to his mother, they invited him to come.

MD – came to stay for eighteen months after their second child was born, and Mrs Hammond was working.

MD – aged eighteen has been staying with them for a year. She helps with the domestic work in the mornings and goes to work in town. Her two year old daughter is with her.

Husband's relatives

MD – has left school and is looking for a job in town.

MZS – brought by his older sister, two and a half years ago from a village to be 'enlightened'. He attends the local middle school.

2 MZS – both stayed in the household for a year while they were working in town. Then one left to attend training college and the other went to be a pupil teacher, while waiting for admission to a college.

MZS – attends a technical school. The husband has paid his expenses and lodged him in his school holidays for over three years.

MZD – attends secondary school and spends all her holidays in the household.

FZS – a school boy who stayed with them for a year to attend school and helped in the house three years ago.

Marriage among a Matrilineal Elite

MR ACQUAH

During several visits paid to the Acquahs' household over a ten months period, the number of relatives living in the house, in addition to the conjugal family, ranged from three to fourteen, the mean being five. The permanent residents included the husband's brother, working in town and two maids, who were distant kin of the wife. (The wife was not aware of the exact relationship.) The couple's young siblings came to spend school holidays with them. The husband's maternal uncles came to visit the town. His sisters and their children came for holidays. His brother stayed with his wife and children, while awaiting accommodation. The largest gathering was at Christmas when there were over twenty people staying in the household.

The result of the giving and receiving of help to and from a variety of co-resident kin and in-laws in the form of food, lodgings, clothing and money, in return for past and present services, is frequently that any tendencies to residential isolation are inhibited. The outcome is that upon close and repeated observation and enquiry into the recent past, the composition and location of many households is seen to be remarkably changeable over a period of weeks, months or years. As a result of several pressures the boundaries of the co-resident household group are often fluid and seldom coterminous with the conjugal family unit.

SPOUSES AND IN-LAWS

The frequent overcrowding and co-residence with kin, in-laws and strangers has undoubtedly varied effects upon the day-to-day relationships between conjugal family members, who are seldom found in their houses without some relatives or maids present. The domestic privacy of husbands and wives may be seriously curtailed. Parents and children may seldom be alone for long in each other's company.

Categories of people live together who would scarcely do so according to tradition, and many customary elements are seen to persist in their relationships, though in modified form. Thus, for instance, an often expressed feeling of restraint and avoidance was noted between Akan husbands and their wives' relatives living in their households. This became particularly obvious at meal-times. Traditionally men do not even eat in the same house as their affines, hence whenever the wife's mother or aunt paid a visit to several of the households observed, she usually remained in the background, often in the kitchen, while her son-in-law ate at the table in the dining-room cum lounge. Similarly several wives' junior kin, such as sisters and nieces, were noted not to eat at the same table as their sisters' husbands, but to dine in the kitchen. One or two wives remarked that their young relatives felt too shy to sit at the same table as their brother-in-law. In fact some wives and their children were themselves observed to continue the customary practice of eating separately from the husband, especially when his time for returning home from his office did not coincide with their own arrival home from school and work.

The innovation whereby some wives live at close quarters with their in-laws on the other hand, was often seen to be associated with both covert and overt expressions of hostility. Wives would complain that husbands' younger brothers and sisters staying in the house did few or no chores, and in a few of the instances in which the husbands' mothers and adult sisters came to stay, both during and prior to the periods of observation, tension reached such a high pitch that open conflict erupted. Some of the issues over which such conflict arose are discussed in chapters 4 and 5.

CONCLUSION

In the latter part of this chapter the ways in which Akan Senior Civil Servants become husbands and householders have been indicated. Becoming a husband is seen to be often a gradual process, which may be spread over a period of months or even years. Some of the Akan customary rites are usually performed before the registration of the marriage. Co-residence of husband and wife may precede the last stages of the wedding procedures and does not always follow them. Childbirth not infrequently occurs before the completion of the marriage rites and the setting up of a co-resident conjugal family household. The travelling involved in the process of getting a higher education and in occupational transfers may lead to spouses and parents and children being temporarily separated.

Before coming to live and work in Accra most of the husbands and wives under study have worked in one or more provincial towns, many have studied abroad, sometimes spending one or two years of their early married life abroad. Once the couple come to live together in Accra, when the husband has been posted to his high ranking government job in the administrative centre, and acquired accommodation in a suburb, their household may shelter one or two or a continual stream of relatives coming to stay with them, to be provided with the necessities of life, to help with the chores or simply visiting. House-room is frequently used to capacity, as it accommodates some of the hundreds of rural–urban migrants, who have swelled the population of the capital in the past ten years. Thus in their modern suburban housing, far from their home towns, couples are often living at close quarters with relatives and in-laws, who would traditionally not co-reside. There is evidence that aspects of the customary relationships of respect, avoidance and hostility found in the rural Akan domestic setting continue, sometimes modified or exacerbated, in the new type of residential context. Examples have illustrated the great difference between households with respect to composition, and the relative isolation, in residential terms, of the conjugal family.

In the chapter which follows, the ways such Akan couples allocate their resources in money and time are considered: how they provide for material needs; how their chores and child-care are carried out and how they make decisions about such domestic matters. The problem central to the discussion is the assessment of the degrees of *segregation* and *closure,* observable in the organization of these areas of marital behaviour; the possible associations of these two variables with each other, and the kinds of conjugal conflicts and strain observed, according to the ways in which domestic rights and duties are allocated, between spouses and their kin. The first consideration is the domestic budget.

NOTES

[1] Central Bureau of Statistics (1969: 197).

[2] This fact was noted more than twenty years ago, Crabtree (1950: 55) and Busia (1950: 41). It has recently been verified in a study of students' attitudes (Oppong, 1972a).

[3] As a sociology graduate in his thirties described the situation, such men have their monogamous 'companionate' marriages at home and keep the other wives outside!

THE ALLOCATION OF RESOURCES

The earning, management and allocation of material resources are tasks with which all husbands and wives have to deal, and ones which may vary considerably in the way in which they are carried out. They fall in an area of activities and decision-making which is of crucial importance, both to the couple concerned and their dependants.

The outline of the customary Akan pattern of organizing the material basis of domestic life, given in Chapter 2, indicated that the Akan conjugal family does not traditionally own, use, manage or inherit any exclusive, substantial property of its own, though husband and wife co-operate to provide for the maintenance of themselves and their children. It is the matrilineage which forms the *closed* economic group, membership of which gives rights in its resources, and members of which may serve as substitutes for each other, with regard to the holding of economic rights and obligations, such as responsibility for debts or co-ownership of property.

Subsequently the discussion of the Akan Senior Civil Servants, their incomes, occupational privileges and kinship obligations, showed that their major sources of livelihood are now individually earned and controlled incomes, though a large minority still maintain shares in jointly held family properties. Recognition of obligations to assist parents, to help brothers and sisters, to educate sisters' children and so on when necessary, means that this income is frequently used to maintain a number of kin. There are signs however, that the extent to which the roles of financial provider and educator are played across the boundaries of the now neolocal and somewhat geographically and socially remote, urban conjugal family, vary very much from individual to individual and region to region. But though the degree of *openness* varies, few conjugal families appear completely financially discrete and *closed*.

The question asked now is what kind of financial relationship obtains between Akan husbands and wives, both in the light of the customary norm and of the conditions of their new urban situation. The problem is to see how they cope with their one or two sources of income in relation, both to their own material needs, and those of their dependants; to what extent they spend, save and own goods jointly or separately, the types of co-operation they practice in managing their financial affairs. An important concern will be to see whether the degree of *segregation*, apparent in couples' financial activities, appears to be associated with the degree of *openness* observed, and which particular types of resource allocation and management appear to be frought with tension or conflict and change in the new urban context.

FINANCIAL PROVISION: SHARING RESPONSIBILITY

Financial provision for the conjugal family and household is in most cases a shared responsibility. Two thirds or more of wives are in paid employment and some of those who stay at home are earning money by trading, sewing or baking. Since all wives who are earning contribute something to their own and their children's support, we may estimate that fewer than one in four husbands are completely responsible for the upkeep of their wives and children.[1] The following comment of Mrs Boadu illustrates a typical attitude of many working Ghanaian women. Few wives feel they can afford to depend upon their husbands for support, because not only is the cost of living high in the capital, but many husbands and wives, as has already been indicated, have more or less extensive obligations to kin in addition to their own children.

MRS BOADU

Mrs Boadu is a trained teacher, aged thirty-five, and has worked ever since she married ten years ago. The only times she has stopped work are for three maternity leaves and for nine months when she went to England with her husband and there took a part-time domestic science course. She says she works for several reasons: to earn enough money to buy what she wants herself (she doesn't have to ask her husband for clothes); to get out of the house and meet people; to avoid doing chores in the house; to help her widowed mother to whom she sends several cedis monthly, and her divorced sister, whose six children she helps to maintain in school. In addition she pays about half of the food bills for her own household of eight, and regularly buys things for her own children, including clothes

The allocation of resources

Table 4. 1. *Percentage of working wives contributing to items of domestic expenditure**

	Item	Contribution		
		Nil	Part	All
I	Own clothes	0	66	34
	Children's clothes	13	79	8
II	Food	21	74	5
	Domestic labour	24	65	11
III	Transport	64	28	3
	School fees	77	23	0
	Rent	84	8	8
	Fuel	87	10	3

* *N* = 43 Akan couples with employed wives.
The survey responses used in this chapter are those of the 61 Akan husbands with Akan wives unless otherwise stated.

and toys. She knows that her husband would not be able to buy them all the things they want, for not only is his salary limited, but he has a number of responsibilities to his own mother and sisters. She feels she cannot rely upon him to supply all her own and her children's material wants.

The types of items for household use which wives are likely to supply can be divided into three categories, those which nearly all working wives provide, those most make some kind of contribution towards and those items they are unlikely to pay for at all (see Table 4. 1).

The items wives are most likely to buy include their own and their children's clothes. Many have numerous dresses and Ghanaian cloths. Funerals, Memorial Services and parties are all occasions for lavish expenditure on new clothes. Styles change rapidly and new social occasions warrant new outfits for those who can afford them. The latest styles in ear-rings, bags, watches, wigs and shoes are all expensive and much sought after, and these are items which most husbands will be either unwilling or unable to provide as rapidly as the changes in fashion occur.

As regards payment for food, husbands often give their wives a regular fixed amount, which may be far below what is really spent, and wives complain that the amount does not always increase as the family grows or when the cost of living rises. It is the usual practice for the wife to add from her own earnings to pay for the additional cost of food, such as buying the vegetables from the market, while the husband not infrequently does some of the store-shopping, and may pay for those provisions.

The way in which domestic servants' wages are paid varies. In some households it is the husband who pays, in others the couple share the cost and in yet others the wife pays. Some wives pay servants' wages because they feel that they ought to do so, since servants are doing work which is felt to be basically a wife's duty. The two items of expenditure, food and labour, lie in an ill-defined area of responsibility, which appears to be a source of potential tension between husband and wife (see Table 4. 1). Each spouse may at some point try to avoid responsibility and shift all or part of it on to the partner. Both items are a perpetual drain upon the monthly income, from which the provider cannot claim a return, unlike the durable moveable goods such as clothes and machines of one kind and another, which are subject to permanent and individual ownership. The cost of transport is a further permanent drain upon limited resources, which may also be a source of friction. More often than not the husband foots the bill, since most husbands, but few wives, own cars. Many wives thus depend upon their husbands for transport, others get taxis or go with friends to work or to shop.

School fees, fuel and rent are normally paid by the husband, the latter two mainly because they are deducted from his earnings. The wife may oblige by helping to pay, but she will not normally feel that she ought to do so, and should the husband omit payment of any of these bills, she is likely to think it a gross neglect of his duties as father and husband. They belong to an area of the domestic budget in which responsibility is fairly well defined.

The financial provision for the Akan Senior Civil Servant's household is mainly a shared activity, in which most wives play an important part. Each spouse however, tends to make a separate contribution, and in a number of fairly well-defined areas. The husband usually adds the most, since his salary and material resources, in terms of accommodation and transport gained through his job, are generally more substantial than those of his wife. Often there is little prior consultation before items are provided. Few discuss how money should be spent together or actually pool their resources. The case of the Takyis provides an illustration of an acute form of friction over money which may arise, developing into open conflict, when the areas of responsibility of husband and wife are not agreed upon or accepted. In this instance temporary resolution of the conflict was only achieved by the intervention of a mutual friend.

The Takyis, both in their late thirties, have five children and work in offices in the town, he as a surveyor and she as a clerk. The husband comes from an interior Akan town and the wife from Akwapim. Ever since they married they have had no regular budget for organizing the purchase of things for their household, nor have they sat down together to discuss what they both earn and how it should best be spent. In fact neither knows what the other earns or spends. The husband gives her ₵20 each month for housekeeping. He also usually goes to the shops on Saturday mornings and buys provisions, such as tinned fish, milk and beer, and the wife passes through the market on her way home from work to buy vegetables, smoked fish, pepper and other things. They both buy clothes for the children at Christmas and birthdays and each buys his or her own clothes and toilet articles.

After a quarrel, in which the husband took the side of his sister who was paying a visit, the wife decided to stop using what amounted to half of her monthly salary on food and other household needs. The husband retaliated by refusing to let her use his car or even to give her a lift to work, if she would not pay half of the petrol, maintenance and insurance costs. He also refused to pay the steward at the end of the month (previously he had paid the steward and his wife had paid the maid). For a whole week the wife was adamant and walked to the end of their avenue to take a taxi to work, which cost her a cedi a day. On the fifth day the husband was suddenly taken to hospital with suspected appendicitis. The car was left locked in the garage. The steward, who had not got his pay, stopped work and the wife still had to walk to get a taxi to go to her office, as well as to get transport to visit her husband in hospital. It was only after the intervention of an old class-mate of the husband's that he relented and began to provide a more adequate monthly sum for food and domestic help, and to give his wife the use of the car. After a few weeks the wife began once again to add a few cedis each month from her salary to buy the luxury items which her children loved, such as margarine, tinned milk and jam.

The fact is that, like the Takyis, most husbands and wives, when they are both working, spend their own separate incomes, each paying

Table 4. 2a. *Financial relationships: openness and segregation*
$(N=58)$

Score on financial closure index	Score on wife's financial provision index*		
	High (4–7)	Medium (1–3)	Nil (housewife)
Open (4–5)	7	4	3
Medium (2–3)	11	5	12
Closed (0–1)	7	5	4

* See Appendix p. 165 for descriptions of the scores used.

for some necessities and, when responsibilities are poorly defined and subject to question, tension may easily develop, as one spouse feels that he or she is shouldering too much of the burden.

A final question we may ask at this point is whether there appears to be any correlation between *joint* provision for household needs – as indicated by the relative size of wives' contributions to the household expenditure – and the extent to which financial relations appear *open* or *closed* – measured in terms of the husband's spending money on maintaining and educating kin and owning property jointly with them. Table 4. 2a above would seem to indicate that there is no obvious correlation between the two. Wives contribute relatively large amounts to household expenditure in situations categorised as both *closed* and *open*. We may next turn to financial management as opposed to provision and assess to what extent the pattern is similar or different.

FINANCIAL MANAGEMENT: SECURITY AND
CONFLICT AVOIDANCE

With regard to the long term management of resources, only a few couples jointly own property, such as houses, cars and farms or possess joint bank accounts. In the survey more than twice as many husbands said they owned property together with their kin, as with their wives, and fewer than one in ten couples were reported to have joint accounts. Moreover, although husband and wife typically both provide for household needs, many wives use their incomes in ways unknown to their husbands and few wives claim to know what their husbands earn and how they spend it.

In discussions spouses commonly admit that they insulate most of their cash and property dealings from observation and control by their partners on purpose, partly so as to avoid conflict. Thus the husband may preserve a measure of secrecy about his own allocation of resources, so as to keep from his wife the extent of his extra-conjugal family commitments, either to matrikin or other 'rivals'. A fear, which may influence either spouse's behaviour, is that of the idea of a potential or actual rival, the second wife or second husband, either already benefiting from the spouse's resources or likely to do so at the termination of the marriage through divorce or death.

The wife, if earning, is likely to keep her own savings accounts and even property, both to avoid criticism about her spending habits from her husband (such as the amount she spends each month on personal adornment), and also to provide that measure of financial security, for herself and her children, both at present and in the future, which she may feel her husband is unable or unwilling to provide for her. Indeed in some cases husbands, aware of their own limitations in this latter respect, are known to encourage their wives to maintain a high degree of financial independence. The extent to which spouses maintain separate money interests does however, vary from couple to couple and while in some cases the separation of interests is itself a matter of mutual agreement by husbands and wives, who consider the arrangement to be the most suitable adaptation to their domestic situation, in other cases the arrangement is a continual source of friction, each spouse repeatedly attempting to gain more knowledge of and control over the other's spending.

The major factors, openly stated by the husbands and wives concerned, to be associated with this general pattern of *segregation*, in particular with the determination of many working wives to maintain control over their own resources, are twofold. The first factor is the persistence of customary Akan norms and practices regarding the financial unity and solidarity of the sibling group and more inclusive matrilineage segment for both the ownership and inheritance of property and, what is crucial, the exclusion from this unit of a man's wife and children.

The matrilineage segment as we have already noted remains in Akan society, in fact as well as customary law, the significant unit for the ownership and control of immoveable property, houses and land. Groups of close matrikin, mothers and their children, sets of brothers and sisters still continue to own and manage property, not only what they have inherited, but also new properties, which they have purchased. Thus if an individual builds a house or starts a farm, there may be the expectation on the part of his matrikin that they will be joint benefactors. In fact they do sometimes eventually live in the house or work on the farm. Individual ownership of such property is not always taken for granted. It may have to be proved. Thus property a wife helps her husband to establish can eventually be considered to belong to his matrikin, his mother and siblings and maternal nephews. Knowledge that this can occur makes a working wife hesitant to enter financial ventures with her husband, unless she knows that her own and her children's rights are clearly stated and incorporated in legal documents. Such a risk may be increased of course if the property in question is in the husband's home town.

This fear of matrilineal inheritance is perhaps the most deep-seated factor affecting the financial activities of wives. There is a sharp awareness that the practice still continues even among educated urban migrants, far from their natal areas, and even in cases where the wives and orphans in question have resort to the legal protection afforded by the provisions of the Marriage Ordinance. This awareness is continually renewed through the circulation of gossip, giving harrowing accounts of the fate of the conjugal families of deceased educated Akan men. It is also reinforced by observations of the fate of their own rural female kin and affines, whose husbands may have died suddenly, before making any provision for them and their children. Such gossip includes tales of young educated widows, whose in-laws come to seize their deceased husband's clothes and personal possessions and to lay claim to insurance benefits, before even the deceased has been buried; or stories of village widows, whose meagre boxes of possessions have been held and searched by their in-laws, before they have been allowed to return to their family homes with their own few cloths and trinkets.

In the light of such facts some wives readily admit that they maintain their own resources, separately from those of their husbands, sometimes refusing to assist the latter in their efforts because of a definite feeling of alienation from the husband and his matrikin, at least as regards financial matters, and the very real fear that at possible widowhood only a very small part of any household property will be theirs. Even, as a wife married under the Ordinance, a women's due share of her husband's property at his death intestate amounts only to two-ninths, unless she has legal evidence that her rights are more extensive, as they may in fact be if she has worked and earned a salary throughout her married life and added her resources to his. A further factor is that few husbands appear to make wills or to take out substantial insurance policies for the benefit of their wives and children. Not only are these new forms of activities against which prejudice may exist, but there is in many cases little immoveable property to inherit and little surplus cash to be invested annually in life insurance. Moreover just as during his life-time the Civil Servant has a number of dependants in addition to his own children, there is likely to be a number of would-be heirs at his decease. The fact that separation of financial interests by husbands and wives is more marked among the Akan couples than among Ewe couples similarly situated, but coming from an area in which patrilineal descent and inheritance are the rule, clearly supports these contentions that *segregation* is in part a reaction to matriliny.[2] The second factor associated with *segregation* is that many husbands and their wives have a far higher standard of living, in terms of accommodation and spending power, as a result of their high educational attainment than their kin, including their own parents and siblings, even though the latter may be richer in terms of property ownership. Thus, as has already been indicated, they may be potentially and actually subject to persistent pressure to assist those with a much lower standard of living, a situation also common among non-Akan Senior Civil Servants, who work in the capital and come from areas in which 'patriliny' is the norm (Oppong, 1969). If the husband has numerous claims made on him for help by people whom he feels obliged to aid, then the wife may be afraid that her personal resources are being used indirectly to support her in-laws, instead of either maintaining her own and her children's comparatively high standard of living, or even helping her own relatives, who may also want her assistance. Thus rather than pool her resources in full, she may only be willing to provide items from which she and her own children benefit directly, such as clothes and food, and she may be determined to try and provide for herself and children the kind of security she feels her husband cannot provide. Thus the survey data indicate in Table 4. 2b that financial management – in terms of shared spending and ownership by husbands and wives – is less likely to be very *joint* when the husband is involved in heavy commitments to maintain and educate kin and owns property with them. Table 4. 2b below illustrates that no couple was found in the cell denoting excessive *openness* and *jointness*. We have now indicated the extent to which customary norms persist, the lack

Table 4. 2b. *Financial relationships: openness and segregation*
(N = 59)

Score on financial closure index	Score on joint financial management index*		
	Joint (3)	Medium (1–2)	Segregated (0)
Open (4–5)	0	5	9
Medium (2–3)	4	12	14
Closed (0–1)	3	4	8

* For mode of calculating scores see Appendix p. 165.

of functional individuation of the conjugal family unit in terms of ownership, maintenance and long term financial security, the continued practice whereby husbands and wives share responsibility for material needs and the widespread separation of spouses' interests which concern money.

THE PANEL STUDY

The next step is to look at aspects of the twelve extended case histories taken from the panel study of Akan couples, to see into what categories their relationships fall with respect to financial management and what are the attitudes, expectations and conflicts expressed by the husbands and wives, both with respect to each other and their kin. The aim of this is partly to probe into the bases of conjugal harmony and conflict, to see which types of economic arrangements appear to be sources of satisfaction and which of dissatisfaction, which types of relationships spouses try to maintain and which they try to change in order to improve their own positions by minimizing any strain or dissatisfaction they experience (See Table 4. 3).

Three of the couples, the Mensahs, Ananes and the Korangs, could be classified as having relatively *joint* knowledge and activities with regard to spending, saving and owning. At the same time their relationships were comparatively *open* in that the husbands recognised considerable obligations as educators and providers, towards their matrikin (See Table 5. 3, p. 124). In the category *segregated/open* were six of the twelve couples, with separate financial arrangements, one spouse knowing little of how the other was spending and saving while at the same time the husbands had considerable financial responsibilities towards their kin. Of the remaining three couples, in which the spouses had minimal obligations to fulfil towards kin, one the Kwasis had a *segregated* relationship, and the other two the Baakos and Menus were *joint*, the Baakos completely combining their two salaries.

Examination of the kinds of comments these several spouses made about each other and about kin and affines, regarding the use of money and property-holding, indicates which sets of relationships appeared to be categorised by tension and conflict, and those which appeared harmonious. In the *joint/closed* category the two husbands and wives Mr and Mrs Baako and Mr and Mrs Menu voiced no complaints about each other or their kin, and no wishes were expressed to change existing financial arrangements.

The husband and wife in the *segregated/closed* category Mr and Mrs Kwasi directed no complaints about finances against kin or affines. However the husband, a lawyer, remarked that,

Women in Ghana like their independence too much! They will not have joint bank accounts with their husbands. A colleague's wife did, but she was unusual and it did not last long. They are always thinking of money and their pension rights from an early age and they do not like to stop work when they have children and lose these rights. One cannot find wives who hand their pay packets over to their husbands!

Meanwhile the wife, a teacher, one day recounted the gist of a serious argument between herself and her husband, concerning the division of financial responsibility in their home. Her husband wanted her to pay the washman, maid and gardener, now that she was working and she had refused, saying that if that was the case, he could sack them all and she would just wash him one shirt each day and nothing else. She said she intended to keep her own earnings to herself. She was willing to buy her own clothes (even though she knew that the well-dressed girls in town did not buy their own!) and she was willing to add a little to the money for food, but she told him to buy the children's clothes. She remarked that when she married it was on the understanding that her husband would clothe and feed herself and her children. Now she exclaimed he even wanted her to pay him for driving her to work, but that is out of the question. Nor did she intend to fall in with his suggestion of helping him to build a second house. She said firmly that she was keeping her own savings intact.

There was thus in this case both conflict as to how responsibilities should be allocated and over the retention of individual rights to personally earned resources. Each wanted the other to shoulder more burdens and to give up some jealously held rights. Both were bent upon increasing their own satisfactions. Each looked around and saw people who appeared to be better treated than they were. Thus the husband referred to a colleague's wife, who agreed to join her resources with those of her husband, so that the latter could have a better chance of getting a loan for a building project. The wife referred to unmarried girls in town, who had their wigs and cloths bought for them by their men friends. The argument which erupted in this household, served to bring to the surface long standing grievances and to point in which direction each spouse wanted changes to be made. No one else was brought into the matter to assist the cause of either partner.

In the category *open/segregated* was an assortment of couples, some spouses apparently fairly satisfied, others dissatisfied, with their existing situations. In these couples both the husbands and wives wanted their partners to accept more financial responsibilities, such as by contributing more to the cost of food, fuel and service and one or two even wanted their partners to go on into new areas, for instance by helping in the building of houses, or even spending money on leisure pursuits enjoyed together. Since their wishes were not met, they complained in the hope of changing their partners' attitudes and behaviour. As these husbands and some of their wives tended to be involved in financial transactions with kin, many of which incurred heavy expenditure, they often either regretted the demands made upon themselves, or voiced oblique criticism of their affines for similar demands made upon their partners.

The Kwapongs, an administrator and nurse, in their early forties, who have been married for ten years provide an example of such a case. They have a large household of thirteen, which includes eight children (five of their own and three older children by Mr Kwapong's first marriage). They have both over the years spent a considerable amount of money on helping relatives and continue to do so, supporting young ones through school (siblings and maternal nephews) and maintaining the old and sick. Each owns property jointly with matrikin, the wife a trading concern in Accra with her mother and sister, the husband a citrus plantation and building project with his three younger brothers. Neither has an active or prosperous father or maternal uncle and so, as their (illiterate) mothers' eldest children, they find themselves asked to give a lot of help.

The allocation of resources

Mr Kwapong does not openly complain of stress, but says that he is very hard pressed, on his present salary, to meet all his commitments. He has to keep avoiding taking on more responsibilities.

He admits that, if his wife did not assist him by paying for many of the household items such as her own and the children's clothes and the food items bought at the market, he would not be able to make ends meet. He even had to borrow ₡40 from her one month to help pay the term's school fees for their two youngest children.

One of his major complaints about his wife is that when he gave her ₡200 two years ago to start some trading at home in cloth and wigs, she handed it on to her mother, who trades with her in town. He hesitated to raise any objections as his mother-in-law was involved! The other subject, to which he makes rueful reference is the fact that his wife will not help him to build a house for them in his village.

Mrs Kwapong is fully aware that but for her own contribution to the weekly budget, they would not be able to make ends meet. She does not openly criticize her husband about this, but she comments that a colleague's husband, on a similar salary, gives his wife twice as much for food each week as her own husband gives her. She also often decries at length the customary Akan system of family relationships, whereby women rely upon their sons and brothers too much and as a result husbands are not prepared to maintain their wives and children adequately. She feels herself particularly deprived, since she has no senior brother or mother's brother to turn to herself. Moreover her own father is dead.

She states quite forcefully that it is because of her personal awareness of the problems involved in matrilineal inheritance that she has no intention of joining her husband in any of his property ventures, either farms or houses. She prefers to join her own mother and sister in starting to put up a small shop in town, so that they can increase their trade in wigs and cloths. She had a very bitter experience when her father died some years ago and her poor mother was turned out of the house she had been living in for fifteen years and her father's two stores and cocoa farm were immediately taken over by his sisters' sons, leaving nothing for her mother or his children. This happened in spite of the fact that her father had promised, sometime before he died, that he would provide for them. As she was the most highly educated of her mother's surviving children, she had to take over some of the responsibility. They call her father's nephew (now in charge of the stores) 'father' when they see him, but he has done nothing for them.

It is because she cannot rely either upon her husband or father or uncle that she is now busy doing so many things. She cannot afford to be idle as she has her children and herself to think of. Thus as well as being a full time nurse, she runs the trading business with her mother and sister, selling cloth and wigs, usually on credit terms, to colleagues, friends and neighbours. In addition she has a little poultry farm of fifty fowls in her back garden and sells the eggs locally.

This example further illustrates how the separation of control over their respective money and properties may be viewed by husbands and wives as an effective attempt both to avoid conflict and to give a measure of security to the wife and children in a situation in which the husband's matrikin are unmistakeably recognized as their rivals for his attentions. The maintenance of a courteous social distance also helps to avoid any unpleasant confrontations. Thus Mr Kwapong's elderly female kin are visited and supported in their home village. They do not come to stay with the wife. Similarly Mrs Kwapong's mother and sisters live in town and seldom pay social calls, as they see her almost every day in the course of their joint business activities. If they do occasionally pay a visit a respectful social distance is maintained by the wife's mother's refusal to dine with her daughter's husband and her staying in the kitchen either helping with the cooking or nursing the baby. An element of dissatisfaction is apparent on the part of both of the spouses. Each would like the other to assume more financial responsibility in the household and to use fewer resources on kin. Both also voice an element of strain in fulfilling their manifold obligations and look forward to a time when these will be reduced, through a decrease in the number of the young and old who depend upon them.

Another couple, the Kwaminas, were in a similar position to the Kwapongs, in that they did not join their respective resources together and each was supporting kin to some extent, but no sign of strain or dissatisfaction was apparent. The husband was at the top of his salary scale and in addition owned a number of properties, farms and houses inherited from his father. He had no difficulty in maintaining his mother and two sisters and their children at the same time as providing adequately for his three children by his first wife, now deceased, and his two sons by his second wife. He approved highly of the 'extended family' system in Ghana, contrasting it with the neglect of widows, orphans, the old and the lonely which he said he had observed when in England. His wife, who used part of her salary to buy food and clothes, part to help her mother and mother's sister, and part to save in her Post Office account, seemed quite satisfied with the arrangement. She herself owned nothing jointly with her husband, but she knew that during his lifetime her husband was well capable of supporting his kin as well as his own and her children and that he had already written a will, as his father did before him. Since he intended to leave some property to each of his children, she has no qualms about their future.

It was among the three financial relationships categorized as *joint/ open*, in which couples were attempting to maintain a relatively *joint* financial relationship and who at the same time were supporting and educating kin and subject to frequent demands from them, that two of the marriages most frought with conflict and stress were observed. The wives in these couples Mrs Mensah and Mrs Anane complained bitterly of their in-laws' demands and pressures and even displayed open hostility with them. They were both annoyed that money they had helped to earn and save appeared to be channelled off to their mothers and sisters-in-law and their children, and also felt very insecure about the future, since neither had a maternal home to go to or had been able to save anything. Moreover, because of the heavy demands made upon them, their husbands had not yet begun to build houses for themselves. In one case the couple attempted to maintain a united front against the husband's relatives. Both complained bitterly of the traditional matrilineal practices and ideas regarding finances in marriage and the position of the wife. The other husband was not so whole-hearted in support of his wife and tried to minimize the conflict between her and his sisters by taking both sides in turn.

These sets of relationships were obviously the most unstable of all and even as they were under observation changes were being made to stabilise them. In one case the couple's *joint* economic relationship became more *segregated*. In the other case the social and financial distance between the couple and the husband's kin increased. Change seemed inevitable, the only question was in which direction. The relationships of the third couple the Korangs classified as relatively *joint* and *open* differed from the other two in several

Table 4. 3. *Financial relationships : the panel study* ($N = 12$)

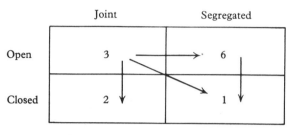

→ directions in which change desired by wives.

ways. Their main joint activity was a house, built entirely from the husband's resources and held in their joint names. Although the wife added something from her trading profits to pay for food and clothes, her husband assumed the major responsibility. Each knew what the spouse did with money and discussed how they should buy things and save, but they kept their accounts separately. With respect to *openness* the husband had helped two nephews through school, but since his own father was still alive, prosperous, and still married to his mother, he had no other responsibilities towards his mother and her children, or grandchildren. Moreover, the couple saw relatively little of their respective relatives, only visiting the husband's parents about once a year. They lived in a small bungalow and kin seldom came to stay. As a result of these several factors neither spouse felt under any compulsion to take on more obligations than they could fulfil, nor did the wife feel financially insecure and threatened by her in-laws, as did the wives in the two previous examples, about whom more will be said in Chapter 5.

DISSATISFACTION AND CHANGE

This classification of sets of relationships is illuminating in that it shows clearly those structural contexts within which conflict and role strain were most apparent, those in which it was latent and those in which there was apparent harmony. It is also helpful in the diagrammatic representation of the directions in which changes were desired, expected or actually took place during observation (see Table 4. 3). With regard to tension and the likelihood of change, in the *joint/open* category any direction of change was welcome to one or both partners in two of the couples. The wives were tense, dissatisfied and insecure, one even to the point of sickness. The husbands, with the many demands on them from several quarters, showed signs of the strain at their inability to cope satisfactorily with their social situations and fulfil all their obligations as husbands, brothers, uncles and sons. They mainly saw a lessening of their external obligations as the solution to their problem. In the *segregated/ open* group some husbands and wives were also suffering under the strain of being asked to shoulder more burdens than they could easily carry and wanted to decrease the pressure. Friction arose between those husbands and wives who wanted to have more control over the ways in which their partners used their incomes, as occurred also in the Kwasi's relationship categorized as *segregated/closed*. The *closed/joint* relationships seemed ones at which several of the dissatisfied spouses were aiming, if unsuccessfully. They were trying to decrease their own obligations and to have a greater knowledge of their partners' economic activities. Significantly the Baakos and the Menus in this last category had no complaints themselves about finances and were attempting no changes in their relationships. Among all the couples in the *open* category, it was in the ones in which resources were felt to be under most pressure, the Mensahs and Ananes, in which the wives suffered from a sense of financial injustice and insecurity, that tension was most apparent. If the husband's resources were ample enough to provide in what was felt to be a satisfactory manner, for the present and future needs of his conjugal family as well as dependent matrikin, or if the wife retained control over her own resources, then disharmony was not so likely to come to the fore.

Examination of these aspects of this limited number of cases has clearly indicated a number of facts including the following: that some spouses are more dissatisfied than others with the financial aspects of their domestic situations and that dissatisfied ones are often making efforts to improve matters by increasing their control of their own resources, by attempting to gain more benefits from the partners' resources and by trying to limit the benefits enjoyed by others either from their own or their partners' resources.[3] The efforts of the individual spouse, to improve his or her own financial position, often result in domestic tension and sometimes conflict between partners and between spouses and kin and affines. This tension and conflict may be minimized to some extent by the separation of resources and the insulation of financial activities from observation by interested parties, including spouse, kin and affines.

CHORES: THE WIFE'S ROLE

The household chores, including the preparation of food, childcare and general maintenance of the home, are seldom carried out by the husband, wife and children alone. In fact there are many homes in which the conjugal family members play a very small part in performing these tasks. As a general rule there are others available to help, either employed maids and stewards, or, relatives, or both, and these helpers do the majority of routine jobs.

Her lack of total involvement in household chores and child-minding, is perhaps the most salient aspect of the urban, educated Akan wife's domestic activities. She is not expected to spend all her time on housework and seldom does. She generally delegates tasks, so as to continue her paid employment. Even in the minority of cases, in which the wife is not working, she usually has some kind of help, often more than one person. It is in fact a customary Akan practice, whether they remain in their maternal homes or join their husbands, for women to be provided with domestic help by their matrikin, throughout their married lives, so that they are supported in carrying out their various tasks as wives and mothers, especially at the time of childbirth. Thus if a women leaves her mother's household to take up residence with her husband, it is usual for a junior relative to be sent with her to help or, among the coastal Akan, a family servant's child or other maid. This is a practice still widely adhered to by Akan in the city, so that one finds many wives with a succession of young female kinswomen and others sent to them by their senior relatives. A few examples have already been noted above, in which kin come to stay in the home to do housework and act as nursemaids, some illiterate teenagers or even younger children, others attending school and doing household tasks in the morning and afternoon. Thus it is that many wives with several small children confidently go out to work, knowing that their housework is being done for them and their children cared for.

The position of educated wives in the town varies considerably however, according to whether their kin are willing and able to continue to supply them with this crucial support in playing their multiple roles inside and outside the home. While some have senior relatives who adequately anticipate their needs and are in a position to provide for them, others have to go to great lengths to get help, sometimes using very distant and affinal links to recruit people

102

into the household for this purpose. Some of the wives' relatives help in the house and also learn new skills part of the time, either in the house or in town. Often more distant relatives are merely fed, clothed and given pocket-money in return for their services. The following case is an illustration of how fortunate those wives are who continue to have a ready supply of domestic helpers coming from their home towns. In this case the range of kin and affines, who have come to help is relatively wide. The wife's father's mother's and husband's kin have provided help. She herself has reciprocated by giving wages, domestic training, board and lodging.

Mrs Attah and her husband are both coastal urban Akan and have been married for six years. The wife is in her late twenties and works as a bank clerk, the husband is in his mid-thirties and a senior administrator. They have three children aged five, four and two and live in a spacious suburban bungalow. The wife, in spite of her three roles as housewife, full-time office worker and mother of three small children never seems harrassed or over-tired. Her house is spotless, her children always neat and she herself becomingly and fashionably dressed. As she admits, she has never done any of the tiring or dirty household chores since she married, such as polishing floors or cleaning windows, nor has she ever had to look after all her children on her own. She has always had a full or part-time steward to do most of the cleaning and washing, and one or more relatives to look after the children. There have always been people in the house to help her, who have given their time and services in exchange for lodgings, food, clothing, pocket-money and sometimes savings in a Post Office book, or simply because they were kin and offered to help, especially during crises such as childbirth. In all, seven female relatives have helped at some time, including her own mother and mother-in-law. She has also employed eight or more domestic servants for varying lengths of time. At the present she has three girls staying with her. Kin and affines who have helped include the following:

WM – came a month before the first birth and stayed about seven months. Then she came about two weeks before the birth of the second child and stayed on for one year while the husband was studying abroad.

HM – she came a week after the third birth and stayed for about eight weeks. She was invited to come because the wife's mother was then ill and could not come.

HZHZD – came when in her late teens after leaving middle school till she found a job in an office a year later. In the meantime she did the cooking and helped care for the children. (Referred to as 'cateress'.)

WMBWZD – the wife's mother's brother sent her when he knew she wanted a maid to help in the house. She has attended school and wants to earn money to buy herself a sewing machine. When she has earned enough she will leave and become an apprentice seamstress.

WFZDDD – she has been with them for six years attending school and helping with the chores. Her father never claimed her and her mother was in financial difficulties, so Mrs Attah took her to help the mother. She visits her mother at holiday times.

WFD – she is in her mid-teens and has stayed with them for a year to attend school in the town. Her father pays her fees. She helps with the washing-up, tidying and cleaning of the house.

WMZD – she came when she had finished middle school for a year and helped in the house before starting work at the nurses' training school.

Employees include the following:

1. A maid servant Akuia from their home town aged about nine, who had never been to school, accompanied the wife after she got married. The latter knew her mother, who was a market trader. The girl stayed about two years and then her mother said that she wanted to perform the customary puberty rites for her and so sent for her to return home. She was given some money when leaving and the wife gave her mother money when she saw her.

2. An illiterate Ga girl from Accra aged about twenty, was contacted through a neighbour's maid, but she only stayed about two weeks as she proved to be pregnant.

3. An Akan girl aged about fourteen, who had been to primary school came after being obtained through a food seller. She was not good with the children and after staying for three months on a salary of ₵2 per week she was dismissed.

4. Subsequently a girl in her mid-teens from the couple's home town was employed. Her parents lived near the husband's family house. She stayed with them over a year on a salary of ₵10 per month and then she left to become apprenticed to a seamstress.

5. The next girl who also came from their home town did the same thing. She stayed one year to save up to buy a sewing machine and then left.

6. When they stayed in the north they had a 'Hausa' boy aged about fourteen to help with the cleaning and washing. He was paid 6 cedis a month and stayed twelve months leaving their service when they went on transfer.

7. Two Ga girls aged eighteen and twenty respectively came one after the other and only stayed for two and three weeks.

The support that the wife receives from kin may be such that she even feels quite confident about assuming sole responsibility for her household, working and caring for her children for a year or two during her husband's absence on transfer or studying. In the case below the wife managed satisfactorily for one and a half years. Conversely, should the wife go away to study abroad or to her maternal home to deliver a child, similar substitutes are likely to be available to step in and cater for the husband's domestic wants. Thus each spouse may become independent of the other.

Mrs Yeboah, a teacher, is managing her household alone for eighteen months and also teaching, while her husband is abroad studying for a further diploma. She continues to receive necessary support from her matrikin who, since she married, have helped her to care for her children and to find reliable domestic help. She in turn has helped them by providing accommodation and paying school fees. Of the seven relatives, who have stayed in the house at some time, four are the wife's matrikin and two others are people sent by them. They include:

WS – came to stay for three months when the first child was born.

WZD – stayed for three months and looked after the children when Mrs Yeboah went abroad to do a course.

WZD – she has been with them for four years. Mrs Yeboah asked for her to come so that there would be a reliable person in the house in the afternoon when the children come home from school. She is paying for her to attend a vocational training school in the mornings.

WZSS – he is in his mid-teens attending school and has been with them about a year.

MBWSD – 'cateress': Mrs Yeboah asked her mother's brother's daughter for sometime to help her with the cooking and she was sent. She has been with them for six months.

WZS – he lived with them for three years. He worked in town and helped with the housework.

A similar case was that of Mrs Ansere, a nurse managing her

household alone for twelve months while her husband was abroad taking a post-graduate diploma. Her sister's daughter and a niece (FBDD) helped her by doing the chores and caring for her children when she was at work.

Mr Mireku's case meanwhile illustrates how a man might also manage to be in charge of his household and go to work at the same time. His wife went to her mother's house for three months at the birth of their fourth child, taking their third child with her. His sister, who had left middle school and was looking for an office job in town, looked after the house with the help of a sister-in-law (WMBD). His wife's younger brother was also in the household attending school.

Wives however, without kin willing and able to come and stay with them to help, and in whose families there are no servants' or farm labourers' children available, are forced to rely upon affines or strangers, the latter either supplied to them straight from the rural areas or employed from the pool of casual labour already in the town. Wives unable to find a reliable source of domestic help find themselves under stress, both physical and mental, as they try to cope with their several duties as mothers, housewives and employees. The following is an example of such a wife, who during ten years of marriage, has employed over twenty maids and five or six stewards and several part-time washmen. Her mother and sister have only been able to give temporary assistance. She has been continually worried by the problem of finding capable helpers, able to take on the responsibility of looking after her small children.

After Mr and Mrs Bonsu married, the wife who had just left training college, continued teaching at Akropong while her husband resumed work in the Volta Region. Within a few months their first baby was born and the wife's mother and sister stayed with her to look after the baby while she was at school. Some of her pupils also helped with the household chores. When the baby was eight months old she managed to get a departmental transfer to the station where her husband was then working. There she was in a difficult situation as her mother and sister did not go with her and she could not find a suitable nursemaid. Six came and left for one reason or another, during their year's stay there. For six months of that period she had no maid and was reduced to leaving her baby with the steward, who gave milk she left in the refrigerator, while she was away at work between 8 a.m. and 3 p.m.

106

The allocation of resources

At the end of that year they left for another station on transfer and the wife taught at the local primary school once more. They got a new steward from the husband's brother, who had gone abroad. He looked after the baby for some time, but then he left and they got a maid through the wife's elder sister. She came from near the wife's home town. She looked after the baby and they also found another steward. Unfortunately within six months that maid had to leave after attempting an abortion.

Soon after that they were transferred to Accra, where they lived in three different lots of rented accommodation. It was there that their second child was born and the wife's mother came and stayed for four months.

When the baby was three months old Mrs Bonsu began to teach again in Accra, but she had only been at work two months, when her husband was transferred to Wa. There she taught for five months until the birth of their third child. During their stay in the north a Dagomba, a Ga and an Ewe maid were employed in succession and stayed for varying lengths of time. She also had a Frafra steward. By then the first child was at nursery school and her brother's wife's daughter of about nine was sent to stay with them and help in the house.

The following year a fourth child was born. Mrs Bonsu stopped work two weeks before the birth and returned to work when the child was two months old. Within six months they returned once more to Accra, bringing no maids or relatives with them.

In the seven months they have been in Accra they have had eight different maids, who have come and gone, none of them giving satisfactory service. At present a middle-aged Ga woman lives out and comes each day, and an Ewe teenage girl lives in. Mrs Bonsu is worried that her children are not being cared for as she would wish. The baby is not gaining weight and is always ailing and the older children are being shouted at. She is looking round for another suitable maid. The alternative of resigning from her job does not appear to have been considered as a possibility.

These several cases indicate the ways in which the exchange of services and time for material rewards in the form of lodgings, food, clothing, pocket-money and training, between a couple and their kin and servants maintain the *open* character of the conjugal family, with respect to chores and child-care, providing maternal and domestic role substitutes for educated Akan mothers. For the wife who is deriving benefit from these exchanges, the main contrast is between some one like Mrs Attah, who, during six years of marriage, has secured the services of as many reliable, even educated relatives to help her care for her children, and Mrs Bonsu, who has had great difficulty in securing anyone at all reliable and who has had to depend upon the chance services of hired women and girls. Whereas the one gives the appearance of happy, confident motherhood, the other is anxious and continually worried by the difficulties of running a home, caring for her family and going out to work.

Household chores may be ranked with some accuracy according to whether or not the wife is likely to do them herself. At the bottom of the list are the cleaning jobs and the sweeping, window-cleaning and dish-washing. Few do the laundry themselves. Even cooking, which in some settings elsewhere is synonymous with the roles of wife and mother, is given a relatively low valuation amongst her wifely duties, by some educated women and much of it is delegated to maids. Those who say that they do their own cooking are often observed to be merely supervising the young girls in their households, who are actually doing the work.

A few wives have mechanical aids, washing machines and electric mixers and grinders in their kitchens, but much of the washing continues to be done by hand and the grinding and pounding of nuts and vegetables is often done with flat stones and wooden pestles and mortars. Similarly charcoal pots are used for much of the cooking, since charcoal is cheaper than gas or electricity, though it involves greater time and care than the methods using the more expensive fuels.

Since the majority are working full-time outside the home, the extent to which most wives can supervise the food preparation and babycare in their homes is limited. When husbands complain about their wives' house-keeping, it is usually to say that they do not like to eat food cooked by maids and therefore the wife either has to stay at home or cook in the evenings and put the food in the refrigerator, or they complain that they do not like leaving their children with illiterate nurse girls. Accordingly the few say that their wives should stay at home, so that these tasks may be done to their liking!

Table 4. 4. *Percentage of husbands performing household tasks by frequency and type* $(N=61)$

Type	Task	Never	Occasionally	Often/Always	Previously
1. Food preparation	Store-shopping	0	45	53	2
	Washing up	29	56	13	4
	Marketing	44	31	20	4
	Table setting	45	51	4	0
	Cooking	49	40	2	9
2. Child care	Buying clothes	4	57	31	2
	Dressing	11	72	15	2
	Bathing	38	52	4	6
	Changing	43	43	12	2
	Food mixing	46	40	10	4
3. General maintenance	Repairs	5	39	55	0
	Car washing	8	39	53	0
	Tidying up	9	62	25	4
	Mending fuses	33	30	37	0
	Washing shirts	30	48	15	7
	Making beds	31	60	6	3

HUSBANDS AND CHORES

Just as in the case of wives, the household tasks husbands perform range from those commonly their responsibility to those which they seldom if ever do (Table 4. 4). The majority play some part in the general maintenance of the house and its contents, seeing that odd jobs get done such as mending broken mosquito-proofing or fuses, but since the houses many occupy are government owned, there is much reliance on the Public Works Department to see to the major repairs and the painting and decorating. Husbands are however expected by their wives to see to it that the appropriate people are called in. The wife, whose screens have been hanging unfixed for weeks or who has needed shelves putting up in her larder for several months, is likely to complain bitterly about the negligence of her husband, for not seeing to jobs considered to lie in his field of responsibility. Not many husbands play a very active part in the general cleaning and tidying of the house, though a few do jobs such as washing their own shirts, a chore to which they may have become accustomed as secondary school boarders.

Husbands, as the main controllers of money and transport, are very likely to do those chores involving travel and spending. Thus all at some time, and some even always, do the store-shopping and nearly all play a part in buying their children's clothes. They drive to the main stores in the centre of town after work, at lunch time and on Saturday mornings, to choose and pay for their own provisions, even those who do little else in the way of household chores. But not many are prepared to do the market shopping. Some wives laugh about this saying that their husbands are only willing to shop in the market when there is no one around to see them. If they go they may be teased by the market sellers. Other activities concerned with the preparation and serving of food, are seldom done by husbands, in particular the cooking.

The extent to which the husband takes an active part in child-care varies very much from couple to couple and according to their circumstances at the time. While very few husbands often do such things as dressing, changing, feeding or bathing their children, less than half admit to never doing these things at all. They are more likely to dress children than to mix baby food or to bath them. Wives whose husbands take an enthusiastic part in the care of babies and young children are of course very pleased and praise them highly. But they consider their husbands to be good exceptions to the general rule. Wives whose husbands object to doing any of these things may regret it, but they scarcely blame them and complain, as they do when they neglect other tasks considered to be more in their areas of responsibilities. On visiting households however, it is not unusual to see husbands playing with their younger children, and sometimes even nursing and feeding babies.

OPENNESS AND SEGREGATION

Few couples can be classified as *joint*, as far as the assumption of responsibility for housework and child-care is concerned. Very few husbands are prepared to act together with, or as substitutes for, their wives in doing or supervising any or all of the chores involved. On the other hand in nearly all households there is regular full-time help of some kind, often from kin, so that work and responsibility can be delegated and in the main relationships can be classified as relatively *open* in this respect, since people come in to take over these aspects of maternal and conjugal role obligations.

The twelve extended case studies mentioned above were examined with reference to these two variables, to see what kinds of attitudes and expressions of satisfaction or otherwise were associated with

Table 4. 5. *Domestic Chores: the panel study* ($N = 12$)

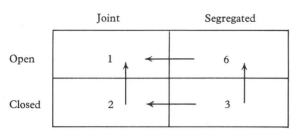

→ Directions in which change desired by wives

the extent to which couples did chores jointly and the extent to which other substitutes, mainly kin, came in to take over tasks (See Table 4. 5). One couple, the Menu's, fell into the relatively *joint/open* category, with husband and wife and kin all participating in domestic duties and acting as substitutes for each other. The wife in this position was well satisfied and content for things to remain as they were. She had both her own kin and husband willing to take on almost any kind of task or responsibility, so that she never felt worried or under a strain in going to work and looking after her children and house.

Two couples fell into the fairly *closed/joint* category the Baakos and the Mensahs in that the husband was willing to take on child-care and jobs, such as laundry and food preparation, when necessary. While help from outsiders consisted mainly of that from maids and stewards, who did not completely take over any of the major areas of responsibility. The wives in this category praised their husbands for their participation, which they realized was more than normal, but they were rather disturbed by the fact that they could not find any of their own relatives to come and give full-time assistance, especially at the times when they had small babies in the house. Both of the husbands were concerned that they should find such help and had also tried to persuade their wives to stop work and stay at home.

Six couples fell in the category of comparatively *open/segregated*, that is the wife and kin and domestics performed the majority of housework, the husband only doing jobs such as shopping and seeing to repairs. Three couples could be classified as relatively *closed* and *segregated*, that is no one acted as a substitute for and jointly with the wife and was ready and able to assume responsibility for her major task areas, though all did have household help of some kind. Several of the wives whose husbands did not give much help complained either overtly or in asides and jokes. The wives with relatives to help them could manage without much strain. But those who had no responsible kin to help felt themselves under stress, as they could not rely upon help from their husbands either.

The arrows of Table 4. 5 show the direction in which dissatisfied wives desired change. They wanted more participation and assumption of responsibilities by both their husbands and kin or paid help. Many, not unnaturally, wanted to lighten their burden of chores and duties. They both wanted the traditional pattern of domestic help from kin to continue and at the same time some were pressing for innovation by trying to persuade their husbands to play a more active domestic role. Both changes would be to their benefit. In the same way it was seen that some wished to maintain the customary pattern of wifely economic independence, while at the same time encouraging their husbands to increase their acceptance of financial responsibilities towards them and their children and also to cut down their financial obligations to kin. Just as by keeping separate financial resources, many spouses maintained a high degree of independence, so in the matter of use of time we have seen that the relative lack of complementary division of labour between them meant that often either spouse was comparatively expendable, that is the household could continue as a viable house-keeping unit, if either man or wife were to be absent for some time, as so many tasks were delegated. Either partner could, if necessary, both earn the living and be in charge of running the household.

A further item for comparison is the range of kin included in the domestic activities. The range of kin educated and supported is relatively narrow. In contrast the range of kin brought into the household to give service is wide. In some cases the relationship is so distant that the spouse is not even aware of its exact nature. While some are making a definite effort to cut down on the former ties, non-kin are brought in when there is no one available to perform the latter function.

DECISION-MAKING

The outcome of numerous domestic decisions, arrived at tacitly or after discussion, together or separately, by Akan Senior Civil Servants and their wives, concerning the allocation of their money and time on household tasks and the maintenance of family members, the structuring of certain conjugal rights and obligations, have now been outlined. Emphasis has been upon the norms, both the prescriptions stated by the actors and the patterns depicted by the survey material. Systems of relationships which differ from the general patterns have also been noted, as well as those involving strain, dissatisfaction and tension, either for the individual husband or wife, in carrying out a number of domestic functions, or between spouses, or between couples and their kin.

There now remains the more complex problem of attempting to demonstrate the processes by which such decisions are made, especially when several alternative choices present themselves: a problem which is notably difficult to investigate.[4] Such decisions for the husband at least, include those concerning which financial requests of kin to accept and which to refuse; whether to open a joint bank account with the wife; whether to build a property in the city in the name of the children or to build a house for the mother and sisters in the home town; whether to invest money in land jointly held with brothers and how many relatives to accommodate and educate. Decisions concerning the use of time include those such as which kind of domestic chores to perform in the home and how much time to spend in caring for the children and so on. These and many more similar small domestic decisions affecting day to day living, are part of the stuff of which are made changes in the structuring of domestic rights and obligations between spouses and between couples and their kin. In particular these choices are associated with the degree of functional individuation of the conjugal family and the amount of sharing and substitution exhibited in activities and responsibilities assumed by husband and wife and kin. Thus the next chapter deals with the power positions of husbands and wives in relation to each other, and the factors which appear to enhance a spouse's ability to make the kinds of choices he or she wishes and by so doing to influence the behaviour of others. Subsequently the ways in which decisions were made in a number of families, in relation both to spouses' power positions and aspirations and those of their kin and affines are examined.

NOTES

[1] Cf. Caldwell (1968: 69–70).

[2] I have discussed this contrast in a paper entitled 'Domestic Budgeting among some salaried Urban Couples', given at a Family Research Seminar held at the Institute of African Studies Legon in February 1971, later published in *Legon Family Research Papers No. 1*. There I indicated that whereas over half of the Akan couples in the Civil Service survey

sample discussed here were found to have financial relationships classifiable as *segregated* fewer than a third of the Ewe couples of similar occupational status had such *segregated* relationships. Clignet has noted a similar difference in budgeting arrangements among the matrilineal Abouré and patrilineal Bété in the neighbouring Ivory Coast. (1970: 336).

[3] As Weber expressed it, 'If...[people] are interested in improving their position through monopolistic practices they will tend to favour a *closed* relationship' (1962: 97).

[4] Caldwell comments upon this difficulty in his investigations among a comparable population (1968: 70).

5

POWER AND DECISION-MAKING

The process of decision-making in the home, how domestic tasks and resources should be allocated, is an admittedly complex sequence of events, taking place between spouses and between them and their kin, affines, colleagues and other significant sets of associates and reference groups, with and about whom they exchange goods, services and communications. It depends to a great extent upon the relative power position of the spouses and their respective aspirations. A spouse's power position may be thought of as consisting in his or her ability to alter the partner's behaviour to conform to that desired, even in spite of counter demands and pressures from outsiders, especially in terms of the use of money and time upon objects persons and interests valued by the spouse. Couples' power relationships have been broadly categorised here as *syncratic*, couples sharing their major decision-making; *autonomic*, spouses each making their own decisions separately, with a minimum of consultation, and husband-dominated or *autocratic*, in which the husband makes the majority of decisions affecting both his own and his wife's use of resources (Herbst, 1954).[1]

The relative power position of husbands and wives has been shown in this and many other urban communities to be influenced, both by the comparative resources which husband and wife bring to marriage, such as education and income and the type of occupational and kinship positions each maintains outside the conjugal family, as well as by the prescribed and traditional authority patterns of the cultures to which they belong (Oppong, 1970). Wherever women have access to strategic resources, being important economic producers and managers of property, their part in domestic decision-making has been shown in numerous studies to be potentially enhanced. The kinds of social and economic resources and obligations, which Akan Senior Civil Servants bring to their marriages, have already been indicated. The various types of resources available to their wives remain to be examined, before the power element of their conjugal relationships is considered.

WIVES' RESOURCES

The customary independence or relative autonomy of Akan wives is widely recognized as the outcome of three factors, their work outside the home, their matrilineage membership and their freedom as women to marry husbands of their own choosing. They are not noted however to have been given much chance to influence their husbands or to control their interests (Danquah, 1928: 155). Their traditional resources as farmers and traders include the use of the produce and profits of their labour, which especially in the latter case may scarcely be subjected to control by their husbands (McCall, 1961: 297). Their resources as lineage members include the permanent security of a family home and farm land for themselves and their children, who are among the heirs to the family estate. Their resources as women include the right to instigate the dissolution of their marriages, should they prove unrewarding, on the grounds that the husband is unwilling or unable to fulfil his duties as a husband satisfactorily and then to remarry a man considered more likely to offer an agreeable marital relationship. The customary extent of the Akan married woman's independence is indicated both by the frequency with which they have continued to live in their maternal homes, rather than going to live with their husbands, and by the frequency with which they divorce and also remarry. In the new urban setting however, a number of radical changes in the sources of security and life opportunities of Akan wives are immediately apparent. Primarily, instead of living in their maternal households, supported to a greater or lesser degree, both economically and socially, by lineage property and matrikin, they are mainly living with their husbands, far from their places of birth and enjoying numerous modern, urban amenities provided for them through their husbands' Civil Service jobs. It is their husbands, not their matrikin, who provide the basis for their comparatively luxurious mode of life, a standard which only few wives would otherwise be able to maintain, either through their resources as employees, as kinswomen or as wives of other men.[2] The majority thus, in a sense, depend upon their husbands in a way they customarily never did.

The reasons for this drastic change in their position are not far to seek. First of all, though having attended school and continuing the traditional pattern of working outside the home, the majority do not possess the level of education which would admit them to occupational statuses equivalent to those of their husbands, for only a minority are university graduates. In nearly every case their salaries are much lower and their possibilities of earning the same or being provided with similar amenities, housing, transport and so on through their own skills and training are fairly remote. Those however, who are qualified nurses or teachers do have potential access, through their work in schools and hospitals, to comparatively well-built accommodation and modern amenities wherever they work, but of the less spacious 'junior service' type and without transport facilities (unless they are graduate secondary school teachers). Thus for instance in many cases in which the wife is working, the cost of the economic rent of the house in which she lives with her husband is several times higher than her own monthly salary. The contrast, between the life of a nurse married to a doctor and a nurse living with her children in nurses' accommodation is a good example of the rise in standard of living and social prestige involved for a woman in marrying a professional man or administrator. The first is likely to be driven about in a large new car and to live in a spacious bungalow, surrounded by lawns and flowers, and her children to attend expensive private schools. The money she earns, if working, is partly used to dress herself in the latest fashion. On the other hand the nurse, living off her own income, may be in a tiny flat, go shopping by lorry or bus and send her children to the local authority school, and unless she finds a second source of income she will have little left over for luxuries.

Secondly, as regards matrilineage membership, their positions tend to be more vulnerable than those of women who have continued living in their family houses, farming or trading in their home towns. Few, in their roles as sisters, daughters and nieces, can expect to have the same social and economic status and privileges in their home towns and villages, as they receive from their husbands in the capital. Indeed their rural relatives, especially if illiterate, may be living a kind of provincial farming life they would not not care to return to, for more than a short visit. Few rural relatives could offer them the type of accommodation, diet and sanitation to which they have grown accustomed. Meanwhile those of their kin in salaried employment, mainly in the urban areas, scattered both in Ghana and abroad, tend to be living in conjugal family households with their own spouses and children, which could scarcely offer a sister or sister-in-law a permanent home, though she might be welcome to spend a holiday with them. The few, with a big well-built family

117

house to go to, are fortunate, but even that is unlikely to offer them the kind of privacy and space to which they have become accustomed during their suburban life in government accommodation.

The fact now is that the position of the educated Akan wife has changed radically. While customarily an Akan wife has a more secure home and source of permanent maintenance with her own mother and siblings than with her husband, those married to educated men look to their husbands to provide them with this kind of security. As one perceptive Akan professional man remarked to me, when considering this question,

The modern Akan wife now expects her husband to be a brother as well as lover and father of her children. She looks to him for the permanent home and security she once found with her matrikin.

We have noted already that wives tend to shift from place to place with their husbands, dependent upon them for social as well as economic support to a much greater degree than in the traditional environment. She may even depend upon him to share with her the responsibility of caring for the children and looking after the house, if she has no reliable kin to help her.

As regards the woman's third resource, the customary sanction of withdrawal from marriage and the possibility of entering a new and more rewarding conjugal relationship, the position has again altered to the detriment of educated wives. Not only does dissolution of a registered marriage incur considerable trouble and expense, far more than in the case of customary marriage, but an educated divorcée, past her early youth, will be unlikely to remarry a man of the same social and economic standing as her first (graduate) husband, an event which is not improbable in the village setting. In particular she will be unlikely to have a second registered marriage. In town educated, 'carful', 'fridgeful' men are at a premium and there is an abundance of female bank clerks, nurses and primary school teachers looking for such husbands. Moreover many of these may be willing to accept a conjugal relationship on terms much less expensive for the man, than the divorcée in question, including perhaps duolocality and customary rites! The avenue of withdrawal and remarriage has thus lost its power, as a potential sanction, for wives to use in marriage. Now it is not wives but husbands, in this category at least, who are scarce. Moreover registered marriage is not a relatively inexpensive relationship which men have no hesitation in contracting. Thus because of their frequent dependence upon their graduate husbands to maintain the standard of goods and services which they at present enjoy, and because of the relative diminution of their other sources of power outside marriage one may view the position of the educated Akan wife as being far more vulnerable than that of the Akan wife in the rural village setting, in which her ultimate source of security is her matrilineage membership, giving access to a permanent home and source of livelihood. Through what they say and do, some wives appear to be acutely aware of these changes. A few express a sense of insecurity which occasionally appears obsessive, repeatedly bemoaning their new lot. The majority make a number of more or less successful constructive adaptations to the novel situation in which they find themselves, the aim of the latter being to increase their own resources, both potential and actual, which are relevant to their domestic situations.

THE STRUGGLE FOR SECURITY

First of all, as was observed above, the majority continue to work, in particular those with vocational training. Holding a job not only provides a monthly salary to raise the standard of living, but it also gives potential access to an alternative mode of livelihood and accommodation especially if the occupation is a semi-professional one, such as nursing. Wives state openly that they cannot afford to rely entirely upon their husbands for support or security and continue to work throughout marriage, in most cases, without any thought of stopping. This happens even in domestic situations in which the onlooker might think that their children appear relatively neglected, due to lack of satisfactory nursing arrangements. Those who for one reason or another are not working, complain and try to obtain jobs as soon as it is feasible. No Akan wives were observed to view the role of housewife as a full-time, permanent and entirely satisfactory one! Her salary may be only one fifth or less of what her husband earns, but it nevertheless gives her an outside resource and a measure of independent security. In addition some wives make tremendous efforts to continue their education, in some cases even after years of marriage and during the pre-school years of their children, to the extent of leaving their husbands and children for months or even years in the process. Few wives were encountered who said they would refuse to leave their families in order to further their own vocational or professional training. During periods of marital stress observed it was to their careers that women looked as a possible source of security should their marriages break down.

Moreover wives were noted to be well aware of their diminishing rights as kinswomen. One or two, who felt their husbands were treating them badly, complained that they had no home to go to, especially those whose mothers were no longer alive, or whose fathers had remarried. Two wives went to stay with their educated siblings during periods of acute marital tension, but they realized from the beginning that their visits were no more than holidays and could not be prolonged indefinitely. Knowing that they had no real homes to go to, other than their husbands' houses, a few determined wives intend to build their own houses in their home towns and one or two do so, either alone or with the help of kin, even when this entails diverting funds from projects planned by their own husbands. As one wife pointed out to her husband, she had not even got a suitable place to sleep for herself, let alone for her five children if she went to her home town. Her mother's and maternal uncle's houses were already overcrowded. Thus wives may sometimes use their salaries to provide the homes in their villages, or elsewhere, which are not adequately provided through matrikinship ties. Again the possibility of instigating divorce and remarrying is not often considered feasible by the dissatisfied wife, as there is seldom a more rewarding marital relationship to which to withdraw. A more realistic alternative, for instance, in the face of competition from another would-be wife or in-laws, is to cling tenaciously to the position held and to marshall the support of friends and relatives to intercede and talk to the husband. Indeed in view of her own weak bargaining position, a wife may be heard to state that she knows many husbands (her own included), have girl-friends and have even set up second wives in houses elsewhere, but she may be prepared to accept this state of affairs, so long as such happenings occur far enough away from the household! Obviously the ultimate sanction of withdrawal and remarriage is maintained as a realistic possibility and also potential female competition is more successfully encountered if the wife preserves her glamour! Thus many wives spend a large part of their monthly salaries on cloth, wigs, cosmetics and seamstresses and hairdressers' charges in order to maintain a fashionable and youthful appearance.

Viewed in these terms then the Senior Civil Servants wife's new position may be a relatively vulnerable one. She is usually well aware that the possession of education, a job and money are some of her main potential assets in the new environment. These not only supply the family with the goods and services need to maintain the relatively high standard of living enjoyed, but may also offer an alternative source of personal maintenance and security, should the need arise. It now remains to be seen how the possession and utilization of these resources appears to enhance the wife's power position *vis à vis* her husband, in both decision-making and task performance in the household. A number of interesting correlations become apparent when reports of the ways decisions are taken are examined in relation both to the comparative resources husband and wife bring to marriage, and to the organization of tasks and responsibilities in the home.

WIVES' RESOURCES, DECISION-MAKING AND
TASK PERFORMANCE

If we consider first the twenty-seven couples in which the husbands reported that they made major household decisions jointly with their wives we find that not only have most of their wives had a higher education but the majority are currently professionally employed, mainly as teachers and nurses. As regards financial provision for the household over half of these wives are making contributions ranked as high (see Table 5. 1). However among the couples in which the husbands report that they and their wives take major decisions separately or that they themselves take the main decisions only a minority of wives have higher education, professional employment, or are making high contributions to household expenditure. Indeed, in terms of average expenditure by wives on household items, the wives in the couples reported to be husband-dominated rank comparatively low, with a mean score of 2 as compared with that of 3 among the other two categories of couples. The survey data thus support the view that the wife's position in decision-making in the home tends to be enhanced when she has educational, occupational and financial resources and also uses these in providing for family needs. Furthermore if we next examine modes of task performance in relation to decision-making we see that while the majority of couples classed as *syncratic* have somewhat joint financial relationships in that they either own property, save or spend together, only a small minority of the remaining couples exhibit such behaviour (see table 5. 2). Moreover the majority of husbands in the couples with *syncratic* relationships play a comparatively extensive and active role in carrying out chores and child-care – tasks which as was seen above their wives like them to do.

Table 5. 1. *Mode of decision-making and wife's resources*
($N = 58$)

Decision making	Wife's resources		
	% With higher education*	% Professionally employed**	% Making high contri-butions to expenditure***
Syncratic ($N = 27$)	82	56	52
Autonomic ($N = 19$)	47	32	37
Husband-dominated ($N = 12$)	50	42	25

   * Higher education included training for teaching, nursing and graduation.
  ** Mainly as teachers and nurses.
 *** Score 4–7 on Financial Provision Index (see Appendix p. 165).

Table 5. 2. *Mode of decision-making and joint task performance*
($N = 58$)

Decision-making	Percentage of couples with joint task performance	
	Financial management*	Chores**
Syncratic ($N = 27$)	74	52
Autonomic ($N = 19$)	16	21
Husband-dominated ($N = 12$)	25	33

 * Couple scored 1–5 on Financial Management Index (see Appendix p. 165).
** Husband scored high (5–8) on the Chore Performance Index (see Appendix p. 165).

Examined from the wife's point of view these facts would appear to suggest that, the more the resources she brings to marriage are equivalent to those of her husband, the more likely is she to have power to influence domestic organization to suit her own interests: namely, by herself entering into the area of control of finances, while at the same time her husband is more likely to assume greater than average responsibility for doing time-consuming household tasks. In other words, equivalence of domestic input in financial and educational terms, appears to be associated with a tendency towards increasing similarity of rights and duties, responsibilities and tasks, assumed in the conjugal relationship: that is a tendency towards overall *jointness*.

Power and decision-making

The norm has been stated, but only with respect to husbands and wives. Decision-making by couples now requires examination in its social context and over time. Husbands and wives may be living at a distance from kin, but we have already noted their comparatively intense social, financial and residential involvement with kin and affines and the extent to which a number of goods and services are exchanged or held jointly by them. The next question considered is what part do kin play in the domestic decision-making process; what happens when husband and wife disagree as to how resources should be allocated between themselves or them and their kin? what happens when an individual and his or her kin or affines beg to differ? Such an analysis may again help to discover which types of conjugal relationships are characterized by a harmonious allocation of tasks and resources, and which by tension and instability, and it may also uncover some of the correlates of change.

The re-examination of the twelve extended case studies aims to provide both this dynamic element and the social context of the decision-making process. The cases illustrate the kinds of domestic power struggle occurring in the relationships characterized by tension and instability, and also the sets of people whose domestic relationships provide the models referred to by the actors as being admired or criticized.

The panel of twelve conjugal case studies were found to include four which could be typed as comparatively *syncratic*, four relatively autonomic, and four characterized by a fair degree of *husband dominance*. These have been tabulated to indicate the kinds of use of resources and the incidence of tension associated with each type of decision-making (see Table 5.3).

The two cases, the Baakos and Menus, in which decision-making could be categorized as *syncratic* and in which the conjugal relationship appeared stable (in the sense that no radical change in the structuring of rights and obligations was being initiated or envisaged by either partner) had several characteristic features. Both couples were markedly home-centred in their interests and activities. They spent much of their time at home, reading and playing with their children, watching television with them, and making toys and things for the house and gardening. The Baakos owned their house jointly, Mr Menu was supervising the building of a house held in his wife's name. Although both Mrs Baako and Mrs Menu worked full-time

Table 5. 3. Couple's decision-making, use of resources, attitudes and domestic tension

Decision making	Use of		Reference models						Attitudes to						Stability/ Tension
	Money	Time	Parental		English		Akan		Spouse		Affines		Spouses associates		
			h.	w.	h.	w.	h.	w.	h.	w.	h.	w.	h.	w.	
Syncratic															
1. Baako	CJ	CJ	—	—	—	—	—	—	A	A	—	—	—	—	S
2. Menu	CJ	OJ	—	X	—	—	—	—	A	A	—	—	—	—	S
3. Mensah	OJ-	CJ-	X	—	A	A	X	X	A	A	—	X	X	—	T
4. Anane	OJ-	OSg-	—	—	—	A	X	X	X	X	—	X	X	X	T
Autonomic															
1. Affreh	OSg	OSg	A	A	—	A	A	X	x	X	x	X	—	x	T
2. Frimpong	OSg	OSg	—	—	—	A	A	—	x	x	x	x	—	—	t
3. Kwapong	OSg	OSg	—	—	—	—	—	X	x	x	—	—	—	x	t
4. Kwasi	CSg	CSg	A	—	—	A	—	—	x	x	—	(x)	x	x	t
Autocratic															
1. Korang	OJ	CSg	A	X	—	—	X	—	—	(x)	—	—	—	—	S
2. Kwamina	OSg	OSg	—	—	X	—	A	—	—	—	—	—	—	—	S
3. Smithson	OSg	OSg	—	X	—	—	X	—	—	—	—	(x)	—	—	S
4. Blankson	CSg	CSg	—	—	—	—	—	—	—	—	—	—	—	—	S

J = *Joint*; Sg = *Segregated*; J- = *Joint* changing to *segregated*; Sg- = *Segregated* formerly *Joint*.
S = Stable (no apparent signs of change in allocation of resources).
T = Tension manifest in open conflict: arguments, accusations, avoidance.
t = Tension latent; covert conflict: attempts to change allocation of resources.
X = Criticism openly expressed.
x = Criticism latent in jokes and complaints; (x) = Mild dissatisfaction expressed.
A = Approval expressed; — = No criticism/praise recorded.
h = husband; w = wife; O = open; C = closed.

they both consciously tried to spend as much time as they could with their children. Significantly both couples commented upon their own comparative social isolation and took pride in the fact that they were to some extent different in their home life from the people they knew in town, since they spent all their time and money upon their children and home. Neither wife maintained extensive social contacts with colleagues, associates or neighbours, though Mrs Baako did attend church regularly and belong to the Women's Fellowship. Their main social activities were visits to kin and friends paid together with their children and husbands who drove them there. They attended a minimum of official social functions, such as cocktail- and dinner-parties. The husbands were members of hobby and pro-fessional clubs and occasionally attended meetings, but were not members of drinking cliques or societies. The few associates they met frequently were known to their wives. Thus, since the activities of both husbands and wives outside the home were comparatively restricted and mainly institutional, each tended to know what the other was doing and where he or she was at any time of the day or evening.

Their financial and social obligations to kin were relatively limited, even with close kin living in Accra. None of them complained or commented about the content of their own or their spouses' relation-ships with kin and affines or associates. Nor were any overt signs of conjugal conflict and tension observed. Indeed the wives praised their husbands for the help they gave in the home and with the children. Both husbands acted as substitutes for their wives in per-forming a variety of chores and child-care tasks, such as bathing the children and making snacks for them. Similarly both couples felt relatively secure financially as they had carefully saved enough to build and buy their own properties, in which both wives, as well as husbands, had a secure stake. In short each husband and wife appeared to spend the major part, if not all, of his or her time and money upon the home and children, which was the object valued by both couples. Each seemed satisfied with the existing state of affairs. Moreover there was no external pressure upon any spouse to conform to a different pattern. The only possible major change mentioned by husbands and wives in both families was that the wife might stop work, when the economic needs of the family were less pressing at some time in the distant future. Free discussion, shared goals, agreement on basic issues, joint interests and activities appeared the keynote of their relationships. The following is an outline of aspects of the relationships of one of the couples.

Mr and Mrs Baako were both born in coastal towns and attended local schools. The husband's education was financed throughout by his father, a teacher, and that of his wife by her mother's kin, after she had been left an orphan. Mr Baako was an early graduate of the University of Ghana and became a senior administrative officer, working for several years at provincial government stations before being transferred to Accra. His wife has a junior administrative post. (Her promotion to a higher grade has been hindered by her atypical reluctance to leave her home and family for a year or two to do any further training.) They have each spent only a few weeks abroad at different times on courses connected with their jobs.

They were married ten years ago and have four children. Apart from occasional visits by educated kin, the husband says that he is cut off from most of his relatives on both his father's and mother's sides. He has not visited his home village since his father's mother died fifteen years ago. His father does not live there, as he is still teaching, though of pensionable age, and subject to transfer from one town to another. Of his few educated kin, his own father's and father's brother's children, there are some he has not heard of for a year or more. Several of them are studying abroad. His own mother died thirty years ago and he has no financial or other claims from his mother's kin, in fact he seldom sees them. The question of matrilineal inheritance does not concern him. His wife also sees relatively little of her kin. Her elderly aunt, her mother's sister, comes to stay with her each time she has a baby and she occasionally goes home for a funeral. Most of her educated relatives are scattered. She hears news of them through her mother's sister.

Both husband and wife report that they discuss everything they do together. They keep a monthly account of their expenditure in a book in which they write down everything they want. They each contribute exactly half of the amount needed for food each month. In the same way, when they bought their present house, they each put down half of the deposit out of the money they had saved prior to marriage. As regards chores some are considered his, such as caring for the rose garden, the car and the general repairs and decorating in the house. The cooking is the wife's responsibility which she does with the help of a maid. Jobs such as bathing the children and helping them with homework they both do. He also helps with the laundry by washing and ironing his own shirts. They go to work together, drop the children at school and return home at lunch time to eat with the children and then they both go back to work together. Each praises the other highly for the part played in the home.

If we presuppose that generally, in the Akan system of kinship and marriage, there is likely to be an element of tension or conflict in relationships between spouses and their respective in-laws, we may diagnose the lack of such apparent conflict in these two cases, as being the result of what Merton (1967: 37) calls, 'the mechanism of differing intensity of role involvement among those in the role set'. In this case neither spouse is intensely involved in relationships with kin. They are therefore not subject to expectations, nor involved in transactions, at variance with the expectations of their spouses. Again in considering the two couples it is apparent that both are satisfied with their relationships. Each sees the partner as fulfilling his or her own needs, and those of their conjugal family group, sufficiently, even more than sufficiently. The wives in each couple also have a sense of security about the future in that they, together with their husbands, have made adequate provision for needs to come.

It is interesting to note the way in which both the Baakos and Menus are aware to some extent of their own detachment or 'deviance', the former in a more articulate and sophisticated manner than the latter. In fact Mr and Mrs Baako are remarkable, among all the couples interviewed, for their objective assessment of the causes and kinds of changes taking place in the family in Accra as a result of 'urbanization' and 'education'. They see themselves as being affected by these changes and suffering losses as well as gaining advantages through them. For instance they note that their comparative social isolation from kin means that they find themselves alone bearing the full responsibilities of housekeeping (some chores are delegated to a maid) and raising and caring for their own children. Because they take the question of child-rearing very seriously, they both consider that the wife may have to stop her work at some point. They have already discussed what other job she might be able to do at home, so as to continue to make some financial contribution, while caring full-time for the children. Both husband and wife have given up very real opportunities to go away on courses of further education, because they realize these would involve splitting up the family, a thing they have not as yet felt prepared to do. Moreover neither feels that he or she has any responsible adult relative who would be both willing and able to take care of their children for them. They thus see the absence of ties in the 'extended family' as being associated with an increasing interdependence of husband and wife and the necessity of spouses assuming alone more social and financial responsibilities for their own children, as well as the cutting down of external financial obligations.

The next two couples the Mensahs and Ananes also followed a *syncratic* pattern of decision-making, but had unstable conjugal relationships. Here neither husband nor wife was recorded as commenting with detachment on the changes they had observed to be taking place in domestic relationships. Perhaps they were themselves too much involved in the ongoing drama of change, and all the tension and conflict it involved for them! They passionately denounced polygyny and matriliny and other aspects of Akan custom affecting traditional and modern marriage relationships, rather than remarking dispassionately the effects of 'urbanization'. Nor were they isolated from conflicting pressures, although they were attempting to become so, just as they were trying, with varying degrees of success, to make their conjugal family units discrete in residential and financial terms, and their marriage relationships *joint* with respect both to deciding and doing things. Whereas however, the *joint* aspects of relationships, noticed in the two previous couples had become routinized, in these two couples a definite effort often had to be made, sometimes in spite of a feeling of mistrust or the warnings of associates.

Both Mr Mensah and Mr Anane were professionals from interior Akan towns. Their fathers were polygynists and they had numerous brothers and sisters ranging from middle age to infancy. Mr Mensah's wife was a teacher and Mr Anane's wife a nurse. According to the separate reports of both husbands and wives, during the several years each couple spent abroad (returning two to three years previously) they had very 'close' marital relationships, deciding everything together and sharing their financial and other responsibilities.

The husbands played active parts in the care of their children, born abroad. Within two years of returning to Accra however, both couples were finding great difficulty in maintaining their usual conjugal solidarity and shared decision-making, in the face of powerful social and economic pressures to the contrary mainly from the husbands' kin.

Mr Mensah's house was the site of frequent gatherings and reunions of his relatives and he was often sent for to spend weekends in his home town, attending funerals and Memorial Services for deceased relatives and friends of his family. His wife became increasingly upset by the way his mother, sisters and brothers exerted influence upon him, through their continual advice about his behaviour (even to the extent of querying his helping his wife in the house). Their continual exhortations resulted in his spending much of his money and time in ways contrary to his wife's wishes and without her prior agreement or even knowledge. Mr Anane had numerous financial claims made upon him by his mother and sisters and their children. The former even threatened on one occasion to come to his office in rags and disgrace him if he would not give her the financial support she thought was her right. Both husbands felt and voiced considerable strain in trying to fulfil their various obligations as sons, brothers and uncles to their matrikin, as well as trying to fulfil the high expectations of their wives and children.

Under the strain of these external pressures, both the Mensahs and the Ananes became increasingly unable to discuss household matters with each other. Each began, partly or wholly, to contract out of some domestic responsibilities, previously shouldered without hesitation. Thus the wives began to think twice about using their incomes to purchase household items, as they watched the way in which their husbands' behaviour was changing. Angered by his wife's attitude Mr Anane stopped helping in the house as he had previously done. As a result of the tension between them, both he and his wife began to spend less time at home after finishing work and there was an increasing tendency to seek solace and advice outside the home. They began to spend much of their time with their colleagues, with whom they discussed their domestic situations. As a result each criticised the other for spending too much time with colleagues and not enough at home.

Both Mrs Mensah and Mrs Anane in conversation, strongly criticised their husbands' relatives for the way they were trying to spoil their marriages. While Mr Mensah attempted to stand united with his wife in the conflicts which ensued, Mr Anane's kin had such a powerful influence over him that he found it impossible to turn squarely upon them and refuse all their requests or to ask them to modify their behaviour. He was ultimately left trying to placate both them and his wife in the subsequent domestic upheaval. He thus earned both his wife's and relatives' displeasure, since each felt they were in the right and should have had his full support.

In the Mensah's case conflict between the wife and in-laws culminated in a poison insinuation directed by the wife against the husband's sister, which precipitated the latter's departure from the house. The sister-in-law swore never to return to her brother's household and thoroughly blackened his wife's name with the husband's relatives in his home town. In the Anane's case a family meeting was held to discuss the issue of conflict between Mrs Anane and her husband's sisters. Dramatic scenes and statements followed in which the sisters again swore never to come to the house. Both marital relationships, once *joint,* in that decisions, responsibilities and tasks were shared, changed through external pressure, mainly from kin but secondarily from colleagues. Each time tension reached its dramatic peak the main protagonists were the wife and the husband's sisters. After the tension had abated somewhat and the outbursts of accusations and threats had died down, attempts were made to return to the previous pattern of *joint* conjugal relationships.

Husbands and wives once more began to consult with each other and to share responsibilities, considering the goods or duties of one to belong equally to the other. Significantly in conversations together, before and after these several events, both the Mensahs and Ananes voiced strong criticism of the Akan system of kinship and marriage and the Mensahs in addition criticized their own parents' marriages, characterized by divorce and polygyny, as examples of the evils of the system. In contrast they praised the European conjugal family pattern, with which they were all familiar from their travels in Europe and from foreign friends. Excerpts from Mrs Anane's statements illustrate some of the underlying causes of discord, showing that tension centres upon what the wife feels to be the unfair allocation of time and money by the husband between competing beneficiaries, essentially herself and children on the one hand and his mother's children on the other.

Mrs Anane objects to her husband's excessive hospitality to his relatives, mainly mother and siblings, and also to the persistent idea that 'what is mine is yours' between him and them. Mr Anane and his brothers share the ownership of property, exchange goods and borrow informally without thought of return. Articles such as cars and radios are passed from one to another without the equivalent exchange of money. Mr and Mrs Anane are often at the losing end of such transactions, perhaps partly because he is the oldest among his brothers and sisters. As the wife bitterly points out, she went to work when she was pregnant and tired to earn money, part of which she now feels is benefiting her in-laws. For example:

(a) ₵1,000 accumulated by the husband when they were abroad has been sunk into a family venture jointly held by the five brothers. This is managed by one of them who is a primary school leaver.

(b) ₵2,000 was spent on a car, which was given to his brother to use while they were abroad. It was wrecked by him and no money has been refunded to them.

(c) ₵30 is spent on average each month for the entertainment of the husband's kin and the expenses of travelling to and from funerals.

(d) ₵250 has been used by her husband to help his father set up a small poultry farm. (What she finds particularly annoying about this is that her father-in-law has recently taken a new young wife, who sits at home and benefits from his help while she, Mrs Anane, works hard!) What she would like her husband to do is to save their money, so that they can build a house of their own. But as a result of the shortage of money her husband has not even done anything to help her in a trading venture she wants to join with a colleague (wax prints and shoes), nor will he take her on a holiday, nor buy her any of the kinds of expensive presents she would like and which she sees her colleagues using.

Not only does she feel he spends too much money on and with his kin, but she also feels that he spends too much time with his friends, including old class-mates and colleagues. He has started to become involved in a clique of heavy drinkers and often he does not get home until late in the evening. The result of this is that he does not spend as much time with her and the children as he used to. He even says he has not got time to go shopping himself or to take her to town. Nor does he see to it that repair jobs in the house are done. Due to the increasing personal friction between them, they no longer go to parties or attend the cinema together. If he goes out at night, it is usually with his brothers or colleagues.

The wife's ill-feeling against her husband is seen to manifest itself in several ways. She voices her discontent to friends and acquaintances, quarrels with him, refuses to speak to him for long periods and eventually threatens to leave. At last her wrath turns away from her husband and is vented upon the people she sees as the basic cause of her discontent, his sisters. The strain of multiple visits of kin, at a period when the wife is in poor health, results in what had been latent tension and complaints to others, becoming an open conflict between herself and two of her sisters-in-law, who are spending their holidays with them. The conflict is sparked off by arguments about the use of kitchen utensils and who should do the cooking and serve the food. The open conflict between them leads to the calling of two family meetings, at which the couple, four of the husbands siblings and one of their wives are present as well as an unrelated couple, a colleague of the husband and his wife, who act as witnesses and try to smooth matters down. The wife and sisters make public their respective complaints concerning the wife's apparent refusal to give them food and her accusation that they are spoiling things in her kitchen. The official end of the meeting is reconciliation, with the wife shaking hands with the husband's sisters and publicly stating regret for the incident and for behaviour the sisters found objectionable. Since the basic cause of conflict has not been mentioned however, the ill-feeling still continues. His sisters resolve never to stay in the house again, but only to call and greet their brother. The wife resolves to ignore and avoid her husband's relatives when they come to her house.

At some stage of the conflict the distraught husband tries to minimize the seriousness of the dispute and to laugh off the situation. The personal reconciliation of husband and wife is ultimately brought about by a short holiday they spend away together.

The situation depicted here between the Ananes and his kin is basically that of a power struggle between the wife and sisters-in-law, for greater influence over the husband's behaviour and resource allocation. The conflicting pressures converging upon the husband in his positions as husband and elder brother are temporarily lessened, as the members of the role-set turn from harrassing him with their demands to struggling with each other. As Merton (1967: 376) notes, in such situations the person in the status subject to conflicting expectations may become during the drama the *tertius gaudens*, 'the third party who draws advantage from the conflict of others'. The husband is fully aware that his wife and sisters have for a long time each wanted a greater share of his time, attention, money and living space. Once they have made their differences of opinion public and decided to practice avoidance and separation of activities and interests, then his position is somewhat improved.

Another of the mechanisms noted by Merton to help articulate roles in a role-set which is at work here, is that of support by others in similar social statuses who are attempting to cope with similar difficulties. Thus the husband and wife feel a sense of moral support prior to the crisis by spending time and discussing problems with their colleagues. What each fears might happen however, is that the other will follow the example of those who, when in similar difficulties, sought a solution by turning their backs on the marital problems and going elsewhere for gratification, for instance by deciding to divorce and remarry.

In both of these cases, categorized as basically *syncratic*, the chronic instability and conflict is seen to be the outcome of the husbands' intense involvement with both their matrikin and wives. Since the demands of each upon them conflict, dissatisfaction and strain are the result. Several mechanisms are adopted in an attempt to stabilize the situations or to shift to a new position. There is an attempt to become isolated from kin, with whom contact is not actively sought. The husbands begin to attempt to keep some of their activities with kin secret from their wives and *vice versa*. The wives similarly begin to think twice before joining their resources with those of their husbands.

On more than one occasion, the conflicts between the wives and their in-laws become public. Since in these conflicts the husbands ultimately stand on the side of their wives, the latter emerge as successful in that the in-laws are forced to retract; that is to visit the house less often, to treat the wives with more circumspection, and to whittle down their claims upon their brothers.

The wives' repetition of gossip about the results of domestic conflicts in other households, show that they are fully aware of the dimensions of the issues at stake. These include remarks about husbands, who have physically thrown their wives and their possessions onto their verandahs; who have separated from their wives and live with their sisters; who have divorced their wives and taken on second wives or who live in an estranged manner with their wives and have one or more mistresses in the town. At the same time both Mrs Mensah and Mrs Anane are aware that they are aiming at a more rewarding type of marital relationship than most women of their acquaintance are fortunate enough to enjoy. The model of relationships they are emulating is far away from their own social circle. They feel however that they deserve it since they, as professionally qualified women (teacher and nurse), are putting all their considerable resources including youth, training, money and time into their marriage relationships. Moreover they have no external sources of security towards which they may look, such as rich brothers, uncles, fathers or mothers to whom they could turn for support. The intensity with which they are bent upon gaining their major life security and gratification as wives, is seen to be partly a matter of choice, partly a matter of chance (including the years of isolation with their husbands, when they become used to relying upon each other for support), and partly a matter of circumstance (the lack of other dependable figures to whom to turn). Both are determined to continue working, partly because they realize this enhances their domestic positions. They can contribute to the household and assist their husbands and also leave the house when there are too many in-laws around. Moreover their jobs give them an added sense of security, when their in-laws demands and confrontations seem particularly threatening.

Thus we see here that two conjugal relationships characterized by *jointness* and shared decisions, systems of relationships which had developed during several years of relative social isolation from kin and countrymen abroad, were observed during the period of study to undergo a period of instability and tension, culminating in open conflict. Withdrawal from sharing of activities and contacts increased, until both wives were completely avoiding their in-laws, and one husband and wife had ceased to communicate. The stages of mutual withdrawal could be viewed as a form of hostile retaliation. Their attempts at post-crisis reconciliation and return to the former position were seen, at least at first, to be marred by a lack of trust. These conjugal relationships are likely to remain conflict prone and unstable, so long as the husbands' ties with kin remain intense, since the interests of the wives and in-laws are destined to be at variance.

AUTONOMIC RELATIONSHIPS: THE PEACEFUL STRUGGLE

The relationships of the four couples categorized as having separate decision-making processes the Affrehs, Frimpongs, Kwapongs and Kwasis had several traits in common, which differentiated them from the remainder. Each husband and wife tended to decide, without reference to the partner, and sometimes quite contrary to the latter's wishes, how a large proportion of his or her time and money should be spent on certain things. This resulted in lack of communication and friction. Financially they had few or no joint budgeting arrangements or property, and neither knew very much about how the other used money. The husbands and to some extent the wives, spent a minimum of time on household chores and child-care. They nearly all had many activities and interests distracting their attention from the home. All voiced the opinions that their spouses should spend more time or money or both in the interest of the home. Thus for instance Mrs Affreh and Mrs Frimpong remarked that their husbands would not even go shopping, while Mrs Kwapong and Mrs Kwasi commented that their husbands avoided bathing or dressing the children. Meanwhile Mr Affreh remarked that he was expected to eat food cooked by maids, and Mr Kwapong said he wanted his wife to spend less time trading and more doing housework. The husbands and wives tended to have similar resources at their command, in terms of independent incomes (three of the wives were working full-time), and support from external sets of kin and associates. All the spouses maintained frequent contact with kin, whom they often visited alone, both those in town and those in their home villages. They gave and received help and support from them, both economic and moral. For instance in several cases spouses had joint economic enterprises with relatives which involved their meeting frequently (e.g. Mrs Kwapong p. 97). As a result, the spouses all had sets of people with whom they were engaged in frequent exchanges of intimate views and news, gaining and giving support and advice of one kind and another, often without the knowledge or approval of the partner. Thus not only did husbands and wives often express some dissatisfaction with each other, but they also tended to criticize each other's kin and colleagues and associates, who were felt to be either using up the partner's time and money, which could have been better spent in the home, or reinforcing opinions with which the husband or wife did not agree, and so widening their own gaps in expectations and ideals.

The four couples varied, both in the extent to which their opinions differed and to which they openly expressed their discontents about each other and their respective sets of associates and kin, and also in how far they were trying either to withdraw from disagreeable situations or actively trying to change them. It was their frequent criticism of each other, and of associates which differentiated them sharply from the *husband-dominated* and stable *syncratic* couples, who made no such remarks.

The relationships of all four couples were apparently based upon a more or less peaceful struggle for dominance or autonomy between relatively well-matched opponents. The result of this struggle was continuous latent tension in the home and conflicting aims and pulls, rather than jointly made decisions, resulting in shared activities and apportionment of responsibility. Each spouse was continually observed to be trying to obtain control over opportunities and advantages which were coveted by others (Weber, 1962: 85).

The Frimpongs provide an example of such a couple whose relationship is characterised by *autonomic* decision-making and continual tension under the surface. There is an obvious lack of trust in the relationship. Since often one does not know how the other is spending time or money, there is a latent fear that the husband or wife is being disloyal in some way, either by giving too much to relatives, spending too much on friends or in the husband's case taking on a girl-friend, as one or two of his associates have done.

The Frimpongs spent their first few years of married life separated either from each other in Ghana or separated from their children, when they were in England. Each gained much moral and also economic support from kin and friends during the periods of separation. The wife lived with her own parents for two years and the husband formed firm friendships with colleagues from his home region.

When they set up house together each had a number of financial and social obligations to kin and friends continuing from this period. The wife has two junior relatives staying with her. The husband still spends much of his leisure time with associates instead of at home. He continues to support one or two matrikin and his children by his previous wife.

Partly as a result of this the wife complains that her husband does not give her enough money for shopping each week, nor does he take her to town at all or discuss the financial situation with her. On the other hand he complains that she keeps her money to herself, though he admits that she has occasionally helped him when he has been in difficulty by lending him money till the end of the month. In addition she regularly adds some of her money to the food bill and buys all her own and the children's clothes.

The wife also complains that her husband does not spend enough time at home with herself and the children. He admits that he prefers to spend his leisure at a hotel bar drinking with friends, rather than coming home to the overcrowding and the noise of the children. They both usually visit their home towns alone once a month or so. If either has a problem he or she tends to discuss it with friends or kin rather than marriage partner.

The tension in this household never reaches open conflict during the period of observation. Criticism is not direct, leading to any confrontations, but rather expressed obliquely in asides, in jokes and comments about others. Both husband and wife give the appearance of being relatively well satisfied with their lot, while attempting daily in numerous small ways to exert pressure for improvement. Thus the wife keeps trying from time to time to persuade her husband to come straight home from work instead of drinking and staying out till evening, to help her with the shopping and child-minding, and to add her own or her children's names to a property he has started to build. Meanwhile he keeps telling her how pressed he is for money in the hope that she will use more of her income on the household needs. Aspirations tend to be just one step ahead of present practice and not much out of line with the people with whom they associate, many of whom, they are aware, have problems similar to their own.

In one of the relationships in this category however, the character of *autonomic* decision-making and action was observed to reach a chronic level. The gulf between the expectations and activities of the husband and wife became apparently so wide that it was only with extreme difficulty they could at one point continue to communicate at all. The extent, to which they decided upon courses of action and carried them out separately, is indicated by the fact that not only did they commonly travel to visit places and people alone, but they often went without consulting or even notifying each other. Thus the husband sometimes disappeared from Friday till Monday and the wife did not know where he was. (She said he might have gone to a Masonic Lodge meeting or to his home town.) Similarly the wife went off to stay with her relatives for several weeks, without discussing the matter with her husband. After two weeks he rang her up and told her to come and look after the children, whom she had left with the 'cateress', as he too wanted to go away for a few days!

Their backgrounds and upbringing were quite different. The wife was a fourth-generation educated teacher, whose father had been a doctor and mother a trained teacher. All her brothers and sisters and parents' siblings were professionally trained. She came from a coastal town. The husband was on the other hand the first among his kin to be educated. He was reared by his maternal uncle, an illiterate cocoa farmer. His mother, a trader, had children by three different marriages. His father died when he was young. From the beginning it was clear that their expectations as to how domestic rights and responsibilities should be distributed between them and their kin were drastically at variance. She expected him to have no financial obligations to his kin and to remain financially dependent upon him herself during the infancy of her three children. He expected to provide for several matrikin and did so, thinking that she should be largely self-supporting. While she expected to live with only her husband, children and servants, he brought his sister and two nephews to stay in the house.

As their mutual dissatisfaction in their home increased, the husband spent more and more time with his men friends and subsequently a girl-friend. His wife went on her own to visit her relatives in the town. Their differences in expectations and opinions about family life were indicated by the fact that, while the husband stated firm approval of customary Akan norms of kinship and marriage, including matriliny, polygyny, financial independence of wives and the security to be gained from matrilineage membership, the wife approved of nuclear family individuation and complementary division of labour between husband and wife. Some of her comments given below present an impression of her dissatisfaction. She sees that the problem of their differences in expectations as one of 'class' and 'culture' and probably insurmountable.

According to Mrs Affreh the Akan can be grouped into two, the 'enlightened' ones from the coastal towns and the illiterates from the villages both on the coast and in the interior. The ideas of the two groups of people regarding marriage and family life are quite different and they should never intermarry. She herself has marriage problems and other urban, coastal Akan women she knows, who have married rural Akan men, especially those from the interior, have had the same kinds of difficulties. That is obviously why her own mother did not want her to get married to her present husband in the first place! People such as members of her family always think one should marry someone of the same 'class' (from another educated coastal family). She did not know what they meant until she had experienced it. The two sets of people have quite different ideas about relationships between relatives and between husbands and wives.

(a) Division of labour

She worked until her third child, now two years old, was born. She no longer works and would like to stay at home until her children have all grown up. She knows that most Akan women keep on working and just have three months maternity leave and then continue, but she herself was brought up by her own mother, who was always at home and never left the house to go to work. (She did some trading in cloth at home.) She raises the question as to how children can love their mothers when the latter are never at home with them. Those who have been brought up by their own mothers appreciate it. For instance her own brothers were brought up like that and they have all followed suit and kept their wives at home for several years, until their children have grown up. This is the type of family of the 'upper class' coastal families, but the Akan farmers from the interior have quite a different pattern. They have no conception of the kind of home life she is referring to. They expect their wives (of whom they have several) to go out to work on their farms and they do not see why mothers should stay at home. In fact her own husband thinks that wives who stay at home are lazy. He thinks she ought to work now, but she does not agree. (A few months later the wife did in fact try to get a job.)

(b) 'Openness'

Not only do the less enlightened category of Akan think that polygyny and working wives are the order of the day, but they also consider even remote kin to be close relatives. The coastal people do not treat relatives in this way. They are more like the English. They do not believe in recognizing many cousins and so on. They think of distant relatives more as friends than relatives. They are only concerned with their closest kin. They visit close relatives, but they do not live with them. On the other hand the interior Akan stick together and that makes marriage difficult.

Moreover there is the question of matrilineal inheritance. Whereas among the coastal people it depends upon the individual whether he makes a will (just like the British system she said), among the others nephew inheritance is taken more seriously and it is the main difficulty in the family system.

A big problem arises when somebody with an educated coastal family marries someone with an illiterate family from the interior. For instance they (the latter) will treat the kitchen and store in the house as their own. They will just take provisions one has budgeted to buy without even asking. They think the husband bought the food and so they can take it without taking any notice of the wife. She is not a relative. They think they are the ones with power. (Note the recurrent reference to food and the kitchen as a focus of conflict and accusations, between wives and in-laws.)

Mrs Affreh thus thinks in terms of generations of education as bringing about two sorts of change, an increasingly complementary division of labour between the husband and wife, as regards provision for the domestic and financial needs of the household and more *jointness* in other areas, such as leisure spending, at the same time a greater degree of *closure* of the conjugal family, in terms of child-rearing, residence, control over property and inheritance. All these are accounted attributes of 'good' families, of which she can cite examples among her own kin. These adjustments are seen by her as bringing the Akan system of family relationships more in line with the 'British model' of which she strongly approves. Such changes, she reasons, reflect an increase in the wife's power *vis-à-vis* her husband and a corresponding decrease in the power of the husband's relatives, as regards the ways in which the man allocates his resources. Since her husband comes from such a radically different type of family background, she fears he will never see her point of view. In fact, to judge by the way he emulates his own maternal uncle at the moment, her fears seem justified. Whether he will in future is open to serious doubt.

In these four couples, categorized as *autonomic*, a number of similarities and differences are apparent. The husbands and wives admit that some tension and strain exist in their relationships with their spouses or kin or affines or all of these. In each case the wife has considerable sources of security, held separately from her husband, such as a job, an income, savings or supportive ties with kin ready to give her help. Some kind of change either major or minor, appears imminent in each set of relationships, as spouses try to adjust their positions. For example Mrs Frimpong is bent upon exerting influence over her husband, so that he will spend more time and money at home. Mrs Affreh on the other hand seems despondent about improving the existing situation and is toying with the idea of complete withdrawal to a job elsewhere. It is noteworthy that three out of these four wives, like the two wives in the unstable *syncratic* category, refer with admiration to the British or wider Euro-American conjugal family model.

HUSBAND-DOMINATED RELATIONSHIPS

The four cases, in which the conjugal relationships could be classified as relatively *husband-dominated*, also shared a number of common characteristics. At the same time they were quite different from those already described.

In terms of relative resources, both financial and educational brought to the marriage, the wives contributions were comparatively low. None had a secondary education and only one had worked for any length of time since marriage. She was a lowly paid clerical worker, whose husband joked that he took a token sum from her income every month, as a sign of domestic authority! The husbands of the other three expressly forbade them to go to work full-time, though they did manage to find ways of making money on a part-time basis, such as by keeping poultry and sewing. Two of these wives would have very much liked to find full-time employment. In one case the wife's father appealed to the husband to let his daughter go to work, but the husband was adamant.

All four wives were expected by their husbands, contrary to the general norm, to play a full-time role in the domestic work of their households, cooking, baby-minding and so on. Even though they all had servants, they were expected to prepare food themselves and not to rely on the nursemaids to look after the children. The three husbands of the non-working wives specifically stated their disapproval of leaving children to nursemaids to be cared for. Nor did the husbands themselves spend much time on the chores or child-care. Thus on the one hand these husbands had successfully limited their wives' working activities outside the home, and at the same time had a large measure of control over how their households should be run, the allocation of tasks. Only the minor details of domestic organization were left to their wives. The major decisions, as to who should do which task, and how the wives time should be spent had already been decided by them.

In comparison with their wives, the husbands' financial and

educational resources were very high. Each had undergone extensive post-graduate training and they were all at the top, or near the top, of one of the Civil Service hierarchies. They all earned over ₡4,000 a year. Thus in terms of financial and educational input into the households, and prestige reflected from their occupational statuses, the husbands' contributions were large in comparison with those of their wives, as was their influence in making decisions affecting the home and their wives' activities.

In terms of kinship roles too, all four husbands maintained intimate contact with many highly educated influential relatives. Three of their fathers had been professional men. Only one of the wives had educated or influential kin, whom she saw frequently. In addition all four husbands had large areas of activities outside their homes, of which their wives knew or heard little. Three had extensive commitments in organizations in the town as secretaries and chairman of various clubs and societies and as members of Masonic Lodges and religious and other organizations. They also tended to maintain close links with colleagues and associates in the town, visiting and being visited by them frequently. Three of the wives were quite often taken to official functions at which their husbands' colleagues and associates were present.

The wives' activities outside the home were relatively restricted, because of their heavy domestic responsibilities. All had small children. They did however visit kin and friends and joined one or two societies, most of which activities their husbands knew about, but did not join. Mrs Korang, the only wife who voiced any kind of oblique criticism of her husband, was the one who had very much wanted to go out to work, but whose husband had refused to allow her. From time to time she felt a little frustrated about this, as all her friends were employed and earning. Again on one occasion she ventured a slightly sarcastic aside about her husband's lack of interest in the house and assumption of any domestic responsibilities. Financially she was quite happy as her husband had put the second of his two houses in their joint names. A significant difference between the spouses in these cases and those categorized as *autonomic,* was the general lack of either criticism or praise voiced by them about each other or their kin and associates. There appeared to be a tacit acceptance of the *status quo.* The systems of relationships, as they existed in the domestic sphere, and those impinging upon them appeared to be relatively stable and tension-free (cf. Oeser & Hammond, 1954). Respect rather than tension characterized the wives' attitudes and serious or jovial confidence, those of their husbands. The references they made to the domestic norms of others were mainly disparaging, or to similar people, demonstrating role satisfaction and self-confidence. No husbands or wives voiced aspirations concerning major changes in their relationships. No models of behaviour, unsuccessfully aspired to, were mentioned. The references were meant to indicate that the actors themselves were doing the right and proper thing in their own domestic lives. These included two wives' criticisms of their own parents for not rearing them properly, in one case by sending her to be fostered by strangers and in the other by thwarting her ambition to continue her education. In addition Mr Kwamina praised the Akan family system for its care of dependants both young and old and criticized the English system for its neglect. In contrast Mr Korang and Mr Smithson criticized aspects of the traditional Akan system, including in their criticism those educated men in town who continued to act by its standards such as polygyny, easy divorce, and matriliny. Mr Korang noted that because of these facts he found he had little in common with his colleagues and associates from the same region.

These *husband-dominated* couples also had several other characteristic features. They had a more or less complementary division of labour, the husbands providing the financial resources, the wives providing the domestic skills and organization. The husbands had extensive areas of extra-domestic activity, much of which was beyond their wives' range of knowledge, while the wives' extra-domestic activities were relatively restricted and known to their husbands. Apparent stability and lack of conflict marked their relationships. If there was any sign of change, it was towards an increase in the wife's extra-domestic sphere of activities, but then only at some distant time in the future, when the children would all be grown up. The husband's financial resources were apparently ample enough for them, simultaneously and without strain, to provide adequately for their wives and children and dependent kin. There were noted tendencies to feel a sense of moral as well as economic self-satisfaction.

We have now seen from the discussions of the panel of twelve case-studies that the association between the spouses' contributions of resources, their relative power positions and modes of allocating tasks and rights followed by and large the pattern depicted as normal from the survey data. There was a tendency that is, for money and time to be kept and used separately among the *autonomic* and *husband-dominated* couples and for *joint* use of money and time to categorize the couples' activities in the first *syncratic* set.

Most of the husbands and wives were noted, either overtly or covertly, to give praise and blame to their spouses for the way in which resources were allocated and decisions were taken. They also in several cases, criticized their spouses' kin and associates for their influence, either in diverting resources or loyalty elsewhere or in influencing their partners' attitudes in a way contrary to their interests. The majority of couples referred, at some point, to the marriage and family relationships of other sets of people whom they knew or whom they knew about, including their own parents and relatives and friends. In addition they referred to a number of ethnic stereotypes including the Akan and English.

Some systems of conjugal relationships were noted to be much more tense and unstable than others. Among the four couples categorized as *syncratic* were two of the most harmonious and two of the most stressful relationships observed. While the former two couples had financial relationships between husband and kin categorized as relatively *closed* the latter couples were classified as *open* and it was this *openness* which was seen to be affecting conjugal behaviour, causing conflict and increasing *segregation*, not only in the financial sphere but also as regards use of time and energy.

We may at this point take a further look at the survey data and examine these three factors simultaneously, type of decision-making, type of task performance and financial *openness*. The result is illuminating. First we are given further evidence of the correlation between *joint* action and *syncratic* decision making (see Table 5. 4). The seven couples whose overall task performance was *joint* are all in the *syncratic* category. But what is more, these couples have the financial relationships classified as the most closed with a mean score of only 2 on the Financial Closure Index. Indeed the mean score of 2.2 for all *syncratic* couples on that index is appreciably lower than that of the *autonomic* and *husband-dominated* couples which is 2.7. In contrast the four *husband-dominated* couples with the most *segregated* task performance also have the most *open* financial relationships with a mean score of 3. Thus both case and survey data give some interesting indications of the complex associations existing between relative *jointness* and *closure* of conjugal relationships in a number of areas and also marital power and decision-making and the apparent stability and harmony of husband–wife relationships. Obviously when couples find themselves to be in

Table 5. 4. *Financial openness by type of decision-making and task performance* $(N = 58)$

| Type of task performance | Type of decision-making | | | | | |
| | Syncratic | | Autonomic | | Husband dominated | |
	N	Mean score****	N	Mean score	N	Mean score
Joint*	(7)	2	(0)	–	(0)	–
Medium**	(13)	2.2	(12)	2.7	(8)	2.5
Segregated***	(7)	2.6	(7)	2.6	(4)	3
Total	(27)	2.2	(19)	2.7	(12)	2.7

* Scores 4–7 on Financial Provision Index. Scores 2–5 on Financial Management Index. Scores 5–8 on Chore Performance Index.
** Scores mixed including some *joint* and some *segregated*.
*** Scores 0–3 on Financial Provision Index. Scores 0–1 on Financial Management Index. Scores 1–4 on Chore Performance Index.
**** Financial Closure Index (see Appendix p. 165).

conflict prone or stressful situations they make appropriate attempts to restructure their domestic rights and obligations so as to make a more harmonious adjustment to family living in their neolocal urban context. Stress and conflict lead to change.

NOTES

[1] We admit with Komarovsky (1962: 220) that such a simple tripartite classification of conjugal power relationships is woefully inadequate, yet the results of the data analysis below would seem to show that it may serve some useful purpose.

[2] Lloyd has made a similar point in his discussion of the African elite wife (1967: 179).

6

TENSION AND CHANGE

At each stage of the foregoing description of the various systems of distribution of domestic rights, duties and resources, the levels of associated conjugal tension and conflict were noted, as well as the directions in which frustrated, anxious and dissatisfied husbands and wives were seeking to make some change. The kinds of rewards they wanted to achieve and the sort of obligations they were attempting to shed were also noted and the people with whom they were competing in order to reach their various goals. In six of the twelve cases discussed above there were no open expressions of conflict (see Table 5. 3). Spouses were apparently fairly contented with the existing allocation of rights and duties, neither seemed to be making any concerted effort towards change. An element of mutual interdependence was observable in their relationships. Thus in the case of the two *syncratic* stable couples, the Baakos and the Menus, each spouse was giving virtually all he or she had in terms of both time and money to contribute to the household. Partners praised each other and seemed satisfied. In the *husband-dominated* category there was an equivalent exchange of a different kind. Husbands were giving one part of their comparatively ample resources in money and some of their time, providing, what was thought to be adequately, for household needs, while the wives were giving all or most of their time to domestic services, housework and child-care. Since the division of labour was a complementary one, each needed the services of the other to maintain the viability of their conjugal family units.

In the six remaining cases in which there was tension however, there was either a struggle to maintain reciprocity or there was a recognized imbalance in the conjugal exchange, at least as far as the actors judged the situation. Moreover in several of the cases, since neither spouse was playing a very active part in domestic work and all the wives but one were in paid employment, they were not so bound together by mutual interdependence upon the exchange of services, as the other couples tended to be. Most of the husbands or wives could conceivably have continued to run their households

144

with the help of kin and maids in a similar way to that in which they were now run. (In the other cases for either spouse to have run the household alone would have required a much more radical adjustment and change in organization.) The tension and struggle was maximum in the cases of the Mensahs, Ananes and Affrehs (see Table 5. 3). In each couple one or both partners voiced feelings of strain, intense anxiety and dissatisfaction. The wives in particular felt that they were the victims of unfair situations and their main antagonists were felt to be their in-laws, who in their opinion were causing the injustice. Meanwhile in the cases of latent tension the remaining three *autonomic* couples, the question as to whether a fair exchange was being maintained appeared to be constantly under review. There was repeated effort on the part of the husbands and wives to gain what was felt to be their proper due and to rectify any imbalance in their conjugal exchange.

RELATIVE DEPRIVATION

The problem now presents itself as to how marriage partners decide what is a 'fair' reciprocal exchange of goods and services, as far as their own conjugal relationship is concerned. The outside observer may see little objectively different in the domestic positions of one spouse, who is thoroughly dissatisfied with his or her lot and either contracting out of it or fighting to improve it, and that of another person quite contented, who, in terms of measurable goods and services allocated to him or her by the spouse, is in a similar position. The question is, what are the factors affecting the levels and types of satisfaction at which individuals are aiming in the marital relationship.

People have frequently been shown to define the levels of gratification to which they aspire partly by comparing their own situations with those of others like themselves, whom they know or about whom they know. Studies such as those of *The American Soldier* (Stouffer *et al.* 1949) have demonstrated that discontent, leading to innovation and rejection of widely accepted aims, is likely to follow when some see their share of rights and goods is smaller than that of other people similarly situated, when they have a feeling of 'relative deprivation'. Reference groups of several kinds are known often to act as standards of comparison for measuring what is felt to be relatively gratifying or relatively depriving for people in particular kinds of social situations.

145

REFERENCE MODELS

Because of the relative 'invisibility' of married life, the range of such domestic reference groups may be restricted. The relationships observed between the parents or parent surrogates is likely to serve as an important focus for comparison and reference, for not only is the young person directly trained and disciplined by them, but as in the matter of unconscious language learning, the child is also 'exposed to social prototypes in the witnessed daily behaviour and casual conversations of parents'. (Merton 1967: 58). It was noted in chapter 5 that a number of husbands and wives referred to their parents' marriages and their ways of managing domestic affairs. The latter provide them both with admirable examples to be copied and questionable behaviour to be avoided. The attempt to copy or avoid such patterns of parental behaviour, observed at an earlier period or during the present, was sometimes quite explicit, sometimes more apparent from actions than from words, sometimes successful, sometimes unsuccessful. Mrs Affreh (p. 137) for instance provided an example of a woman for whom a minimum standard of expectation had been laid down in early childhood, which she herself was now unsuccessfully trying to copy. Her own brothers however, as she pointed out, had been able to follow the parental example. Again one or two wives referred to their own parents' mode of rearing their children, which they considered unsatisfactory, and pointed out in contrast how they themselves were improving upon their examples, by looking after their own children and giving them every encouragement to continue with their education.

Not only did spouses' own parents serve as reference points, however, but also other kin, who had been socializing agents, grandparents, uncles, aunts and foster parents. Thus husbands were noted to look back with pride on the way a grandfather or maternal uncle had reared them and to be consciously trying to emulate them in the way they cared both for their own children and children of kin (see Chapter 3).

Again it was noticed that a minimum standard of expectations might have been laid down in early marriage, as well as childhood, when the type of social rewards a spouse would consider necessary for his or her future satisfaction had been defined. Thus it was interesting to note that in the two unstable *syncratic* cases, in which conflict was acute and erupting openly, the wives referred to a recent time when they had lived alone with their husbands and been able to organize their marital lives in a way which suited them. They had become used to *joint* and *closed* relationships.

As has already been observed however, husbands and wives did not confine themselves to references to their own parents and guardians and their own past experiences. They also referred to their kin of the same generation, to their colleagues, to their neighbours, to 'people in town'. In addition they mentioned items of gossip about marital relationships, which had been passed on to them by the people with whom they associated. These were often cautionary tales of crises, such as the fates of widows, divorcées, couples in conflict, a common source of gossip circulated among people familiar with each other (Epstein, 1961: 59). Some of these tales appeared to exert an influence upon spouses to adjust their behaviour. For example a wife who recounted several stories of widows and orphans being disinherited, as well as the activities and attitudes of her in-laws, was observed to separate her savings and property from those of her husband, thereby falling more in line with the general social norm for management of domestic finances.

As well as referring to the behaviour of specific people in this way, kin, colleagues and associates, these twenty-four spouses and the others included in the study also made mention on numerous occasions of ethnic stereotypes of systems of family relationships. These included Akan subgroups, especially the contrast between coastal and interior people. They also included references to the neighbouring groups such as the Ga and Ewe, among whom they had all lived and worked for many years and in addition the English and other Europeans and Americans with whom they were familiar from many sources, from school, from work and often because they had lived abroad.

These spontaneous references to domestic relationships among neighbouring and known ethnic groups also varied. Some were disparaging. Some were approving. Thus for example Mrs Affreh contrasted the 'good' educated, coastal families and those with less education from the interior and rural areas. References were made to the lack of matriliny (as practised by the Akan), among the Ewe. Fewer direct contrasts were made between the Ga and the Akan, as the former were felt by one or two to be, as one wife put it, 'somewhat betwixt and between' with respect to inheritance.[1]

Significantly five out of the six wives in couples with tense relationships with their husbands and affines, wives who felt particularly 'deprived' and dissatisfied, referred to the Euro-American conjugal family ideal as being the model they aspired to copy. Previous writers have often noted the importance of the Europeans as a normative reference group for this educated Ghanaian population (Foster, 1965: 5, 8). The attraction of this particular family stereotype for women and for the dissatisfied in general, has also been noted. The aspects of this model which the dissatisfied wives commonly referred to included the sharing by husbands and wives of tasks, responsibilities and leisure, such as shared child-care and chores and holidays and evenings spent out together.

The husbands who mentioned the Euro-American model spoke of the wife's increased loyalty to her conjugal tie in such a system, her decreasing reliance on other sources of support, such as her job and the greater expectation of permanence and the narrower range of dependants supported. As was noted in Chapter 4 the changes mentioned were in directions which would benefit the actors concerned, directions which would serve to 'maximize their own gratifications'; a judicious selection of traits rather than a switch to a different 'model' entirely.

Living and working, both at present and in the past in ethnically, educationally and economically heterogeneous societies, with face to face relationships with people from a striking variety of family traditions, and moreover, having in most cases standards of living, types of residences and social statuses, vastly different from those of the members of the parental generation who reared them, the majority found it appropriate, even necessary, to refer spontaneously to the domestic norms of others. Sometimes these references were to confirm that what they were doing themselves was the right or best thing. Sometimes it was to justify their plea for improvement in their domestic situations. Thus among the couples categorized as lacking signs of apparent domestic tension and instability, references were only made to aspects of domestic relationships considered similar or worse than the actors' own. No models aspired to were mentioned. Such references were used for instance by men successfully continuing the family traditions set by their own fathers and grandfathers.

On the other hand many references to what was considered a preferable allocation of rights and rewards were made by the dissatisfied spouses in the couples with tense and unstable relationships. Such references highlighted their own feelings of 'relative deprivation' and served to justify their aspirations and attempt at change to others. Justification was particularly necessary when their aspirations were thought by their own associates to deviate too radically from the recognised norm. Thus in some cases references to the European model were made to support what some observers considered overweening ambition. For example a married friend of Mrs Anane remarked that she was unrealistic, two or three generations ahead of her time! Meanwhile a woman related to her by marriage, and satisfying herself with a more 'normal' pattern of domestic relationships, queried on what grounds Mrs Anane should have such high aspirations for herself. References to the family norms of foreign reference groups then were used to provide a charter and to justify attempts at domestic revolution!

THE PARENTAL MODEL: THE OBSERVER'S VIEW

There were important indications in Chapter 3 that having been reared by an educated father was probably an important factor associated with the kinds of expectations and obligations attached to Akan Senior Civil Servants' relationships with their kin, there were also signs that paternal education might be correlated with a lessening of financial strain. It is pertinent now to examine evidence regarding the extent to which members of the sample appeared to benefit from the past experiences of their educated parents, with regard to their conceptions of their own conjugal relationships and the relative ease with which they have adapted to neolocal urban marriage.

Two kinds of data point towards a comparative absence of tension experienced by couples in which the husbands had mobile, educated salaried fathers. Out of the six couples labelled as having fairly harmonious relationships, five of the husbands' fathers were salaried mobile men, while among the six with comparatively tense and conflict-prone relationships, this applied to only one of the fathers.

There is a further indication of the likelihood of the absence of strain amongst those whose parents and even grandparents had the benefits of education and salaried employment. This time it is evidence of avoidance of a structural situation frought with conflict. In Chapter 4 separation of financial resources by spouses was shown to be a means of obtaining a measure of material security for wives and children and to be often associated with the degree of *openness* in financial relationships between the husband and his kin. The examples of most acute tension between spouses and wives and in-laws were seen to arise as a result of an attempt to maintain a *joint* financial relationship in an *open* economic situation (e.g. Mrs Anane pp. 130ff.) – an attempt recognized in retrospect by the actors as naive. In the survey only one out of those couples in which the husband's father was educated fell into this conflict – prone, relatively *joint/open* category with respect to financial management (score 2 or more on the Financial Closure Index and score 2 or more on the Joint Financial Management Index). Survey data thus appears to indicate that couples with accumulated experience from the past, from their educated parents, are less likely to enter such tension-prone situations than are first generation educated 'newcomers' to the salary-based life of the city, whose guides to urban marital behaviour may, for lack of closer examples, tend to be taken from a very different foreign setting and not be directly applicable to their own situations. The latter may sometimes thus be idealistic rather than realistic in their aims, when they lack appropriate models to refer to from their own experience (for example Mrs Mensah and Mrs Anane). An interesting indication of the ways in which education in the parental generation, with its associated social and geographical mobility, significantly affects people's norms regarding conjugal and kin ties, has been provided from a recent survey of the Ghanaian university student population. This evidence demonstrated clearly that the second and third-generation educated were far more likely than their first generation educated counterparts to state that the conjugal family should be a functionally *closed* unit (Oppong, 1972c).

Several sorts of evidence then support the contention that attitudes and patterns of adaptation to urban life vary, partly according to previous parental experience. One variation is an apparent tendency towards reduction of strain and tension caused by the changes involved. The final task is to examine how parental and even grand-parental experiences with respect to education and its associated mobility, appear to have actually affected the behavioural content of conjugal and kin ties, not merely attitudes and the amount of domestic tension experienced. First, with regard to finances the cases and tables given in Chapter 3 indicated that men, who had been reared by educated, mobile fathers from regions longest subject to economic change, were least likely to have heavy financial commitments to kin. The second and third generation educated were apparently both more intent upon cutting down financial obligations outside the conjugal family and more successful in avoiding them, partly because expectations of help had diminished, as had feelings

150

Table 6. 1. *Percentage of Akan Senior Civil Servants educating children of kin by generation educated* (*N* = 59)

Generation educated	% Educating children	Mean number of children	Total
First	67	1.2	(22)
Second	60	1.2	(22)
Third	50	0.6	(15)

of obligation to matrikin. Table 6.1 supports these observations by showing that the percentage of men educating children of kin decreases with each successive generation of education and its consequent social and spatial mobility, an observation in line with comparable data collected over thirty years ago (Fortes, 1963).

Apparently with mobility, both spatial and social, comes a cutting down of kinship obligations, that is of obligations which tend to detract from the resources of the shifting conjugal family unit. The question now arises as to whether there is at the same time any evidence of a move towards greater financial cooperation between the co-resident married pair than there was in the customary setting. Tables 6. 2 and 3 indicate that there is. With subsequent generations of education, husbands and wives increasingly hold joint properties and accounts, and when the wives are also educated and working they increasingly share the financial provision for the household. The couples in which the husbands are third-generation educated exhibit this trend to the greatest extent.[2] These are at the same time the couples in which the husbands have the least obligations as parental figures in other households. This difference by generations of education is also apparent between the coastal and interior peoples, since it is the former who most frequently have educated parents and grandparents, thus supporting actors' contentions that the former expect and maintain 'closer' conjugal relationships.

Throughout the discussion of the setting up of conjugal family households and the description of the division of labour in the home, there was seen to be a great deal of dependence upon kin to maintain the viability of the domestic unit, since the majority of wives were not full-time housewives and mothers, even at the periods of their lives when they had several small children and babies. The normal pattern was observed to be that educated wives continued to work

151

Table 6. 2. *Percentage of Akan couples with joint financial relationships by husband's generation educated* ($N = 59$)

Joint financial relationship	Generation educated		
	First (21)	Second (23)	Third (15)
Property	12	20	25
Accounts	5	9	13
Financial provision*	10	27	50

* Wife scores 5–7 on financial provision index (see Appendix p. 165).

Table 6. 3. *Couples' mean scores on financial management index by husband's generation educated**

	Generation educated				
	First	Second	Third	Total	N
Mean score	0.8	0.8	1.3	1	(59)

* For mode of calculating score see Appendix p. 165.

throughout their early years of marriage, only taking a three-month leave from work to facilitate their physical recovery from childbirth. They therefore depended to a very great extent upon help from kin. Moreover instances were noted in which the conjugal family members lived apart for months and years and then the dependence upon kin was even more marked. Sometimes this involved wife or children or both actually staying with relatives, sometimes it involved dependence upon two or more co-resident kin, and affines. The range of relatives and affines called in to help in these ways was seen to be wide in contrast to the range of kin given financial help. Wives without such domestic assistance were seen to be in very difficult situations, unless they could get reliable help from paid servants and from their husbands. The solution in a small minority of cases was for the wife to stay at home and be a full-time housewife. One or two couples saw this as a final solution to their problem, but one not sought for the time being. The preoccupation of relatives with their careers or education was often said to be the cause of lack of kin willing and ready to help. There were therefore indications

Table 6. 4. *Akan Senior Civil Servants' chore participation scores by generation educated* (percentages)*

Chore participation score	Generation-educated			
	First ($N=21$)	Second ($N=23$)	Third ($N=15$)	Total ($N=59$)
Low (1–4)	62	70	47	61
High (5–8)	38	30	53	39
Total	100	100	100	100
Mean score	4	4	5	4.3

* For calculation of score see p. 165.

that couples from educated families tended to be less well supplied with assistance in this respect, unless they had family servants sent to help them. There is however evidence that the husbands in such families are more likely to play an active part in household tasks when necessary. For as Table 6. 4 indicates the husbands who had both educated fathers and grandfathers were more likely to be playing an active part in housework and child care. These fifteen husbands were all either coastal Fanti or Eastern Akan. Change is thus in the directions expected, towards *closure* and towards *jointness* and these changes appear most marked among the southern people longest exposed to the effects of the unitary market system.

CONCLUSION

It is by now a commonplace observation on social systems that strain, tension and conflict both produce and are produced by change (Coser, 1967: 20, 30, 32). It is accordingly not surprising that in the foregoing description of aspects of the conjugal and kin relationships of Akan Senior Civil Servants and their wives, the themes of stress and conflict have continually recurred. For on many accounts the couples under study are in social situations subject to change. Indeed many of the changes which affect them at both the personal and national level are revolutionary in dimensions. Not only are the majority among the first in their families to have a higher education, but they are all migrants, in the sense that they have travelled widely in the process of getting an education and promotion in their jobs, and are now living far from their home towns and separated from most of their relatives. In addition the context in which they live is one of far-reaching demographic and economic change including massive rural–urban migration, and a rapidly changing occupational structure. As a result, the resources to which they have access, relatively high salaries and spacious accommodation, are scarce and much sought-after in the town. They and their immediate dependants form part of the new urban elite enjoying standards of living available only to the few. In addition they originate from areas in which a notoriously conflict-prone mode of reckoning descent and inheritance is current, areas which have themselves been subject to the manifold effects of economic revolution for varying spans of time.

In the domestic domain change and contrasts surround them on every side: between one generation and the next, between colleagues from different ethnic groups; between fellow countrymen and foreigners; between members of the several Akan sub-groups; and between rural relatives and urban associates. Everyone in varying degrees is aware of and alive to the implications of these differences. Moreover, as the foregoing account has indicated, there are even marked variations in the relationships of a narrowly selected category of men and their wives, who all come from the same Akan group and who are in broadly similar occupational and age categories. These variations include both the extent to which couples depend upon kin to maintain the viability of their urban domestic units and conversely the extent to which their relatives depend upon them for maintenance, in addition the degree to which husband and wife cooperate with and rely upon each other in supporting and managing their urban households. In other words there are considerable differences in the extent to which conjugal families are *open* and conjugal relationships *joint*.

With rich storehouses of varied personal experiences acquired at home and abroad to draw upon, and a range of relatives, colleagues, friends and acquaintances from several ethnic groups and walks of life, they are knowledgeable about variations in human domestic organisation. They have, as was seen, many references with which to illustrate their descriptions and support their contentions when discussing various forms of family relationships and conjugal ties. Moreover, women as well as men are highly articulate in the discussion of such topics, especially in so far as they impinge upon their own domestic situations.

The tension and conflicts described at such length were seen to be the outcome of several kinds of situations, in which people were attempting, with varying degrees of success, to restructure their existing sets of domestic rights and obligations. Thus husbands and wives who felt a sense of strain because of their inability to fulfil certain domestic obligations to the satisfaction of their own or other peoples' expectations, were trying to do a number of things. They were whittling down the obligations through simple avoidance or rejection, or through trying to shift the burden of the obligation onto someone else who could be cajoled or coerced into helping in this way. For instance, women harrassed by trying to perform too many tasks at the same time, to fulfil simultaneously their obligations as mothers, wives, housewives and employees, selected those responsibilities which they could not afford to neglect, and then delegated or attempted to delegate the rest to substitutes, including kin, maids and their husbands. In the same way husbands, under stress because of the manifold pressures upon them for financial support, both from their own households and those of matrikin, rejected outright some requests for help, in particular those where they felt no sense of prior obligation and tried with various degrees of success to shift some of their household responsibilities onto their working wives.

The dissatisfied, who felt 'relatively deprived', looked around and saw others in comparable positions with a greater share of rewards of various kinds allotted to them, and struggled to increase their own shares accordingly. Dissatisfaction was particularly apparent and developed into anxiety or open conflict between wives and their in-laws, when the former wished to deny the latter the rights and privileges accruing to them in the traditional domestic setting, including the rights to co-residence, maintenance and joint rights in property. They accordingly cited examples they wished to follow from *closed* conjugal family systems. In each case the would-be innovators, trying to improve their own positions, were resisted to some extent by those who had benefited from the *status quo,* whether spouse, kin or affines. Not unnaturally individuals were seen to be clinging to old rights as well as demanding new ones, to be whittling down old obligations and also being reluctant to take on new responsibilities. Thus for instance wives retained the services of kin as much as they could, to help them in the performance of domestic chores, a customary pattern. At the same time they tried to persuade their husbands to help in the home, a new pattern of behaviour. Meanwhile men enjoyed the continuity of the traditional pattern whereby wives contributed to the household's upkeep, but were reluctant to enter the area of domestic chore performance in return.

Such were the areas of stress and strain in domestic life and the struggles and conflicts which ensued as individuals tried to improve their positions *vis-à-vis* their conjugal families and kin. Two of the most important considerations with regard to these conflicting pulls were the relative power positions of the respective spouses and also their aspirations and expectations. In each case the levels of education attained in both the parental and present generation were seen to be crucial intervening variables, since they both implied social and spatial mobility and possession of a resource potentially useful in the domestic situation. In other words education was likely to affect both the type of premarital family experience of the individual and the occupational position or employment opportunities. Throughout the description of the allocation of domestic resources and the discussion of strain-producing and unstable situations, the focus was continually upon the basic family functions which serve to maintain the ongoing viability of the household unit; the process of physical maintenance including the provision of food and shelter; the education of the young and the maintenance of the home, including the performance of vital household tasks such as cooking and cleaning and baby-care. The stresses felt by the spouses were seen to concern its continued viability; the concern of the wife as to who would care for her baby while she worked; the concern of the husband that his wife should help him to pay the food or school bills and so on. The task was to show how the conjugal family unit maintained itself in the relatively isolated context of the suburban bungalow or town flat. To preserve its viability two kinds of input were needed, money and time. These needed to be allocated to suit the expectations of both spouses, if tension and conflict in the home were to be avoided. Thus we examined in some detail the contributions and allocation of these resources. Crises occurred when either obviously was, or was feared to be, insufficent or was threatened in some way.

The demands of the husband's matrikin were viewed as the most serious threat to the financial viability in the urban conjugal family and were the source of the most acute domestic conflicts and struggles. Akan Senior Civil Servants' conflicting obligations as financial providers for matrikin and wives and children were more likely to result in chronic strain when the contradiction between matrilineal and conjugal rights became apparent through the overlapping of the two fields of activity. Since the actors themselves were only too well aware of the likelihood of tension and conflict in such situations of confrontation, there was a marked tendency to avoid them and for a separation of the two types of interests. As Fortes remarked of an earlier period, 'men were endeavouring more deliberately than in the past to *segregate* their conjugal and parental from their fraternal and lineage commitments and responsibilities' (1970a: 215). Thus not only were husbands seen to stand 'balanced between two different sets of people differentiating their roles according to their involvement' (Nakane, 1962, 27), but they were also seen purposefully to separate their divergent economic interests to a more marked extent than their non-matrilineal colleagues, especially when financial ties with kin were strong. There were important indications that the second and third generation, educated with spatially and socially mobile parents, were more apt to avoid such conflict-prone sets of relationships than were those with little parental experience of such new social situations.

It was observed in the introduction that considerable evidence from all over the world has been amassed to demonstrate that, wherever agricultural communities with matrilineage organization become involved in market systems with consequent migration, spread of private property ownership and private accumulation of wealth, the conjugal family emerges as the key kinship group with regard to residence, economic cooperation, legal responsibility and socialization. Inheritance, however, is noted as tending to lag behind in this change process. The material presented in this account has shown a similar pattern. Our concern has been to document the extent to which the conjugal family is in fact residentially isolated, economically individuated, and the precise allocation of responsibility for household tasks. We have indicated that it is among the third generation educated people that these processes of functional individuation and conjugal cooperation appear to be most marked. We have at the same time noted that anxieties, and conflicts over the use and ownership of property and the expression of fears regarding its transmission to the next generation indicate that there is a definite lag in change as regards inheritance of property. The residentially, and in many ways functionally individuated conjugal family may be using property which ultimately will prove subject to the traditional laws of matrilineal inheritance. This is shown to be the area of domestic behaviour most subject to change and conflict at the present time.[3] Whereas in the customary setting latent tension tended to centre upon control over people, in a context of abundance of land and shortage of labour, and subsequently in the case of rich plantation owners and merchants, centred upon litigation over inheritance rights to property, tension in the modern urban setting is seen to focus increasingly upon provision of adequate standards of *maintenance*, education of children and provision of financial security for the future. Regarding the division of domestic labour our data with respect to change, its causes and correlates, follow the trend of findings of studies elsewhere. For many studies of the interchangeability of the roles of husband and wife have shown that the strictness of the division of labour inside and outside the home is related to spouses' class positions, occupations and education (e.g. Blood and Wolfe, 1960: 61; Haavio, 1967). A less strict division of labour has been seen to obtain among the more highly educated and wealthier couples (Mogey, 1955; Thompson & Finlayson, 1963; Klein, 1965: 139). Ethnic differences have also been demonstrated as significant correlates (Harrell-Bond, 1967). What has been strikingly demonstrated in many studies of this type is that the socio-economic position of women is changing rapidly in many sectors of urban society. One notable fact is that men are not very willing to adapt their own roles accordingly, when their wives are also salary-earning members of the household (Jeffreys, 1952; Colson, 1958: 138; Axelson, 1963). Working wives everywhere are potentially subject to strain. Significant shifts have been noted too in the conjugal balance of power with changing access to resources.

With regard to the content of relationships between spouses and their kin, measurement of the financial nexus of exchanges of goods and services has frequently been used both to test the theory that the conjugal family in contemporary urban society (in the United States and Europe in particular) is 'isolated' and the alternative proposal that the 'kin family network' is still viable (e.g. Sussman & Burchinall, 1965). Evidence from many communities shows that educated urban salary earners generally feel some financial and other obligations to kin, as well as maintaining social contacts with them, and these persist in spite of geographical and occupational mobility (Litwak, 1960a, b and c; Ostereich, 1965; Piddington, 1965; Berardo, 1967; Tilly & Brown, 1967: 163). As several writers have pointed out it is the element of obligation and a sense of positive concern which is likely to differentiate kin ties from those of friends (Adams, 1967). In spite of evidence of such exchanges however, the majority of data still support the contention that most middle-class urban conjugal families are financially *closed*. The roles of financial provider and educator are not normally played across the boundaries of the conjugal family unit, as we have seen they continue to be in many educated, urban Akan households. Although aged parents may be maintained or accommodated by their own children, or parents may assist their married children to set up house when they are young and ill-equipped, yet the idea is widespread that even children and their parents should be quite financially independent, once the former have started their own conjugal families (e.g. Hubert, 1965: 60–80). Thus according to the evidence the changes in the financial content of ties of Akan Senior Civil Servants and their kin are in the expected direction, that is economic obligations outside the conjugal family are dwindling, with increasing social and spatial mobility.

The study of strains and tensions involved in the redistribution of domestic rights and duties between Akan Senior Civil Servants and their wives and kin has thus uncovered important changes taking place in both conjugal and kin relationships, which appear to follow world-wide trends recorded elsewhere in urban environments. At the root of the domestic changes seems to be the recruitment through higher education of individuals into the ranks of the salary-earners, and the social and spatial mobility and dependence upon a fixed income entailed by this. Comparison of survey data from coastal, eastern and interior Akan men, and from men who are first, second and third-generation educated, indicates that both the dwindling of matrilineal obligations (increasing *closure*) and the increased sharing of responsibilities and tasks between husbands and wives (increasing *jointness*) are associated to some extent with the social and spatial mobility consequent upon education and urban occupations. Those from families longest exposed to these phenomena exhibit the most marked tendencies towards *closure* and *jointness* in a number of ways. Gough (1952: 85) in her study of changing kinships usages among the Nayar of the Malabar Coast documented a similar trend away from the traditional matrilineage system towards a small bilateral family, adapted to spatial and social mobility and involving a greater intimacy and equality of husbands and wives. Like Gough we do not see such changes to be simply the result of 'Christian influence', 'Culture contact' or the 'copying of European models', as a number of previous commentators appear to have believed, but as explicable in terms of adaptations within the system of domestic relationships, serving to adjust it to the economic and demographic changes, which have been taking place and are still continuing.

159

NOTES

[1] This ambiguous aspect of the Ga kinship system has recently been discussed by Woodman (1969).

[2] Note also that it is the second and third generation educated husbands who most frequently have wives with higher education.

[3] Inheritance was found to figure prominently in an inventory of norms for domestic behaviour areas collected from samples of male and female university students which were listed to show those most subject to conflict and change (Oppong, 1972a).

APPENDIX

THE SENIOR CIVIL-SERVICE QUESTIONNAIRE

Here are some questions concerning yourself and your family. Would you kindly put a circle round the number preceding the right answer in each case or give the correct information in the space provided.

1. (a) What secondary school did you attend?...............
   (b) What are your present academic/professional qualifications? ....

2. Where did you receive your professional training/degree?
   (a) In Ghana   (b) Partly abroad   (c) All abroad

3. Where is your home town?...............   Region?...............

4. What is the ethnic group of your:

	1 Ga	2 Ewe	3 Fante	4 Ashanti	5 Akwapim	6 Other Ghanaian (specify)	7 Non-Ghanaian (specify)
(a) father	1	2	3	4	5	6.........	7.........
(b) mother	1	2	3	4	5	6.........	7.........
(c) wife	1	2	3	4	5	6.........	7.........

5. What schooling have the following had:

	1 None	2 Primary	3 Middle	4 Secondary	5 Training	6 Other (specify)
(a) father	1	2	3	4	5	6.........
(b) mother	1	2	3	4	5	6.........
(c) father's father	1	2	3	4	5	6.........
(d) father's mother	1	2	3	4	5	6.........
(e) mother's father	1	2	3	4	5	6.........
(f) mother's mother	1	2	3	4	5	6.........
(g) wife	1	2	3	4	5	6.........

6. Of what type were the following marriages:

	1 Customary	2 Customary and church blessing	3 Ordinance (registered)
(a) your own	1	2	3
(b) your parents	1	2	3

161

7. When did you marry your present wife?
   (a) Customary rites – month......... Year.........
   (b) Civil/church ceremony – month......... Year.........

8. What is the age group of:

	1	2	3	4	5	6	7	8
	Under 20	20–25	26–30	31–35	36–40	41–45	46–50	50+
(a) yourself	1	2	3	4	5	6	7	8
(b) your wife	1	2	3	4	5	6	7	8

9. What is the religious affiliation of:

	1	2	3	4 Roman	5	6 Other
	Presbyterian	Methodist	Anglican	Catholic	Muslim	(specify)
(a) yourself	1	2	3	4	5	6.........
(b) your wife	1	2	3	4	5	6.........
(c) your father	1	2	3	4	5	6.........
(d) your mother	1	2	3	4	5	6.........

10. How many of the following have you?

Has been to school

	Yes	No
(a) full brothers and sisters	....
(b) half brothers and sisters (father's side)	....
(c) half brothers and sisters (mother's side)	....

11. How often do you see one or more of your brothers and sisters?
    (a) daily   (b) weekly   (c) monthly   (d) less than once a month.

12. How often do kin come and ask for financial and other help?
    (a) never   (b) occasionally (2 or 3 times a year)   (c) often (once a month or more).

13. How long is it since you gave a relative financial help?
    (a) A week   (b) A month   (c) A few months   (d) 6 months or more.

14. Do you make regular monthly remittances to relatives?
    (a) Yes   (b) No.

15. About how much do you spend each month on helping relatives apart from school fees?
    1. Nothing. 2. Up to ₵5 per month. 3. ₵5–10. 4. More than ₵10 per month.

16. Circle the number of children whose education you have paid for in the following categories:

Type of education

	No. of children	Primary	Middle	Secondary	Other post–Middle
(a) own child	0 1 2 3 4 5 6 7	P	M	S	O
(b) sister's child	0 1 2 3 4 5 6 7	P	M	S	O
(c) brother's child	0 1 2 3 4 5 6 7	P	M	S	O
(d) parent's child	0 1 2 3 4 5 6 7	P	M	S	O
(e) maternal cousin's child	0 1 2 3 4 5 6 7	P	M	S	O
(f) other (specify)	0 1 2 3 4 5 6 7	P	M	S	O

17. What is your wife's occupation? 1. housewife   2. part-time worker...............
3. full-time worker...............   (specify)
        (specify)

18. If your wife is earning an income how much does she contribute to the following items of expenditure? Circle the appropriate figure

Amount

Item		Nothing	Part	All
(a) Food	....	0	1	2
(b) Rent	....	0	1	2
(c) Transport	....	0	1	2
(d) Children's clothes	....	0	1	2
(e) Her own clothes	....	0	1	2
(f) Domestic labour	....	0	1	2
(g) Children's school fees	....	0	1	2
(h) Electricity/gas	....	0	1	2

19. How do you reach major decisions in your household?

    (a) Both discuss all issues together then decide.
    (b) Husband decides some, wife decides others.
    (c) Husband decides all main issues.
    (d) Wife decides all main issues.
    (e) Other............................
          (specify)

20. Do you and your wife keep
    (a) a joint current bank account?   1. Yes   2. No
    (b) a joint savings bank acount?   1. Yes   2. No.

21. If your wife earns an income do you know how she spends her money?
1. Yes.   2. No.

22. If you do know how she spends do you and your wife also pool your incomes together and jointly plan your household expenditure?
1. Yes.   2. No.

23. Do you own any of the following properties jointly with your wife, brothers and sisters or other kin? Please circle the right answers:

	With wife	With brothers and sisters	With other kin
(a) farm land	Yes/No	Yes/No	Yes/No
(b) house	Yes/No	Yes/No	Yes/No
(c) car	Yes/No	Yes/No	Yes/No

24. How many children have you?......... Circle their ages

1 2 3 4 5 6 7 8 9 10 11 12 13 14 15 16 17

25. On what date was your first child born?   Month......... Year.........
On what date was your last born child born?   Month......... Year.........

26. Do you expect your wife to do all her own housework?
1. Yes. 2. No. If No, who helps her?.........

27. Have you any paid domestic labour in the house? 1. Yes. 2. No.

28. Do you ever get time to help in the house yourself? 1. Yes. 2. No.

29. Household tasks: Please indicate by circling the appropriate figures how often you have done the following tasks since you married:

	Never	Occasionally	More than half the time	Always	Previously but not now
(a) gardening	0	1	2	3	4
(b) tidying up	0	1	2	3	4
(c) washing up	0	1	2	3	4
(d) marketing	0	1	2	3	4
(e) store-shopping	0	1	2	3	4
(f) buying children's clothes	0	1	2	3	4
(g) bathing children	0	1	2	3	4
(h) dressing children	0	1	2	3	4
(i) mixing food for baby	0	1	2	3	4
(j) changing nappies	0	1	2	3	4
(k) mending fuses	0	1	2	3	4
(l) setting the table	0	1	2	3	4
(m) cooking	0	1	2	3	4
(n) making beds	0	1	2	3	4
(o) washing shirts	0	1	2	3	4
(p) washing car	0	1	2	3	4
(q) petty household repairs	0	1	2	3	4

INDICES

(a) The Wife's Financial Provision Score
The coded responses regarding the relative amounts wives contributed to the payment of eight household expense items were totalled (Question 18). The possible range of scores was from 0–16. A score of 16 would have meant the wife was providing all the money for the items listed. The actual range recorded was 0–8. Zero and low scores meant that the wife was contributing nothing or little to the cost of the items, higher scores meant she was contributing something to several or all items.

(b) The Financial Management Score
A number of responses concerning financial management were alloted scores, which were subsequently added up to give an overall indication of the degree to which husband and wife managed their finances together.

	Score
1. Husband knows how wife spends income	1 or 2
or Couple pool incomes and spend jointly.	
2. Couple own joint property.	1
3. Couple keep a joint savings bank account.	1
4. Couple keep a joint current bank account.	1

The possible score range was 0–5. Scores from 0 to 4 were recorded.

(c) The Husband's Chore Participation Score
To achieve an indication of the husband's overall degree of participation in domestic tasks responses to all the answers to question 29 were totalled ($0 = 0$, $1 = 1$, $2 = 2$, $3 = 3$, $4 = 1$) and divided by four, giving scores ranging from 1 to 8.

(d) The Financial Closure Score
A number of responses concerning the financial content of husbands' relationships with kin were given scores. These were added up to give an overall indication of the extent to which husbands were educating and maintaining kin and owning property jointly with them, as follows:

	Activity		Score
(1) Education of children	Nil	......	0
	One child	......	1
	Two or more	......	2
(2) Remittances to kin	Nil	......	0
	₵1–9	......	1
	₵10 +	......	2
(3) Co-ownership of family property	No	......	0
	Yes	......	1

These scores were added up giving a range of 0–5.

165

BIBLIOGRAPHIES

SELECT AKAN BIBLIOGRAPHY

ARHIN, K.
1968a   The Missionary Role on the Gold Coast and in Ashanti. *Institute of African Studies, Research Review.* Legon. Vol. 4, No. 2, 1–15.

ARHIN, K.
1968b   Status Differentiation in Ashanti in the Nineteenth Century: A preliminary Study. *Institute of African Studies, Research Review.* Legon. Vol. 4, No. 3, 34–52.

BOSMAN, W.
1705   *A new and accurate description of the coast of Guinea.* London: J. Knapton and D. Midwinter (reprinted 1967, 4th ed. London, Frank Cass).

BOWDICH, T. E.
1819   *Mission from Cape Coast Castle to Ashantee.* London, J. Murray.
(3rd ed. W. E. F. Ward (ed.) 1966 London, Frank Cass, Reprint of 1819 ed.)

BUSIA, K. A.
1951   *The position of the chief in the modern political system of Ashanti: a study of the influence of contemporary social changes on Ashanti political institutions.* London, Oxford University Press.
1954   The Ashanti of the Gold Coast. In Daryll Forde (ed.), *African worlds: studies in the cosmological ideas and social values of African peoples.* London, Oxford University Press.

CHRISTENSEN, J. B.
1954   *Double descent among the Fanti.* Behavioural Science Monographs. New Haven, Human Relations Area Files.

CLARIDGE, W. W.
1915   *A history of the Gold Coast and Ashanti: from the earliest times to the commencement of the twentieth century.* 2 Vols. London, J. Murray.
(2nd ed, 1964, London, Frank Cass.)

DANQUAH, J. B.
1922   *Akan Laws and Customs.* London, Routledge and Sons.
1928   *Cases in Akan Law.* London, Routledge and Sons.
1944   *The Akan Doctrine of God.* London, Butterworth Press.

FIELD, M. J.
1948   *Akim Kotoku.* Crown Agents for the Colonies.
1960   *Search for security: an ethno-psychiatric study of rural Ghana.* London, Faber & Faber.

FORTES, M.
1948   The Ashanti social survey: a preliminary report. *Rhodes-Livingstone Journal,* 6: 1–36.
1949b   Time and social structure: an Ashanti case study. In Meyer Fortes (ed.), *Social Structure: Studies presented to A. R. Radcliffe Brown.* Oxford, Clarendon Press.
1950   Kinship and marriage among the Ashanti. In A. R. Radcliffe-Brown and Daryll Forde (eds.), *African Systems of Kinship and Marriage.* London, Oxford University Press.
1963   The 'submerged descent line' in Ashanti. In I. Schapera (ed.), *Studies in Kinship and Marriage.* Occasional Papers of the Royal Anthropological Institute, no. 16. London: Royal Anthropological Institute.
1970a   *Kinship and the Social Order.* London, Routledge and Kegan Paul.

GOODY, J.
1957   Anomie in Ashanti? *Africa,* 27: 356–63.

166

Bibliographies

HAGAN, G.
1968   An Analytical Study of Fanti kinship. *Institute of African Studies, Research Review.* Legon. Vol. 55, No. 1, 50–90.

HILL, P.
1963   *The Migrant Cocoa-Farmers of Southern Ghana : a Study in Rural Capitalism.* Cambridge, Cambridge University Press.

LYSTAD, R. A.
1959   Marriage and Kinship among the Ashanti and the Agni: A study of Differential Acculturation. In W. R. Bascom and M. J. Herscovits (eds.), *Continuity and Change in African Cultures.* University of Chicago Press.

McCALL, D.
1961   Trade and the role of wife in a Modern West African town. Chap. XV. 286–304. In A. Southall (ed.), *Social change in Modern Africa.* London, Oxford University Press.

MORTON-WILLIAMS, P.
1969   Habitat and Trade in Oyo and Ashanti. In M. Douglas and P. M. Kaberry (eds.), *Man in Africa.* London, Tavistock Publications.

RATTRAY, R. S.
1916   *Ashanti Proverbs.* Oxford, Clarendon Press.
1923   *Ashanti.* Oxford, Clarendon Press.
1927   *Religion and Art in Ashanti.* Oxford, Clarendon Press.
1929   *Ashanti Law and Constitution.* Oxford, Clarendon Press.

SARBAH, J. M.
1897   *Fanti Customary Laws.* London, Clowes & Sons.

WARD, B.
1956   Some observations on Religious Cults in Ashanti. *Africa,* 26: 47–61.

GENERAL BIBLIOGRAPHY

ACQUAH, I.
1958   *Accra Survey.* London, University of London Press.

ADAMS, B. N.
1967   *Kinship in an Urban Setting.* University of Wisconsin, Markham Publishing Co.

ALDOUS, J.
1962   Urbanization, the Extended Family, and Kinship Ties in West Africa. *Social Forces,* 41, 6–12.

ALLAND, A.
1965   Abron Witchcraft and Social Structure, *Cahiers d'Etudes Africains,* 5: 495–502.

ALLOTT, A.
1960   *Essays in African Law with special reference to the Law of Ghana.* London, Butterworth.

AXELSON, L. J.
1963   *A study of the Marital Adjustment and Role definitions of Husbands of Working and Non-working Wives.* Washington State University, Ph.D.

BAKER, T. and BIRD, M.
1959   Urbanization and the position of women. Special Number on Urbanism in West Africa. K. Little (ed.) *Sociological Review,* Vol. 7, No. 1.

BANTON, M.
1957   *West African City—a Study of Tribal life in Freetown.* London, Oxford University Press.

BARNES, J. A.
1951   *Marriage in a Changing Society :* R.L. Papers. 20. London, Oxford University Press.

BARTELS, F. L.
1965   *The Roots of Ghana Methodism.* Cambridge, Cambridge University Press.

BELL, N. W. and VOGEL, E. F. (eds.)
1960   *A Modern Introduction to the Family.* Glencoe (Illinois), The Free Press.

BERARDO, F. M.
1967   Kinship Interaction and Communication among Space Age Migrants. *Marriage and Family Living,* Vol. 29, No. 3, 541–554.

Bibliographies

BERNARD, G.
1968   *Ville Africaine, Famille Urbaine. Les Enseignants de Kinshasa.* Paris, Mouton.

BIRD, M.
1958   *Social change in Kinship and Marriage Among the Yoruba of Western Nigeria.* Unpub. Ph.D. Thesis, Edinburgh.
1963   Urbanization, Family and Marriage in Western Nigeria. In M. Ruel (ed.), *Urbanization in African Social Change.* Centre of African Studies, Edinburgh University.

BIRMINGHAM, W., NEUSTADT, I. and OMABOE, E. N.
1967   *A Study of Contemporary Ghana. Vol. 2. Some Aspects of Social Structure.* London, Allen and Unwin.

BLAU, P.
1964   *Exchange and Power in Social Life.* New York, J. Wiley and Sons.

BLOOD, R. O. and WOLFE, D. M.
1960   *Husbands and Wives.* Glencoe (Illinois), The Free Press.

BOTT, E.
1955   Urban Families, Conjugal Roles and Social Networks. *Human Relations,* Vol. 8, No. 4.
1956   Urban Families: The Norms of Conjugal Roles. *Human Relations,* Vol. 9, 325–41.
1957   *Family and Social Network, Roles, Norms, and External Relationships in ordinary Urban Families.* London, Tavistock Publications.
1960   Conjugal Roles and Social Networks. In N. W. Bell and E. F. Vogel (eds.), *A Modern Introduction to the Family.* Glencoe (Illinois), The Free Press.

BUSIA, K.
1950   *Report on a social survey of Sekondi Takoradi.* Accra, Government Printer.

CALDWELL, J. C.
1965   Extended Family Obligations and Education: a Study of an Aspect of Demographic Transition amongst Ghanaian University Students. *Population Studies,* Vol. XIX, No. 2, 183–99.
1966   The Erosion of the Family: A Study of the Fate of the Family in Ghana. *Population Studies,* Vol. XX, No. 1, 5–26.
1967   Population Sections of Walter Birmingham, I. Neustadt and E. N. Omaboe (eds.), *A Study of Contemporary Ghana, Vol. II, Some Aspects of Social Structure.* London, Allen and Unwin.
1968   *Population and Family Change in Africa, The New Urban Elite in Ghana.* Canberra, Australian National University Press.
1969   *African Rural–Urban Migration: The Movement to Ghana's Towns.* Canberra, Australian National University Press.

CLIGNET, R.
1970   *Many Wives, Many Powers.* Evanston (Illinois), North Western University Press.

COLSON, E.
1958   *Marriage and the Family among the Plateau Tonga of Northern Rhodesia.* Manchester, Manchester University Press.

COMHAIRE, J.
1956(a)   Some Aspects of Urbanization in the Belgian Congo. *American Journal of Sociology,* 62.
1956(b)   Economic change and the extended family. *Annals American Academy Political and Social Science,* 305, 45–52.

COSER, L. A.
1967   *Continuities in the Study of Social Conflict.* Glencoe (Illinois), The Free Press.

CRABTREE, A. L.
Marriage and Family Life Among Educated Africans in Urban Areas of the Gold Coast. Unpublished M.Sc. Thesis, University of London.

DOUGLAS, M. and KABERRY, P. M. (eds.)
1969   *Man In Africa.* London, Tavistock Publications.

DOUGLAS M.
1969   Is Matriliny Doomed in Africa? In M. Douglas and P. M. Kaberry (eds.), *Man in Africa,* 121–36. London, Tavistock Publications.

168

Bibliographies

EPSTEIN, A. L.
1961   The Network and Urban Social Organization. *Rhodes-Livingstone Journal*, xxix, 29–62.
1964   Urban Communities in Africa. In M. Gluckman (ed.), *Closed Systems and Open Minds*, 83–102. Edinburgh, Oliver and Boyd.
1967   *The Craft of Social Anthropology*. London, Tavistock Publications.
1969   Gossip, Norms and Social Network. Chap. IV. In J. Clyde Mitchell (ed.), *Social Networks in Urban Situations*. Manchester University Press.

EVANS-PRITCHARD, E.
1940   *The Nuer: a description of the Modes of Livelihood and Political Institutions of a Nilotic People*. Oxford, Clarendon Press.
1951   *Kinship and Marriage among the Nuer*. Oxford, Clarendon Press.

FAGE, J. D.
1959   *Ghana: A Historical Interpretation*. Madison, University of Wisconsin Press.

FARBER, B. (ed.)
1966   *Kinship and Family Organization*. New York, J. Wiley and Sons.

FORDE, D. (ed.)
1956   *Social Implications of Industrialization and Urbanization in Africa South of the Sahara*. U.N.E.S.C.O.

FORTES, M.
1945   *The Dynamics of Clanship among the Tallensi*. London, Oxford University Press.
1949(a)   *The Web of Kinship among the Tallensi*. London, Oxford University Press.

FORTES, M. (ed.)
1949(b)   *Social Structure: Studies presented to A. R. Radcliffe Brown*. Oxford, Clarendon Press.
1962   *Marriage in Tribal Societies*. Cambridge Papers in Social Anthropology, No. 3. Cambridge University Press.
1970(b)   *Time and Social Structure and Other Essays*. L.S.E. Monographs on Social Anthropology No. 40. London, The Athlone Press.

FORTUNE R.
1932   *Sorcerors of Dobu*. London, Routledge and Kegan Paul.

FOSTER, P.
1965   *Education and Social Change in Ghana*. London, Routledge and Kegan Paul.

GARDINER, R.
1970   *The Role of Educated Persons in Ghana Society*. J. B. Danquah Memorial Lectures. Third Series. Accra.

GIL, B., ARYEE, A. F. and GHANSAH, D. K.
1964   *Special Report E. Tribes of Ghana*. Census Office Accra.

GLUCKMAN, M.
1964   *Closed Systems and Open Minds: The Limits of Naivety in Social Anthropology*. Edinburgh, Oliver and Boyd.

GOODE, W. J.
1963   *World Revolution and Family patterns*. Glencoe (Illinois), The Free Press.

GOODY, E.
1966   Fostering in Ghana: A Preliminary Report. *Ghana Journal of Sociology*, 3, 26–33.
1969   Kinship fostering in Gonja. In P. Mayer (ed.), *Socialization: The Approach from Social Anthropology*. A.S.A. 8. London, Tavistock Publications.

GOODY, J.
1956   A Comparative Approach to Incest and Adultery. *Brit. J. Sociology*, 8, 286–305.
1958   *The Developmental Cycle of Domestic Groups*. Cambridge Papers in Social Anthropology, No. I. Cambridge University Press.
1959   The Mother's Brother and the Sister's Son in West Africa. *Journal of the Royal Anthropological Institute*, 89: 61–88.
1961   The classification of double descent systems. *Current Anthropology*, 2: 3–25.
1969   *Comparative Studies in Kinship*. London, Routledge and Kegan Paul.

GOODY, J. and E.
1966   Cross-Cousin Marriage in Northern Ghana. *Man*. Vol. 1, 343–55.
1967   The Circulation of Women and Children in Northern Ghana. *Man*, Vol. 2, No. 2.

Bibliographies

GOUGH, K.
1952 Changing Kinship Usages in the Setting of Political and Economic Change among the Nayars of Malabar. *Journal of Royal Anthropological Institute,* 82: 71–88.
1959 Is the Family Universal? The Nayar Case. *Journal of the Royal Anthropological Institute,* 89, Part I.
1961 The Modern Disintegration of Matrilineal Descent Groups. In D. M. Schneider and K. Gough (eds.), *Matrilineal Kinship,* 631–54. Berkeley, University of California Press.

GUTKIND, P. C. W.
1962 African Urban family life. *Cahiers d'Etudes Africaines,* Vol. 3, 149–217.
1965a Network Analysis and Urbanism in Africa. The use of micro and macro analysis. *The Canadian Review of Sociology and Anthropology,* 2, 123–31.
1965b African Urbanism, Mobility and the Social Network. *International Journal of Comparative Sociology,* Vol. VI, No. I, 48–60.
1965c African Urban Family Life and the Urban System. *Journal of Asian and African Studies.* Vol. I, No. I.

HAAVIO, E.
1967 Sex Differentiation in Role Expectations and Performance. *Journal of Marriage and the Family,* Vol. 29, No. 3, 568–78.

HARRELL-BOND, B. E.
1967 *Blackbird Leys: A Pilot Study of an Urban Housing Estate.* Oxford. B. Litt. Thesis.

HELLMAN, E.
1948 Rooiyard. *Rhodes-Livingstone Papers.* No. 13.

HERBST, P. G.
1952 The Measurement of Family Relationships. *Human Relations,* Vol. 5, No. 1, 3–36.
1954 Conceptual Framework for studying the Family. Chap. XXII of O. A. Oeser & S. B. Hammond (eds.) *Social Structure and Personality in a City.* London, Routledge and Kegan Paul.

HUBERT, J.
1965 Kinship and Geographical Mobility in a Sample from a London Middle-Class Area. *Internation Journal of Comparative Sociology,* Vol. VI, No. 1, 61–80.

HUNTER, M.
1936 *Reaction to Conquest.* London, Oxford University Press.

JAHODA, G.
1958 Boys' Images of Marriage Partners and Girls' Self-Images in Ghana. *Sociologus,* New Series, Vol. VIII, No. 2, 155–69.
1959 Love, Marriage and Social Change: Letters to the Advice Column of a West African Newspaper. *Africa,* Vol. XXIX, 177–90.

JEFFREYS, M.
1952 Married Women in the Civil Service. *British Journal of Sociology,* III.

KILSON, M. D. de B.
1967 Continuity and Change in the Ga Residential System. *Ghana Journal of Sociology,* Vol. 3, No. 2.

KLEIN, J.
1965 *Samples from English Culture.* Vols. I and II. London, Routledge and Kegan Paul.

KLUCKHOHN, C. and LEIGHTON, D.
1946 *The Navaho.* Cambridge (Mass.), Harvard University Press.

KOMAROVSKY, M.
1962 *Blue-Collar Marriage.* New York, Random House.

LA-ANYANE, S.
1963 *Ghana Agriculture: its Economic Development from early times to the middle of the twentieth century.* London, Oxford University Press.

LANCASTER, L.
1961 Some Conceptual Problems in the Study of Family and Kin Ties in the British Isles. *British Journal of Sociology,* Vol. 12, 317–33.

LAWRENCE, A. W.
1969 *Fortified Trade Posts. The English In West Africa, 1645–1822.* London, Jonathan Cape.

Bibliographies

LEVY, M. J. and FALLERS, L. A.
1959   The Family: Some Comparative Considerations. *American Anthropologist*, Vol. 61, 647–51.
LINTON, R.
1936   *The Study of Man*. New York, Appleton Century Crofts.
LITTLE, K.
1959   Some Urban Patterns of Marriage and Domesticity in West Africa. *Sociological Review*, New Series, Vol. VII, 65–97.
1965   *Social Anthropology in Modern Life*. Inaugural Lecture No. 23. University of Edinburgh.
1966   Attitudes Towards Marriage and the Family among educated Young Sierra Leoneans. In P. C. Lloyd (ed.), *The New Elites of Tropical Africa*, 139–62. London, Oxford University Press.
LITTLE, K. and PRICE, A.
1967   Some Trends in Modern Marriage among West Africans. *Africa*, Vol. XXXVII, No. 4.
LITWAK, E.
1960a   The Use of Extended Family groups in the Achievement of Social Goals: Some Policy Implications. *Social Problems*, 7, 177–87.
1960b   Occupational Mobility and Extended Family Cohesion. *American Sociological Review*, XXV, 4–21.
LLOYD, B. B.
1966   Education and Family Life in the Development of Class identification among the Yoruba. In P. C. Lloyd (ed.), *New Elites in Tropical Africa*. London (for International African Institute).
LLOYD, P. C. (ed.)
1966   *The New Elites in Tropical Africa*. London (for International African Institute), Oxford University Press.
LLOYD, P. C.
1967a   The Elite. In P. C. Lloyd, A. L. Mabogunje and B. Awe (eds.), *The City of Ibadan*. Cambridge, Cambridge University Press.
1967b   *Africa in Social Change*. Harmondsworth, Penguin Books.
LONG, N.
1968   *Social Change and the Individual*. Manchester, Manchester University Press.
MADAN, T. N.
1962   The Joint Family: A Terminological Classification. *International Journal of Comparative Sociology*, Vol. III, 7–16.
MAIR, L.
1953   *African Marriage and Social Change*. London (International African Institute), Oxford University Press.
MALINOWSKI, B.
1926   *Crime and Custom in Savage Society*. London, Kegan Paul, Trench, Trübner & Co. Ltd.
MARRIS, P.
1961   *Family and Social Change in an African City*. London, Routledge and Kegan Paul.
MARWICK, M. G.
1965   *Sorcery in its Social Setting: A Study of the Northern Rhodesian Cewa*. Manchester, Manchester University Press.
MAYER, P.
1961   *Townsmen or Tribesmen*. Cape Town, Oxford University Press.
MAYER, J.
1967   The Invisibility of Married Life. *New Society*.
McCALL, D.
1961   Trade and the Role of Wife in a Modern West African Town in A. Southall (ed.) 286–304. *Social Change in Modern Africa*. International African Institute.
McWILLIAM, H. O. C.
1959   *Development of Education in Ghana*. London, Longmans.

171

Bibliographies

MERTON, R. K.
1967   *Social Theory and Social Structure.* (Rev. ed.). Glencoe (Illinois), The Free Press.
MILLS-ODOI, D. G.
1967   *The La Family and Social Change.* Legon. Institute of African Studies unpublished M.A. Thesis.
MINER, H. (ed.)
1967   *The City in Modern Africa.* New York, Praeger.
MITCHELL, J. C.
1956   *The Yao Village: A Study in the Social Structure of a Nyasaland Tribe.* Manchester, Manchester University Press.
1957   Aspects of African Marriage on the Copperbelt of Northern Rhodesia. *The Rhodes-Livingstone Journal,* No. 22.
1962   Marriage Matriliny and Social Structure among the Yao of S. Nyasaland. *International Journal of Comparative Sociology,* Vol. III, 29–42.
1969 (ed.)   *Social Networks in Urban Situations.* Manchester, Manchester University Press.
MOGEY, J. M.
1955   Changes in Family life experienced by English workers moving from Slums to Housing Estates. *Marriage and Family living,* 17, 123–8.
MURDOCK, G. P.
1949   *Social Structure.* New York, MacMillan Co.
NAKANE, C.
1962   The Nayar Family in a disintegrating matrilineal system. *International Journal of Comparative Sociology,* Vol. 5, 117–28.
NIMKOFF, M. and MIDDLETON, J.
1960   Types of Family and Types of Economy. *American Journal of Sociology,* 66, 215–17.
NORREGARD, G.
1966   *Danish Settlements in West Africa 1658–1850.* Boston, Boston University Press.
NUKUNYA, G.
1969   *Kinship and Marriage among the Anlo Ewe.* London, The Athlone Press.
OESER, O. A. and HAMMOND, S. B. (eds.)
1954   *Social Structure and Personality in a City.* London, Routledge and Kegan Paul.
OLLENU, N. A.
1966   *The Law of Testate and Intestate Succession in Ghana.* London, Sweet and Maxwell.
OPPENHEIM, A. N.
1966   *Questionnaire Design and Attitude Measurement.* London, Heinemann.
OPPONG, C.
1967   The Context of Socialization in Dagbon. *Institute of African Studies Research Review, Legon,* Vol. 4, No. 1, 7–18.
1969a   *Matriliny and Marriage.* Paper presented at a Conference on Networks, Leiden Afrika-Studie Centrum.
1969b   Education of Relatives' Children by Senior Civil Servants in Accra. *Ghana Journal of Child Development,* Vol. 2. No. 2.
1970a   Conjugal Power and resources: An Urban African example. *Journal of Marriage and the Family,* Vol. 32, No. 4, 676–80.
1970b   *Aspects of Conjugal Relationships among Akan Senior Civil Servants in Accra.* Ph.D. Thesis, Cambridge.
1971a   Urban Household Budgets. Paper Presented at an interdisciplinary Seminar on the Family among the Akan & Ewe. Forthcoming in *Legon Family Research Papers No. 1.* C. Oppong (ed.)
1971b   Family Change in Africa: A Review. *Institute of African Studies Research Review,* Vol. 7, No. 2, 1–17.
1971c   'Joint' Conjugal Roles and 'Extended Families': A Preliminary note on a mode of classifying conjugal Family Relationships. *Journal of Comparative Family Studies,* Vol. 11, No. 2, 178–87.
1972a   Norms & Variations: A Study of Ghanaian Students' Attitudes to Marriage and Family Living. Paper presented at the second interdisciplinary Seminar on the Family. Forthcoming in *Legon Family Research Papers No. 3.*

Bibliographies

OPPONG, C. (*cont.*)
1972b Education and Change: The Domestic System of an Educated Urban Elite. *Institute of African Studies Research Review*, Vol. 8, No. 1, 31–49.
1972c The Conjugal Family 'Open' or 'Closed' Changes in Prescribed Norms for family relationships among Ghanaian University Students. *Institute of African Studies Research Review*, Vol. 8, No. 2.
1974 *Growing up in Dagbon*. Ghana Publishing Corporation.

OSMOND, M. W.
1969 A cross-Cultural Analysis of Family Organization. *Journal of Marriage and the Family*, 302–10.

OSTERREICH, H.
1965 Geographical Mobility and Kinship – a Canadian Example. *International Journal of Comparative Sociology*, Vol. VI, No. 1, 131–44.

PARSONS, T.
1943 The Kinship system of the Contemporary United States. *American Anthropologist*, 45, 22–8.

PAUW, B. A.
1963 *The Second Generation: A Study of Family Life Among Urbanized Bantu in East London*. London, Oxford University Press.

PHILLIPS, A.
1953 *Survey of African Marriage and Family Life*. London (International African Institute), Oxford University Press.

PIDDINGTON, R.
1965 The Kinship Network among French Canadians. *International Journal of Comparative Sociology*, Vol. VI, No. 1, 145–98.

PLATT, J.
1969 Some Problems in Measuring Jointness of Conjugal Role-Relationships. *Sociology*, Vol. 3, No. 3, 287–98.

PONS, V.
1969 *Stanleyville. An African Urban Community under Belgian Administration*. London, Oxford University Press.

PRIESTLY, M.
1969 *West African Trade and Coast Society: A Family Study*. London, Oxford University Press.

RADCLIFFE-BROWNE, A. R. and DARYLL FORDE (eds.)
1950 *African Systems of Kinship and Marriage*. London, Oxford University Press.

READER, D. H.
1961 *The Black Mans' Portion*. Cape Town, Oxford University Press.

REDFIELD, R.
1947 The Folk Society. *American Journal of Sociology*, LII, 293–308.

RICHARDS, A.
1939 *Land, Labour and Diet in Northern Rhodesia: an Economic Study of the Bemba Tribe*. London, Oxford University Press.
1940 Bemba Marriage and Present Economic Conditions. *Rhodes-Livingstone Papers*, 4.
1950 Some Types of Family Structure Amongst the Central Bantu. In A. R. Radcliffe-Brown and D. Forde (eds.), *African Systems of Kinship and Marriage*. London, Oxford University Press.

RUEL, M. (ed.)
1963 *Urbanization in African Social Change*. Proceedings of the Inaugural Seminar held in the Centre of African Studies, University of Edinburgh.

SAFILIOS-ROTHSCHILD, C.
1970 The Study of Family Power Structure. A Review. 1960–1969. *Journal of Marriage and the Family*, Vol. 32, No. 4, 539–52.

SCHAPERA, I.
1939 *Married Life in An African Tribe*. London, Faber and Faber Ltd.
1949 *Migrant Labour and Tribal Life*. London.

Bibliographies

SCHAPERA, I. (ed.)
1963 *Studies in Kinship and Marriage*. Occasional paper of the Royal Anthropological Institute. No. 16.
SCHNEIDER, D. M. and GOUGH, K. (eds.)
1961 *Matrilineal Kinship*. Berkeley, University of California Press.
SMITH, N.
1966 *The Presbyterian Church in Ghana, 1835–1960*. Accra, Ghana University Press.
SMYTHE, H. & M.
1960 *The New Nigerian Elite*. Stanford.
SOUTHALL, A. and GUTKIND, P. C.
1957 *Townsmen in the Making*. Kampala.
SOUTHALL, A. (ed.)
1961 *Social Change in Modern Africa*. London, Oxford University Press.
SPIRO, M. E.
1954 Is the Family Universal? *American Anthropologist*, 56, 839–46.
STOUFFER, S. A. *et al.*
1949 *The American Soldier*. Princeton, Princeton University Press.
SUSSMAN, M. B.
1953 The Help Pattern in the Middle Class Family. *American Sociological Review*. XVIII.
1959 The Isolated Nuclear Family, Fact or Fiction. *Social Problems*, 6, 333–60.
SUSSMAN, M. and LEE BURCHINALL
1962 Kin Family Network: Unheralded Structure in current conceptualizations of Family Functioning. *Marriage and Family Living*, 24, 231–40.
THOMPSON, B. and FINLAYSON, A.
1963 Married Women who work in Early motherhood. *British Journal of Sociology*, 14.
TILLY, C. and BROWN, C. M.
1967 On Uprooting, Kinship and the Auspices of Migration. *International Journal of Comparative Sociology*, Vol. VIII, 139–64.
TURNER, V. W.
1957 *Schism and Continuity in an African Society*. Manchester, Manchester University Press.
VELSEN, J. VAN.
1967 The extended case method and situational analysis. In A. L. Epstein, (ed.), *The Craft of Social Anthropology*. London, Social Science Paperbacks in Association with Tavistock Publications.
WATSON, W.
1958 *Tribal Cohesion in a Money Economy*. Manchester, Manchester University Press.
WEBER, M.
1947 *The Theory of Social and Economic Organization*. London, Oxford University Press.
1962 *Basic Concepts in Sociology*. Translated and introduced by H. P. Secher. London, Peter Owen.
WILLMOTT, P. and YOUNG, M.
1960 *Family and Class in a London Suburb*. London, Routledge and Kegan Paul.
WILSON, G.
1941 *Economics of Detribalization in Northern Rhodesia*. R.L.I. Papers 5 and 6.
WILSON, M.
1936 *Reaction to Conquest*. London, Oxford University Press.
WOODMAN, G. R.
1966 *The Development of Customary Land Law in Ghana*. Ph.D. Thesis, Cambridge. 2 vols.
1969 Some Realism about Customary Law – The West African Experience. *Wisconsin Law Review*, No. 1.
1971 *The Rights of Wives, Sons and Daughters in the Estates of Their deceased Husbands and Fathers*. Paper Presented at I.A.S. Family Seminar Legon, February; published in *Legon Family Research Papers*, No. 1.
YOUNG, M. and WILLMOTT, P.
1957 *Family and Kinship in East London*. London, Routledge and Kegan Paul.

174

INDEX

abortion, attempted, 107
Abouré, 4, 113
abroad, 35–6, 53–4, 56, 58, 60–1, 72, 77, 79, 126, 128, 133, 147
abusua, 48. See matrikin and matrilineage
accommodation, 4, 6, 8, 31, 52, 58, 72, 76, 82, 93, 105, 117, 119, 154; claims to, 31; government, 118; living space, 9; of relatives, 8, 113; rented, 107; search for, 77; small, 10; temporary, 8, 78
accounts, 90, 113, 126; joint, 90; savings, 99; separate, 100
Accra, 1, 3, 37, 41, 48, 50, 58, 68–70, 73–4, 76, 78–9, 83, 107, 125, 126; City Council, 51; High Court, 50
accusations, 124, 138; between affines, 12, 129, 131
achievement, of ambitions, 55, 66, 69
activity, areas, 34; fields, 22–3
Adams, B. N., 20, 158
administrative centre, 83; employees, 41; experience, 5; post, 58, 68, 126
affines, 6, 69, 95, 106, 124–5, 128–9; accusations by, 12, 129, 131; affinal ties, 34, 158; conflict with, 131, 138, 153; coresidence of, 73, 152
African, 35, 40; conjugal family, 11; educated, 2; elite wife, 143; family life, 4, 10; minister, 50; systems of kinship and marriage, 14; towns, 9, 11; domestic organization
age, school, 55; of spouses, 15
agriculture, golden age of, 37; institutions, 37; women's role in, 32
Ahanta, 28
Akan, 2, 4, 15, 19, 28ff., 34, 39, 40, 42, 45, 49, 70, 137, 142; area, 32, 37, 39; coastal, 2, 32, 35–7, 39; chiefs, 43; couples, 15, 27, 84, 93; (panel of), 94ff., 113; community, 47; conjugal family, 85; customary marriage, 5; customary norms, 48, 91, 97; customary rites, 83; divorce, 45; family system, 126, 130, 138, 141; families, 15; home, 126; husbands, 20, 44, 82; interior, 34–5, 42, 79, 89, 128, 137, 147, 151, 159;

institutions, 25; kinship norms, 3, 137; men, 33 (employment of) 38; mothers, 64; marriage, 3, 25, 48; matriliny, 25; population, 5, 46; professional men, 118; regions, 25; sisters, 64; subgroups, 5, 53, 147, 154; society, 91; traditional practices, 61; senior civil servants, 3, 5, 20, 48, 54, 62, 64–6, 73, 83, 85, 112, 115, 149, 159; reference model, 124; wives, 6, 20, 33, 38, 51, 102, 116, 118–19; youth, 53
Akim, Akyem, 15, 28, 37, 43, 50–1, 57; State Council, 43
akpeteshi, 56
Akwapim, 15, 28, 37, 39, 41, 43, 48, 50, 51
Alland, A., 26
allocation of resources, 85, 115, 124, 130, 133, 142, 156; decisions regarding, 112; harmonious, 123; of husband, 138; secrecy about, 91
allocation of tasks and responsibilities, 95, 144, 157; control over, 139
Allott, A., 26, 51
ambition, 33, 57, 62, 149; occupational, 69
amenities, of modern urban life, 52
ancestor, 21, 29
ancestral property, 50
Anomabu, 50
anomie, 9
anxiety, 144–5, 155, 157
Arhin, K., 26
artisans, 35, 37
Asantehene, 43
aseda, 49
Ashanti, 15, 28, 38, 41, 46, 51, 53; chiefship, 25; court, 38; court records, 50; king, 38, 43; mother, 60; region, 46. See interior Akan
aspirations, 18, 113, 136, 141, 148, 156; of spouses, 115
attitudes, 18, 94, 96, 110, 124, 150; change of, 26; to illegitimacy, 49; to roles, 17; of spouses, 142; study of students', 84; of wives, 141; of working woman, 86
authority, 27; British, 50; domestic, 39; traditional patterns, 115

175

177

179

Index

Index

Index

nephew, 58–9, 60, 64, 77; support of, 96, 97, 100; inheritance, 138
niece, 60, 64, 76, 79, 80, 117
norms, 123, 150; customary, 48, 85; domestic, 141, 160; inheritance, 36, 51; prescribed, 112; traditional, 34ff.
Norregard, G., 50
nuclear family, 80; emergence of 11–12; functioning, 27; individuation of 137, 148; solidarity, 14; system, 7
nurse, 62, 68, 70, 72, 74, 75, 78, 96, 98, 104, 117, 121, 128, 132
nurse maids, 102; reliance on, 139
nursery school, 79, 80, 107
Nzima, 28, 39

obligations, 2, 62, 65, 73, 123, 144, 149, 155; assumption by kin, 22, 27, 110; avoidance, 9; changes in, 11; conjugal, 9, 30ff., 80; extension of, 21; family, 9; financial, 54ff., 63, 135, cutting down of, 150; fulfilment of, 98, 101; kinship, 9, 73, 85–6, 125, 128, 136, 158; to matrikin, 33ff., 46, 151; persistence of, 47; repayment of, 55; social and economic, 5, 6, 47; of wife, 49
occupation, 38, 51–2, 119, 158; of spouse, 7; of wives, 71
occupational, goal, 75; mobility, 158; privileges, 85; position, 156; status, 48, 52, 66; system, 11; structure, 154; transfers, 83
Oeser, O. A., 22, 140
office, 33, 68, 83, 89, 128; worker, 103
old people, 55; maintenance of, 96; neglect of, 99
Ollenu, N. A., 50
open relationships, 4, 21, 34, 44, 94; chores, 107; finances, 90, 99, 100, 143; *open/segregated*, 110ff., 111
openness, 93, 96, 99, 101, 124, 142, 149, 150, 154; definitions of, Farber and Weber, 27; degree of 85. See *closure* and indices
Oppenheim, A. N., 19
Oppong, C., 25, 27, 84, 93, 115, 150, 160
Ordinance marriage, 42, 46, 50, 65
orphans, 32, 92, 126; neglect of, 99; disinheritance of, 44, 147
Osterreich, H., 158
'outside' children, 44, 59
overcrowding, 80, 120
ownership, 34, 35, 85, 86, 88, 91, 93, 94, 98; by kin, 130; private, 47, 52, 92

'parasitism', 9, 26
parents, 5, 34, 53, 55, 58, 61, 75, 93, 146; assistance of, 64, 85; coresidence of, 73; commitments of, 157; marriage of, 31,

130; maintenance of children, 21; role of, 21, 27; siblings of, 5; surrogate, 21, 63, 146
parties, 68, 131
paternal, half brother, 67; responsibility, 47, 49, 64, 88; role, 33
paternity, 31; acknowledgement of, 72; recognition of, 49
patrikin, 9, 63, 126
patriliny, 13, 93; trend towards, 14
pay, 69, 95
payment, for food and clothes, 86–7, 99; of school fees, 46, 56, 58, 105; to kin, 61
pension, 52; rights to, 95
Phillips, A., 25–6
Piddington, R., 158
plantations, 96; cocoa, 38; owners, 158
Plateau Tonga, 13
Platt, J., 23
poison accusations, 12; insinuation, 129
polygyny, 31, 45, 51, 56, 60–1, 65–6, 72, 127–8, 130, 137, 141
Pons, V., 26
population, 3, 28, 48, 83; change, 6, 41, 154
power, 1, 6, 9, 115ff., 122, 138; balance of, 158; of descent groups, 8; distribution of, 7; of kin, 8; to pawn, 29; position, 7, 113, 115, 156; sources of, 119; struggle, 131; type of relationship, 22; wife's position, 121; of wife, 138; of witches, 50. See decision-making
praise, 125–6; lack of, 140; of spouse, 142, 144
pregnancy, 104, 130
pressure, 69, 135, 155; decrease of, 101; economic, 61; of in-laws, 99; external, 129; lack of, 125; of matrikin, 59; on resources, 101
prestige, social, 65, 117, 140
Priestley, M., 36, 42, 50
primary school, 39, 56–9, 60, 67; teacher, 81
privacy, domestic, 82, 118
privileges, 5, 52, 85, 117
problems, domestic, 136–7
procreation, 31, 33, 59, 65
professional clubs, 125; course, 56–7, 74; employment of wives, 121; experience, 5; training, 39, 61, 119, 136; man, 3, 10, 15, 36–7, 41, 51, 77, 117–18, 128, 140
profits, 29, 116; of trading, 99
promotion, 53, 126
property 2, 31, 33, 45, 50, 64, 67, 68, 85, 91–2, 147; acquisition of, 37 (individual), 29; control of, 33, 34, 138; dealings, 90; disposal of, 30 (*inter vivos*) 42, (by will), 42; of father, 65; family, 29; holding, 37; lineage, 29; immovable, 91; inheritance of,

Index

Sahwi, Sefwi, 28

salaried employment, 2, 5, 12–13, 45, 117, 149; benefits of, 39; increase in opportunities, 48

salary, 6, 52–3, 58, 89, 97, 117, 119, 120, 140, 154; combination of, 95; earners, 54; earning, 13, 93; limited, 87; rises, 47; scale, 98; use of, 99; wife's, 120

sample, of Ashanti school-children, 46; case studies, 15; Senior Civil Service Survey, 3, 15ff., 19–20, 26, 63; size, 20; of students, 27

sanctions, customary, 9; domestic, 118; marital, 120; plurality of, 9

Sarbah, J. M., 31–2, 41–3, 48–50

satisfaction, 94, 110, 127, 135; marital, 125, 144

saving, 13, 57, 95, 100, 103, 125–6, 130, 138, 147; account, 91, 99; joint, 24, 86; long-term, 6; money, 75, 99; unit for, 10

Schneider, D. M., 4, 14, 49

scholarship, 53, 56–7, 60–1, 76

school, 5, 37–8, 40, 47, 56–7, 59, 76, 81, 83, 96, 117, 126, 147; in Ashanti, 38, 46; attendance, 61, 79, 104, 116; boy, 61, 80; Catholic, 35; certificate, 58; demand for, 38–9; expansion of, 39; expenses, 81; fees, 46, 61, 88, 97, 105, 156; master, 50; primary, 56, 58; secondary, 19, 39, 53, 56–8, 60–1, 70, 81

security, 6, 10, 93, 98, 116, 121, 133, 137; for children, 33; of conjugal family, 44; financial, 2, 52, 54, 90, 94, 125, 158; material 149; for orphans, 65; sense of, 127; social benefits, 10; sources of, 132, 138; struggle for, 119ff.; of wife, 118; for women, 33, 65

segregation, 2, 22–3, 33–4, 84, 94–6, 101, 142; degree of, 22; of finances (spouses), 49, 90–1, 98; variaton in, 23. See jointness and indices

separation, of activities (conjugal) 93, 124, 136; chores, 111; conjugal, 34, 57, 59, 60, 64, 68, 105–6, 118–19, 135; of decision-making processes, 121ff.; financial, 98–9, 112, 149; of interests, 33, 93, 157; residential, 77; of resources, 101; of spouses and children, 73

servants, 73, 102, 106, 139, 152–3; coming and going of, 16; quarters, 80

services, 82, 120; domestic, 96, 104, 144

sewing, 51, 62, 68, 72, 79, 86, 120, 139; course, 79; machine, 55, 104

sharing, activities, 113, 133–4; cost, 88; decision-making, 133; expenses of wedding, 69; leisure, 74; property, 64 (after death), 92; responsibilities, 113, 130, 159; responsibility for financial provision, 86ff.; tasks, 148. See jointness and syncratic decision-making

shopping, 88–9, 109, 111, 130, 134–5

siblings, 56, 62–4, 82, 92–3, 118, 128, 130, 136; children of, 73; group of classificatory, 21, 29; group solidarity, 91; half, 54, 61; residence with, 120; support of, 96

sick, 61; maintenance of, 96

sisters, 33, 55–7, 62, 64, 68–9, 79; child of, 57, 59–60; education of, 63; elder, 56; inheritance by, 97; inheriting group, 42; in-law, 99; obligation to, 46; as potential heir, 13, 29; residence of, 79; son of, 76

Smythe, H. H., 26

social, activities, 125; calls, 98; change, 34; contacts, 63, 125, 158; distance, 99; maintenance of, 98; field of spouses, 22; functions, 125; isolation, 125, 127, 133; maintenance of status, 52; mobility, 47–8, 54, 151, 156; obligations, 47, 52, 125, 135; pressures, 128; prestige, 117; rewards, 146; rights, 52; status, 65, 117; survival, 34

socialization, 12, 34, 157; agents of, 146

solidarity, conjugal, 6, 126. See jointness

son, 49, 59, 61, 62ff., 69–70, 75; in-law, 83; obligations of, 2, 6; reliance on, 97; rights of, 31

sorcery accusation, 12

Southall, A., 25–6, 51

spatial mobility, 47, 54, 151, 156

spending, 89–90; joint, 86; power, 93; resources, 133, 135, 139; shared, 93; time, 124; spouses, 82ff.; associates of, 124; independence of 112; residence of 8, 46; roles of, 27; separation of interests, 33; sharing of responsibilities, 22, 34

spouse, choice of, 9, 10, 65, 116; cooperation with, 85

stability, 124, 140–2, 143; of conjugal relations, 123

standard of living, 13, 52, 93, 118–19, 154

status, 69; ascribed, 11, 28; achievement of, 11, 48, 55, 66; birth-rights, 31; educational, 73; high, 35; occupational, 48, 52, 54, 73, 117; Senior Service, 72; of wives and children, 31, 66

stereotypes, ethnic, 64, 142, 147

Stouffer, S. A., 145

strain, 3, 66, 84, 98, 101, 111, 113, 128–9, 132, 138, 145, 153, 155–6, 159; engendered by change, 12; expression of, 98; financial, 64, 149; minimization of, 33, 94; paternal bond as source of, 26; psychological & social, 26; role, 12, 100 (lack of)

185

Index